Saga of a Kayasth Family

Raja Girdhari Pershad Mahbub Nawazwant

Saga of a Kayasth Family

Unique Family of Seven Generations and Its Contribution to Literature

Dr NARAYAN RAJ

GYAN

The Publication of this Book has been financially supported by the Narhari Pershad Charitable Trust. The responsibility for the facts stated and or opinions expressed is entirely of the author and not of the Narhari Pershad Charitable Trust.

First Published, 2018

Published by

Gyan Publishing House
5, Ansari Road
Daryaganj, New Delhi-110002
Phone: 9811692060
E-mail: books@gyanbooks.com

Printed at: G. Print Process, Delhi.

Cataloging in Publication Data—DK
Courtesy: D.K. Agencies (P) Ltd. <docinfo@dkagencies.com>

Nārāin Rāj, author.
Saga of a Kayasth family : unique family of seven generations and its contribution to literature / Narayan Raj.
pages cm
Includes bibliographical references.
ISBN 9788121214230 (HB)

1. Kayasthas—India—Hyderabad—History. 2. Kayasthas—India—Hyderabad—Genealogy. 3. Hyderabad (India)—Genealogy. 4. India literature—History and criticism. I. Title.

LCC DS432.K29N37 2018 | DDC 929.072054 23

Dedicated to:

Rai Daulat Rai

Who came to Hyderabad from Delhi along with

Nizam-ul-Mulk Asaf Jah-I

Contents

Foreword

It gives me immense pleasure to introduce the book entitled, "Saga of a Kayasth Family: Unique Family of Seven Generations and Its Contribution to Literature", written by Dr Narayan Raj- a descendant of the Saxena family of Hyderabad. He is the Great Grandson of the illustrious Raja Girdhari Pershad and in this book he wrote about the literary contribution of the members of his family for over more than seven generations. It is comparable to the Novel "Roots" written by Alex Hailey, tracing the genealogy of his ancestors who migrated to America. In this book Dr Narayan Raj examined the contents of important literary works of his ancestors and highlighted their contribution to the evolution of composite literary culture in the Hyderabad State. It is a valuable contribution to the literary history of the Asaf Jahi dynasty, as no other scholar so far has undertaken research on the topic relating to the literary works of Kayasthas of Hyderabad. Undoubtedly, it is a welcome addition to the theme of cultural history of the Deccan in general and Nizam's State in particular.

Kayasthas are a distinguished community in India and have traditionally worked as keepers of public records and accounts, writers, and administrators of the State. Historically, they have occupied the highest government offices, served as ministers and advisors of the rulers, and held important administrative positions during the British Raj. In modern times, Kayasthas have also performed multifarious activities and excelled in various professional fields. Originally they mostly belonged to the Hindi-speaking States of U.P., Bihar,

Madhya Pradesh and Delhi. However, they were a mobile social group and migrated to various other parts of the country. Most of the Kayasthas who came to Hyderabad from Delhi and U.P. in the early eighteenth century got employment in the court of the Nizam rulers of the Asaf Jahi dynasty and also held highest positions as *mansabdars, Diwans* etc and occupied many hereditary positions. The praiseworthy feature of the Kayasthas of Hyderabad was their ability to adopt/adapt/adjust themselves amicably with the changing circumstances and wishes and orders of the Asaf Jahi rulers. The rulers of Hyderabad State since the time of the First ruler Nizam-ul-Mulk recognised their services and bestowed distinctions, awards, and titles on them. In return many Kayasth officials remained loyal and grateful to their masters. The family of the Raja Girdhari Pershad is a case in point. Their contribution to the overall development of Hyderabad State is noteworthy and they worked with dedication and sincerity for its modernisation in all sectors. Scholars like Karen Leonard have written the ethnographic history of the Kayasthas of Hyderabad and documented their achievements in various fields and professions. In particular, this community produced many illustrious personalities who made their presence felt in several fields, including administration and literature by virtue of their abilities and competence.

This book is divided into 11 chapters and contains detailed description of the literary works of leading scholars in chronological order. Although the ancestors of Saxena family migrated to Hyderabad in the 18th century as administrators, it also produced illustrious litterateurs like Raja Girdhari Pershad 'Baqi' alias Bansi Raja. The most distinguishing feature of the Kayasth scholars were that they not only well-versed in the court languages of the rulers, viz., Persian or Urdu but also acquired mastery over other languages. They were multi-linguists and produced valuable works in several languages like Hindi, Sanskrit, Braj Bhasha, besides Persian and Urdu. To begin with, members of Daulat Rai family, like Raja Ram was a scholar of Persian, Hindi and Braj Bhasha.

He also composed *Chitragupt Mahatm* in Braj Bhasha. The early scholars like Rai Swami Pershad composed religious texts (*Bhagawat Puran*) in multiple languages like Persian/ Sanskrit, and Braj Bhasha. Later, Narahari Pershad continued family tradition and translated texts like *Yog Vashisht* from Sanskrit to Hindi, it was great accomplishment. He was a multi-linguist and wrote five books. Among them, *Narahari Prakash* represented his literary accomplishment and Dr Narayan Raj remarked that "it is an outstanding gift to the mankind."

Raja Narsing Raj, the worthy son of Bansi Raja was known for his literary contribution. Following the footsteps of his father, he authored five books in Persian and Urdu languages and composed *Ghazals, Rubaiyat and Qatas*. Raja Narsing Raj's poetry and couplets have elegance, lofty ideas and thoughts, grandeur of imagination and comprehensible approach. Like his ancestors, he wrote Bhajans in Urdu on important Hindu Festivals like *Ekadashi, Siva Ratri, Deewali* etc. He also was a poet of high caliber and esteem and had developed expertise in Urdu and Persian. It is remarked by the author of this book that Aali's "poetical works and couplets have elegance, lofty ideas and thoughts, grandeur of imagination and comprehensible approach." The nineth generation of Hyderabadi Kayasthas, beginning with Rai Narhar Raj 'Saqi', the eldest son of Raja Narsing 'Aali' continued the family tradition of literary contribution. Though they held responsible positions in the Nizams' government under Mir Osman Ali Khan, their passion for writing poetry, *Bhajans*, organising and participating in Mushairas, composing Ghazals continued. It has been observed that in Narhar Raj Saqi's poetry "there is glimpse of mysticism and knowledge of God". Dr Bhaskar Raj Saxena, being a professional graduate authored several books in Urdu, Hindi and English. The twentieth century Kayasth litterateurs wrote mainly in Urdu and English, which became the prominent languages of the elites of Hyderabad. Mahabub Raj, a product of Madrasa-e-Aaliya, was intelligent and quick-witted.

He was an expert in martial arts and a public activist. He wrote Urdu poetry and it was remarked that the main characteristic of his poetry is simple language. He wrote in plain and chaste Urdu. He also used small meters and the construction of his couplets is much organised.

Among the prominent Kayasth scholars of Hyderabad, the name of Dr Sheela Raj is unique and stands as an exception. She was an accomplished scholar of Urdu and History, a rare combination. Her intellectual distinction lies in the fact that being well-versed in Urdu language she was able to write authentic works on the social and cultural history of Hyderabad. Her *magnum opus* "Medievalism to Modernism: Socio-Economic and Cultural History of Hyderabad from 1869-1911" is a path breaking study on modern history. It deals with the processes and the characteristic features of the making of modern Telangana since the rule of Mir Mahabub Ali Khan, who is considered as the liberal, progressive moderniser of Hyderabad State. The book of Dr Sheela Raj is original and innovative as it is based on original Urdu sources. It is different from many scholarly works, which are based mainly on government documents in English. Dr Raj authored nine books in both Urdu and English languages. Her book entitled, "Portrait of an Era" deals with the history of Asaf Jahi dynasty under Mir Mahabub Ali Khan and the biographical history of Bansi Raja on the basis of his diaries. She has thrown new light on the entrepreneurial qualities of Raja Girdhari Pershad and attempts made by the British to scuttle the programme of industrialisation under the Nizam rulers. It is a valuable book on the economic history of Hyderabad State in the nineteenth century, the reign of the sixth Nizam, Mir Mahaboob Ali Pasha, was also significant in bringing about major changes in the political, administrative, socio-economic and cultural fields. He was a popular ruler of Hyderabad who became the beloved of the people. Dr Raj's work mentions that the Sixth Nizam was a liberal ruler and a visionary. The multi-sided progress in the fields of administration, industry, trade and commerce and education have transformed the Hyderabad State from medievalism to modernity. Her works very vividly portray the evolution of composite culture, Hindu-Muslim unity, religious tolerance, communal harmony, *Ganga-Jamuni tahazeeb* under the Asaf Jahis.

Dr Narayan Raj has collected valuable materials on the literary and cultural history of Hyderabad State in the nineteenth-twentieth centuries. He has unearthed hitherto neglected areas of the history of Asaf Jahi dynasty and thrown new light on the neglected aspects. His work reinforces the fact that the Nizam rules continued the Deccani traditions of religious tolerance, communal harmony and cultural synthesis. Although the Nizams rulers encouraged many Muslim poets and scholars from North India, they also encouraged the Hindu Kayasths and facilitated the growth of literary works. The Kayasths known for their loyalty, trustworthiness gained the confidence of the rulers and pursued their literary activities without any hindrances. This fact proves that the Deccani culture flourished in the Hyderabad State during the nineteenth to twentieth centuries. The historical information provided in this book amply proves it.

Therefore, I congratulate Dr Narayan Raj for bringing out a valuable work on the socio-cultural and literary history and the contribution of Kayasths in the making of secular modern Hyderabad.

Professor Adapa Satyanarayana
(Retd)
Department of History
Osmania University
Hyderabad

Family Group of Bansi Raja

L TO R: Sham Raj, Ram Raj, Raja Narsing Raj, Mahbub Raj, Janak Raj, Girdhar Raj
Standing: Narhar Raj

Preface

Ot'they Ai'hl Kamal Ai Shad Ek Ek Karke Duniya Se
Na Hain Voh Ai'hl Mahfil Aur Na Voh
Raunaq Hai Mahfil Ki

Maharaja Kishan Pershad 'Shad'

The entire period of Asaf Jahi dynasty had undergone tremendous changes. The fall of the Moghul Empire and British impact was felt in every sphere of life, such as, Administration, Politics, Economy and overall growth.

However, the most significant period of growth in Hyderabad was from 1869 – 1948 when Mir Mahbub Ali Khan – Nizam-VI and His Exalted Highness Mir Osman Ali Khan – Nizam-VII (1911-1948) were the rulers of the state. This was the period when there was development in the field of administration, industry, education and communication.

Literary activities were at their peak during this period. Literature got a boost. Though, the literary activities were progressing during the earlier period, but they were at a slow phase.

History is witness to the fact the Kayasths played a valuable role in the promotion of Hindi, Urdu and Persian languages. Many great writers, poets, journalists were born, the pages of History of Literature is full of their contribution. Kayasths like Prem Chand, Mahadevi Varma, Ram Babu Saxena, Raja Girdhari Pershad 'Baqi' etc. contributed to Urdu, Hindi and Persian languages.

In fact, Kayasth Community is spread all over India and it is known by its last name and *'Als'*. It is a practice that the marriage within the same *'Als'* was not permitted. But this was not operated strictly. These days family within the same *'Als'* have married with one another. The *'Als'* were stated to be purely nominal and no longer relevant in arranging marriages which has become acceptable.

In the Northern India, there are different 'Als', from the East India. The *'Als'* are used by all Kayasths, such as, Mathurs, Saxena, Bhatnagar, Nigams, Srivastav and Asthana etc.

Kayasths were holding important positions in Pre-Independent Era. Some of them were *Diwans* or the Prime Ministers of the Princely States. Their contributions in different fields are noteworthy. Some of them were the hearts of the rulers. They are famous for their contribution, honesty, dedication, ability and sincerity.

In Pre- and Post-Independent Era, Kayasths were in politics. Some of the renowned Kayasths are Dr Rajendra Pershad, Lal Bahadur Shastri, Netaji Subhash Chandra Bose and many others.

Among the renowned spiritual Kayasth leaders, Swami Vivekananda and Sri Aurobindo Ghosh need special mention. Their contribution is immense and noteworthy.

The contribution of Shanti Swaroop Bhatnagar in the field of Science and Technology is unparallel. Among the Kayasths historians Shri Jadunath Sarkar, Banarsi Lal Saxena occupied prominent position. There are many other renowned historians of the Kayasth Community. The Kayasth community has produced most efficient bureaucrats, lawyers, financial experts as well.

The Kayasths moulded themselves according to the requirement of their rulers and masters. For instance, during the Moghul rule in India, Kayasths mastered themselves in Persian language, which was the official language of the

Moghul Court. It is an established fact that the Kayasths are peace loving community and they never indulge in any unnecessary disputes.

It is said that when *Eshwar* (God) formulated languages, He distributed the languages to every nation of the world. Arabic was given to Arabs, Persian to Iran and Chinese to China and other languages to various countries.

After distributing the languages to every nation, hundreds of languages remained undistributed with *Eshwar* (God). There was no one to take these languages. Thus, God put all these languages in the basket of Bharat that is India.

Among these literary classes, Kayasths were prominent. This community was in the forefront due to its natural ability to bring to light its literary talent. It can be said with authority that Kayasths played a prominent role during every period of civilisation. Peace and tranquility were their motives.

In Hyderabad, many renowned persons were born. Kayasths of Hyderabad made their presence felt in every field of life with their abilities. They took keen interest in the promotion of cultural traditions. They led a peaceful life and encourage the passion among others to lead the life of tranquility.

Hyderabad is a reflection of love and affection with its peculiar cultural values. There was harmony among various communities in the State especially during the Asaf Jahi period.

In Deccan, many learned men were produced who were veterans and great scholars, due to the influence of these personalities, Hyderabad became the centre of Deccani Art and Literature. Poets like Mohammed Khan 'Imaan', Maharaja Chandulal 'Shadan', Hafiz, Mir Shamsuddin Mohammed 'Faiz', Raja Girdhari Pershad 'Mahboob Nawazwant' 'Baqi', Ahmed Hussain 'Mayal', Bachulal 'Tamkeen', Maharaja Kishan Pershad 'Shad', Biharilal 'Ramz' were the renowned personalities of that era.

History is witness to the fact that this period was the era of promoting literary taste. They were not judged on the basis of their apparent criteria but on the basis of individual talent and merit. Therefore, the Hindus also contributed as much as Muslims in the development of Urdu and Persian languages and did not give room to narrow-mindedness and anti-religious feelings.

It is important to study the past in its true perspective to understand the present India which is facing unique problems because of the number of religions which are practiced in our country. Communal harmony and national integration were the tools of Mir Mahbub Ali Khan – Nizam-VI with which he won the hearts of the people. Religion was neither used by the Asaf Jahi Rulers nor the nobility to humiliate communities.

Asaf Jahi rulers who were the Muslims, appointed the Hindus on the key positions in the government and in their palaces. They not only appointed them but trusted them as well. The Asaf Jahi rulers gave prime importance to religion, cultural integration, communal harmony and tolerance.

Among the most trusted Hindu families of the Asaf Jahi rulers, was the family of Rai Daulat Rai. Five generations of this family was incharge of household affairs of the Asaf Jahi rulers. Daulat Rai was appointed Superintendent of His Highness Household and continued in this position till his death. His son, Raja Ram was then given this post by Nawab Nizam Ali Khan – Nizam-II. He served in this post till his death. Nawab Sikandar Jah– Nizam-III then appointed Swami Pershad, son of Raja Ram to succeed him as the Superintendent of the Royal Household. Later, Narhari Pershad was made the Superintendent by Nasir-ud-Dowla-Nizam-IV. He made him Sarishtedar of *Sarf-e-Khas* and awarded him *'Jewels and Khillat'*. Raja Girdhari Pershad the son of Narhari Pershad was also looking after the Royal Household of the Nizam. He was entrusted with the task of formulating regular and irregular troops, *Jamiat-e-Nizam*. He was incharge of many departments of the Nizams Palace including the Royal kitchen. This family served the Asaf Jahi rulers for over hundred years.

It can, therefore, be concluded that five generations of Daulat Rai's family were incharge of the Royal Household of the Nizam's and various departments of the government they served the rulers with utmost sincerity and dedication. This is a rare example which needs special mention.

I lack suitable words to express my grateful thanks to Professor Adapa Satyanarayana, former Head, Department of History, Osmania University, for his invaluable foreword to this work.

I appreciate the contribution of Dr Susheela Vyapari, former Principal, Hindi Maha Vidyalaya, Hyderabad and Dr Sheela Raj, a historian and scholar of repute, whose writings about this family helped me immensely in shaping this book.

I am thankful to Dr Mohammed Ziauddin Ahmed ***'Shakeb'***, (London), for his guidance and help in this work which I often needed and cherished.

I appreciate the cooperation and help of Mr Syed Rafiuddin Qadri, (son of Syed Moinuddin Qadri *'Zore'*) in this work. I am thankful to him for taking keen interest in my work.

My thanks are due to Professor Syed Khaja Moinuddin of the Department of Translation, Maulana Azad National Urdu University, Hyderabad, India, for his help from time to time which was a great source of inspiration to me.

I am also thankful to Sri Jeevan Raj Saxena for his assistance in the compiling of the data.

Dr Narayan Raj

Chapter – One

Introduction

Mir Qamar-ud-Din Chin Qilich Khan Bahadur Fatheh Jung Asaf Jah was a distinguished soldier and a Provincial Governor in the Mughal's reign. He rose to the position thereafter of prominence, which he never lost till his death. Aurangzeb Alamgir recognised his services and offered him high command, such as, Sadar-i-Kul. He continued to serve with distinction in Deccan.

History is witness to the fact that the early decades of the eighteenth century witnessed rapid disintegration of the Mughal Empire. Mir Qamar-ud-Din, son of Ghazi Uddin Firoz Jung, a notable noble in the court of Aurangzeb was the Viceroy of Deccan in 1713 and had the title of Nizam-ul-Mulk Asaf Jah. He was planning various strategies and awaiting the opportunity to establish his rule in Deccan.

He fought with the Governor of Khandesh. Mubariz Khan who had the secret instruction of Delhi Court to oppose Nizam-ul-Mulk by force of arms. The battle was fought at Shakarkheda, Berar in 1724 where Mubariz Khan was defeated and lost his life. This was the beginning of the establishment of the Asaf Jahi dynasty for generations to come. It speaks volumes of Nizam-ul-Mulk's grit and resourcefulness. Instead of adjusting himself to Delhi, he decided to push further to establish his own dynasty. Thus, a new chapter began in the history of Deccan.

It is a known fact that Nizam-ul-Mulk established his authority and shifted his capital from Aurangabad to Hyderabad. Thus, Hyderabad became the cradle of his family. Hyderabad remained the capital of Asaf Jahi dynasty for more than two hundred years.

The founder of the Asaf Jahi dynasty Nizam-ul-Mulk Asaf Jah-I followed the Mughal traditions in administration. The fact remains that when he left for Deccan, he took along with him many distinguished families from the north. Some of them were nobles from the Mughal Court, distinguished administrators and commanders of the army, learned scholars both from the Hindu and the Muslim communities. Among the distinguished families who came to Hyderabad along with Nizam-ul-Mulk were the *Paigah* Nawabs, who were the head of the infantry and cavalry. The ancestors of Kayasth Mathur family of Raja Shiv Raj Dharamwanth were the hereditary revenue administrators. The ancestors of Raja Rai Rayan were the treasurers and accountants in the government of Shah Jahan. The family of Raja Rao Rambha, the Nimbalkars, who were the shatriyas by caste of Suraj Bansi clan a warrior class. Among such distinguished families was also a Kayasth Saxena family which was not only in the army but also in administration. This family of Rai Daulat Rai subsequently produced the great Persian scholar and statesman Raja Girdhari Pershad 'Baqi' alias Bansi Raja.

The literary and cultural history is witness to the fact that the Kayasth family not only participated in the literary activities of Hyderabad but also promoted the cultural activities in the State. The series of the traditions of culture is still continuing. The Kayasth community is leading its life in a dignified manner with their special cultural identity. They are very modest, cultured and intelligent. The members of the Kayasth families especially noted personalities have always been loyal to the government in power. They held many prestigious positions. The ladies and gentlemen of the Kayasth family are identified in society with their peculiar

THE FAMILY TREE OF RAI DAULAT RAI

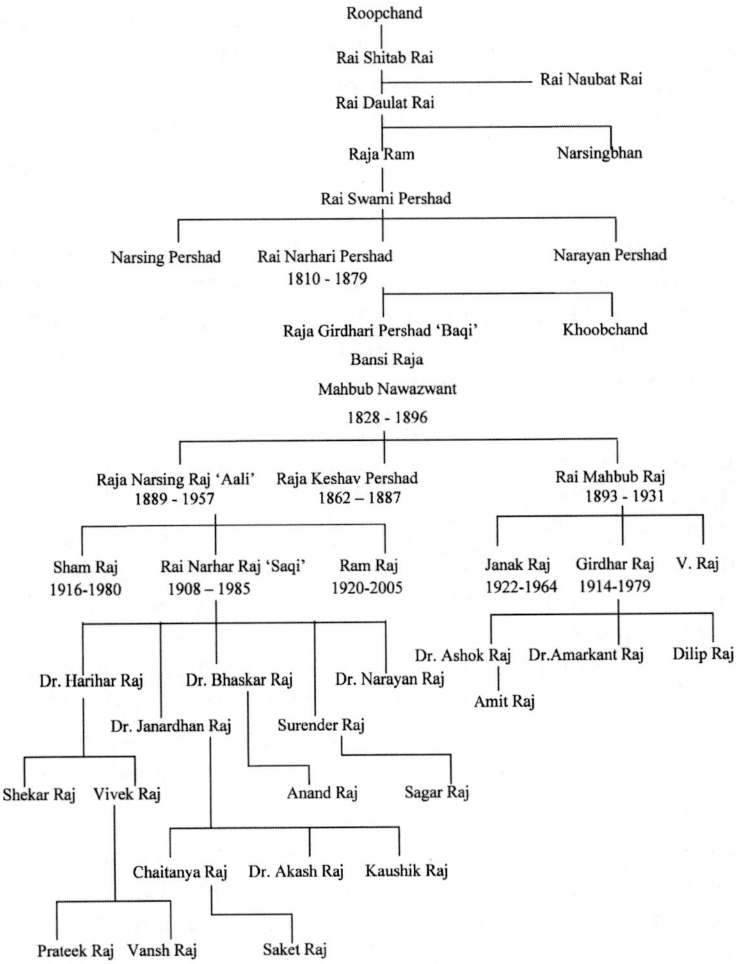

traditions, modesty and style of living. They have admiration for Urdu language and culture. The members of the Kayasth family have made their presence felt in every field of life. They occupy esteem status in society.

The ancestral history of the family of Rai Daulat Rai, a Kayasth Saxena dates back to early eighteenth century. The forefathers of Bansi Raja were engaged in administration of Nizam-ul-Mulk.

In appreciation of their services, the Nizams bestowed distinction, title, awards on them. In return, the family of Bansi Raja always remained grateful and loyal to their rulers and the people of the erstwhile Hyderabad State.

Hari Sharan Chhabra while acknowledging the services and status of the family wrote:

> **"In nobility, greatness, simplicity and modesty, no other feudal house can compete with Raja Bahadur Narsing Raj and his forefathers in Hyderabad State. Loyalty to the State and to the people in a modest way has been their motto".**

The history of the family of Rai Daulat Rai dates back to the time of migration from Chhabramau, district Farukhabad in Uttar Pradesh, when Rai Daulat Rai, son of Shitab Rai accompanied Nizam-ul-Mulk to Hyderabad, via Aurangabad. Rai Daulat Rai got married in Hyderabad in the year 1770. He had a brother Naubat Rai. Shitab Rai was a highly religious person and spent most of his time in meditation and visiting pilgrimage centres. When he visited Jwala Mukhi in Punjab, he decided to detach himself from the worldly affairs and proceeded to the Himalayas never to return. He intimated his intensions to his son Daulat Rai through a letter.

Daulat Rai was Musharif-e-Dewdi (a high position in the Nizam's palace). In 1782, he marched with an army to lay siege to Jagtial. He left behind him two sons Raja Ram and Narsing Bhan. Raja Ram was a distinguished administrator in the Nizam's government and Narsing Bhan was in military service. Narsing Bhan accompanied Nizam-ul-Mulk during the wars and on one such occasion he died in Pangal.

Raja Ram was incharge of thirty six departments of the Nizam's government which includes finance and kitchen. It was indeed a great responsibility and indicates that Raja Ram was one of the trusted employees of the Nizam.

This establishes the foundation for successive generations to enjoy generosity and patronage of the Asaf Jahi rulers.

In the year 1783, Raja Ram permanently settled down in Hyderabad with his family. He purchased a palace in Chandrikapur, which was later renamed as Hussaini Alam, in the heart of the city. Raja Ram was a poet and a writer in Hindi, Braj Bhasha and Urdu. He was a scholar of Persian. He translated Persian books into Braj Bhasha. He wrote Chitragupt Mahatm. After leading the most successful and comfortable life, Raja Ram passed away. He left behind him Swami Pershad, the only son. Swami Pershad was brought up by his maternal grand father Rai Chimna Lal Munshi, a noted scholar of his time. Swami Pershad became the son-in-law of Kumari Lal, *Peshkar* of the Muslim noble Himmat Yar Khan.

Swami Pershad was a poet and wrote in Hindi, Urdu and Persian languages.

Swami Pershad had three sons namely, Rai Narayan Pershad, Rai Narhari Pershad (who was the second son) and Rai Narsing Pershad. Narayan Pershad and Narsing Pershad passed away at the young age without leaving any heirs.

Narhari Pershad was born in the year 1810. Soon after the death of his father, the responsibility fell on the shoulders of young Narhari Pershad at the age of eleven. Nawab Sikandar Jah Nizam-III made Narhari Pershad incharge of the Royal kitchen and *Mashal Khana.*

Rai Narhari Pershad was a learned scholar of Hindi and Sanskrit languages and could converse in these languages fluently. He wrote in Braj and Awadi languages also. He was a distinguished poet and wrote several books. He witnessed the establishment of the British Residency and saw the British interference in day-to-day administration of the state. He passed away in the year 1879. He had fourteen children of whom Khoobchand and Raja Girdhari Pershad 'Baqi' alias Bansi Raja survived. Rai Khoobchand had four sons namely Ganesh Pershad, Madhav Pershad, Siri Pershad and

Parmeshwari Pershad. Out of these, Siri Pershad only survived. Later, Khoobchand passed away during the lifetime of Narhari Pershad.

Raja Girdhari Pershad 'Baqi' alias Bansi Raja was born in the year 1828. It is an established fact that his forefathers were very well settled in Hyderabad. They had earned good name and fame in Administration and Literature. The fact cannot be denied that the Kayasths are known as a literary class throughout India, in the field of Persian and Urdu literatures. Raja Girdhari Pershad was an Administrator, Industrialist, Philanthropist, Reformer and Adviser. He was a poet of repute as well as a Philosopher. He wrote in Persian, Urdu, Hindi, Awadhi and Braj Bhasha. Raja Girdhari Pershad passed away in the year 1896. He had four sons Bhagwan Pershad, Keshav Pershad, Raja Narsing Raj and Mahbub Raj. Bhagwan Pershad died at an early age and Keshav Pershad died at his prime age when Raja Girdhari Pershad was alive. Raja Narsing Raj and Mahbub Raj were alive when Bansi Raja passed away. He had four daughters, Gajra Rani, Jagdamba Rani, Lalita Rani and Durga Rani.

Raja Narsing Raj was born in the year 1889. After completing his early education, he looked after his personal estate. He was bestowed with the title of 'Raja Bahadur' by Nizam VI. He was a scholar and a poet of repute. He wrote in Persian, Urdu, Hindi and Braj Bhasha. He composed in all the principal forms of verses recognised in poetry, such as, *Gazal, Qasida, Rubai, Qata,* Chronogram, *Nazm, Marsia, Masnavi* etc. Many of his works indicated the diversity of thoughts.

Raja Narsing Raj had three sons and two daughters. Both the daughters passed away at the very young age. His sons were Rai Narhar Raj, Sham Raj and Ram Raj. Raja Narsing Raj passed away in the year 1957.

Rai Narhar Raj was born in the year 1908. He had his early education in the Kayasth Pathshala. Later, he continued his education in New English School, Poona. He studied at

Nizam's College, Hyderabad for Intermediate in which his optional subject was Persian. Later, he went to Poona and joined Agriculture College for a Landlords Diploma course in Agriculture.

Rai Narhar Raj was a poet and wrote in Urdu and Hindi. Rai Narhar Raj passed away in the year 1985 leaving behind five sons namely; Dr Bhaskar Raj, Dr Harihar Raj, Dr Narayan Raj, Dr Janardhan Raj and Surender Raj. He has two daughters Ms. Meena and Naveena.

Dr Bhaskar Raj was born in the year 1934 and had his early education in Hyderabad and did his graduation in Veterinary Science from Osmania University. Later, he did his Law from Osmania University and post graduate Diploma in Marketing from Bombay.

He wrote several books in English, Urdu and Hindi languages. He was an orator of repute and participated in many debating competitions and won several awards. He has one son Anand Raj and three daughters Ms. Asha, Nisha and Lata. Dr Bhaskar Raj passed away in the year 2014.

> **It can therefore be concluded that the seven generations right from Raja Ram to Dr Bhaskar Raj contributed to literature in six different languages namely, Hindi, Awadhi, Braj, Urdu, Persian and English. It is not only unique but the rarest of the rare contribution of a family.**

Besides the above personalities, there are two members of this family who not only contributed to literature but the history of Hyderabad and need special mention. They are Mahbub Raj and Dr Sheela Raj.

As mentioned above, Mahbub Raj was the son of Raja Girdhari Pershad 'Baqi'. He was born in the year 1893. He had early education in Madrse Aliya. He was a poet and his Diwan has been published. He had three sons namely, Girdhar Raj, Janak Raj and Vishveshwar Raj. Girdhar Raj was the member of Indian Administrative Service. Mahbub Raj had six daughters.

Dr Sheela Raj is the daughter-in-law of Rai Narhar Raj and wife of the author of this book. Dr Sheela Raj did her MA. in Urdu, B.Ed. and M.A. in History from Osmania University. She did her Ph.D. in History from SNDT Women's University, Bombay.

She is a historian and a scholar of repute and is considered to be an authority on the Asaf Jahi rulers.

She was a staunch believer in Hindu-Muslim unity. She wrote:

> **If civilisation is to survive, the tussle between the Hindus and the Muslims must be resolved. It is, therefore, essential for us to trace the history and find out how the problems were tackled in the past. The remedies and essence of philosophy, customs and traditions need a special mention in the present context. Fanaticism has no place in a civilised or cultured society. Religious tolerance and respect for each other's religion is the need of the hour. The policies adopted by the Asaf Jahi rulers and nobility of the nineteenth century Hyderabad are a shining example of Hindu-Muslim unity and tolerance, which should serve as the guide for the present day society.**

Dr Sheela Raj passed away in the year 2008.

It is a known fact that, this family was always against the British Raj. Girdhari Pershad was against the policies of the British. In the year 1877 a Durbar was held in Delhi for which Nawab Mir Mahbub Ali Khan Nizam-VI was invited. Raja Girdhari Pershad accompanied Nizam-VI to attend Delhi Darbar. He circulated his poem, *Latifa Darbar*, composed by him in Persian against the policies of British Raj. All the rulers and dignitaries who attended the Durbar appreciated it very much.

Communal harmony and integration were the two important tools through which Nizam-VI won the hearts of the people. The Asaf Jahi rulers and the nobility of Hyderabad never exploited religion to humiliate communities. They did not take religion to the streets as is being done by the politicians of the independent India. The rulers and nobles of the erstwhile state of Hyderabad gave prime importance to religious cultural integration, communal harmony and tolerance. They maintained these practices throughout their tenure, as a result of this, the Hindus and the Muslims participated wholeheartedly in each other's religious festivals. Bansi Raja also participated in *Eid* and *Muharram* etc.

While referring to the socio-economic conditions of Hyderabad, the history is witnessed to the fact that since the establishment to the Asaf Jahi rule, the State witnessed many ups and down throughout the eighteenth century and the first half of the nineteenth century. The social life of the people was far from satisfactory. However, the most noticeable feature of the late nineteenth century Hyderabad was the development of a heterogeneous society represented by different communities, castes and classes. It is a fact that Bansi Raja won the heart of the turbulent class of the Arabs who had advanced money to the State. Bansi Raja settled the dispute between the Arabs and the Government of Nizam for the repayment of loans. Bansi Raja enrolled the Arabs into Regular and Irregular troops and *Jamiat-i-Mahbub*. The services of Bansi Raja in this regard were recognised by one and all including the Nizam and the Government.

The titles bestowed by the Nizams were classified into various categories and were generally conferred on the occasion of the Nizam's birthday and also on the occasions of festivals, such as, *Nauroz, Dassehra, Diwali, Holi, Eid* etc. in a *Darbar* organised on these occasions.

These titles were awarded in recognition of services. These titles were Jung, Rai, Raja Bahadur, Khan Bahadur etc. In fact, historically these titles and honours were the legacies which the Nizams inherited from the Mughal Emperors. The titles of Jah, Mulk, Daula and Vant etc. were meant for the nobility.

Beside the above mentioned titles, there were many others which were awarded to the relatives of the rulers, Nobles of the highest rank, Prime Minister, nobility etc. In addition to these, Nizam used to bestow honours in the form of jewellery, awards, emblems of distinction, *Ambari, Naubat Roshan Chowki, cash awards* etc.

Most of the family members of Bansi Raja were bestowed with the titles of Rai, Raja, Raja Bahadur and Vant. Raja Ram's original name was Ram Pershad. When Nizam bestowed the title of 'Raja' on him, he was called Raja Ram. The title of Rai was bestowed on Swami Pershad and Narhari Pershad; hence they were called Rai Swami Pershad and Rai Narhari Pershad. Girdhari Pershad alias Bansi Raja was awarded the title of Raja Bahadur and later, he was elevated to the status of nobility, when he was awarded the title of Mahbub Nawazwant. Bansi Raja was also awarded *Ambari and Naubat Roshan Chowki.* Narsing Raj, the son of Raja Girdhari Pershad was awarded the title of Raja Bahadur.

Bansi Raja also started many industries such as, paper, leather, gun powder, arms and ammunition, clothes etc. His arms and ammunition factory caused a great deal of anxiety to the British and the paramount power. It had shaken the high officials of Government of India and the British. He started his gunpowder factory in the year 1864. The garment stitching unit was established in the year 1868. He started his arms and ammunition factory in the heart of the city during the year 1868. He wrote in one of his books, *Kalam-i-Mutafarikhat,* that he started these and many other factories on the insistence of Sir Salar Jung–I.

As mentioned earlier, when Nizam-ul-Mulk left for Deccan, he took along with him many distinguished personalities and the families. They belonged to both the Hindu and the Muslim communities and the learned scholars.

The Persian language and literature had become the language of administration in the Mediaeval India. It was the language of culture also. It served also as a link between the

Hindus and the Muslims. The Hindus and the Muslims played an important role in development of the Persian language. This was a notable feature of the Mediaeval Indian history. Persian language rose to glory during the Mughal period. A large number of Muslims contributed to the development of Persian, such as, Amir Khusro, Faizi, Maulana Mulla Masih and a host of others. This continued till the period of Mirza Asadulla Khan 'Ghalib' and later came down to Dr Sir Mohammed Iqbal.

The fact cannot be ignored that the Hindus also contributed wholeheartedly in the promotion of Persian language along with their Muslim brethren. Among them Munshi Ram Singh and Bhimsen Saxena need special mention. It is the responsibility of the historians to highlight the contribution of the Hindus for the development of Persian literature in India. If they neglect this fact, these historians will not be doing justice to the Persian scholars of the Hindu community.

When Nizam-ul-Mulk Asaf Jah shifted his capital from Aurangabad to Hyderabad many Persian scholars accompanied him. Lala Mansa Ram's (a peshkar of the Asaf Jah-I) son, Laxminarayan 'Shafeeq', was a reputed poet in Persian and Urdu languages. His book '*Chamanistan-i-Shaura*' is considered to be an important contribution to Persian literature.

Persian remained the language of the Court of Asaf Jahs for nearly two hundred years. Asaf Jah-I himself was a Persian poet of distinction. He left two *Diwans*.

Maharaja Chandu Lal '*Shadan*' who was the administrator and the *Peshakar* at the Nizam's Court was a renowned poet in Persian and Urdu languages. His contribution to these languages is immense. There were about three hundred poets who were connected with the house of '*Shadan*'. '*Shadan*' left two *Diwans* in Urdu and one in Persian.

The fact cannot be denied that the Hindus contributed as much as Muslims towards the development of Persian language and literature. The last distinguished Indian Hindu Persian scholar of the nineteenth century was Raja Girdhari Pershad *'Baqi'*, who was a courageous and bold writer.

It is an accepted fact that Urdu poetry first blossomed in the courts of Deccan under the Qutub Shahi rulers of Golconda and Adil Shahi rulers of Bijapur. They not only patronised literary and distinguished personalities but themselves were writers of verses in Persian and Deccani Urdu. During that period Urdu was known as Deccani.

Nizam carried forward the tradition of learning and literature, subsequently, in Hyderabad. Poets, scholars and philosophers migrated to Hyderabad enjoyed and the patronage not only from the Nizam but also from the nobles of Hyderabad. It was the period of Mir Mahbub Ali Khan Nizam-VI, which is characterised by the literary and cultural renaissance, Urdu literature developed under Nizam-VI who was himself a poet of distinction. Hyderabad became a centre of scholars and poets after their disintegration from Delhi, following Mutiny of 1857, Bahadur Shah Zafar, the last Mughal ruler was deported from Delhi. After the death of Nawab Kalb Ali Khan of Rampur the hopes of the poets and scholars were shattered and as a result, they were attracted towards Deccan.

These poets who came to Hyderabad from Delhi and Rampur enjoyed the court favours, hospitality and royal patronage. As a result of the royal magnanimity many books were written on different subjects in the Court of the Nizam.

The poets who enjoyed the favours of the Nizam, no doubt, were men of literary merit and whose language was chaste. They contributed much to the Persian and Urdu literatures, religion, law and history.

His Exalted Highness, Mir Osman Ali Khan, the last ruler of the Asaf Jahi dynasty was not only a liberal patron of art and literature but was very much interested in Urdu poetry. He himself was a distinguished poet and scholar.

He left behind him as many as seven *Diwans* of Urdu *Ghazals*. The noted Urdu Poet, Nawab Fasahat Jung 'Jaleel' was his *Ustad* (guide) in poetry.

During the reign of Mir Mahbub Ali Khan, Raja Girdhari Pershad 'Baqi' held a prominent place in the literary field and was considered to be one the best poets of Hyderabad. It may be mentioned here that 'Baqi' was a leading literary figure and one of the best Persian poets, Hyderabad had ever produced.

It is a known fact that the Nizams never interfered in other religions. The family of Bansi Raja consisted of writers and poets of distinction. They wrote in Hindi, Urdu, Persian, Braj Bhasha and Awadhi languages. They also wrote on diversified subjects including religion. Eventhough, the family was close to the Nizams, right from the beginning; neither they had any interference from the Nizams nor any restrictions. This was the greatness of the Asaf Jahi rulers to give free hand to the writers to write about their own religion.

The family of Bansi Raja wrote verses in Hindi language. They followed the pattern laid down by Tulsidas and thus wrote *Chaupai, Doha, and Sarota.* In Urdu and Persian, they composed all principal forms of verses such as, *Ghazal, Qasida, Masnavi, Salam, Hamd, Naat, Qita, Rubai.* Some of them were experts in writing '*Tariq*' (chronogram). They were known for their quick and befiting verses. Their works indicated the diversity of thoughts. They wrote *Bhajans* in Urdu using mainly the words of Hindi, Braj and Awadhi languages. It is a known fact that *Bhajans* are written on *Devi, Devta and Bhagwan. Bhajans* are also written on festivals, such as, Navratri, Shivratri Ekadasi etc. They were written in many languages but writing *Bhajans* in Urdu is a rare phenomenon. Very few poets have attempted to write *Bhajans* in Urdu, however, some family members of this family had written *Bhajans* in Urdu language and left behind them a large collection of Urdu *Bhajans*.

The *Mushairas* are very common in the literary circles. *Mushaira* is the gathering of poets where *ghazals* (poems) are recited on set of topics. These *Mushairas* has their own glory, culture and traditions in the past from which one gets an opportunity to see and learn mannerism and etiquette unlike the present day *Mushairas.*

'Baqi' used to organise *Mushairas* in honour of Hazrat Hafiz Mohammed Shamsuddin 'Faiz' his tutor. Raja Narsing Raj Aali organised annual *Mushairas* in memory of Maharaja Kishen Pershad 'Shad'. Rai Narhar Raj organised an All India *Mushaira* in the honour of his *Ustad* (tutor) Fasahath Jung 'Jaleel' Manikpuri.

It is a fact that the family of Bansi Raja has no equal for its sincerity, loyalty and affection to their sovereign, the example of which can rarely be found in the entire history of the Asaf Jahi rule. This can further be elaborated by the fact that Sikandar Jah, Nizam-III (1803-1829) made Narhari Pershad incharge of the *Bowerchi khana* (Royal Kitchen) and this continued during the period of Nasir-ud-Daula, Nizam-IV (1829-1857), Afzal-ud-Daula Nizam V (1857-1869) and Mir Mahbub Ali Khan Nizam-VI (1869-1911). During his tenure, after Rai Narhari Pershad, Raja Girdhari Pershad was made incharge of the Royal Kitchen. Therefore, the *'Bawarchi Khana'* or the Royal Kitchen was under the charge of his family during the period of four successive Nizams. This is indicative of the fact that the Nizams had great confidence and trust in this family. This also shows that the Nizams never differentiated between the Hindus and the Muslims and made Hindus incharge of the Royal Kitchen for over a centuary that is right from the time of Raja Ram.

However, during the second half of the nineteenth century Mir Mahbub Ali Khan, a progressive ruler and thereafter Maharaja Sir Kishen Pershad, the then Prime Minister (1901-1911), were the two outstanding personalities who contributed much to transform antiquated feudal structure into a modernize one. It was because of the administrative reforms and the re-organisation carried out by these towering personalities, the state witnessed administrative, cultural, social and economic development which was unprecedented in the history of Hyderabad.

Hyderabad has presented the most spectacular picture of Hindu-Muslim unity in its real sense. This is due to the fact that it was difficult to differentiate between a Hindu and a Muslim as they dressed alike, their food habits were similar, the marriage and death ceremonies had similarity and above all, Urdu was the common language. In fact, it will not be incorrect to say that Hyderabad was a wonderful State in India. The ancestors and the subsequent generations of Bansi Raja maintained the customs and traditions of not only Asaf Jahi rulers but also of Hyderabad.

This family is highly pious and religious. The ancestors of Bansi Raja were not only strictly the followers of *Sanatan Dharm* but they equally respected other religions as well. It is a fact that the rulers of Hyderabad were the Muslims but they never interfered in the religion of other communities. Everyone was given the choice to follow their own religion. It is also a fact that eventhough this family was closely associated with the Nizams, the rulers, but the members of this family were not afraid of following their own religion freely. This was a unique feature of that era.

As mentioned earlier this family is pious and religious. This can be established with the fact, that the ancestors of Bansi Raja visited religious places in India. They wrote religious books, such as, Bhagwat in Awadhi language, Sanskrit and Braj Bhasha. One of them translated Yog Vashisht from Sanskrit into Hindi. They wrote *Bhajans* etc.

Bansi Raja himself travelled to religious places extensively in India, so also his future generation. Bansi Raja and his ancestors wrote religious books such as, Bhagwat in Persian, Shiv Puran in Urdu, and translated Shambu Puran from Sanskrit into Hindi. His son, Raja Narsing Raj and grandson, Rai Narhar Raj wrote *Bhajans* in Hindi using Braj Bhasha and Awadhi languages. The outstanding contribution of Bansi Raja was the composition of the book *Rubayat-e-Babarkat* in Persian in which he highlighted the significance of 99 names of 'Allah'. This book contains one *qasida, haftband and marsia* on Hussain.

This composition of 'Baqi' is indicative of the fact that he was deeply influenced by Sufi thoughts as well.

Raja Girdhari Pershad not only constructed temples in and around Hyderabad but also renovated the old ones. The temple at Keshavgiri and Damagundem were renovated. He constructed a Ram temple at Sabzimandi, Hyderabad, Tulja Devi temple at Puranapul and Durga Devi Temple at Keshavgiri. Annual *Jataras* of these temples were organised by Bansi Raja and after his demise, his son Raja Narsing Raj and grandson, Rai Narhar Raj continued the tradition and conducted *Jataras.*

The present generation of this family followed the footsteps of their forefathers and constructed small temples of Duttatreya Maharaj Sri Sri Manik Prabhu (2012), Chitraguptji (2013), and Sri Hanuman (2015), and Sri Krishnaji Temple in 2018. It is pertinent to mention here that even the present generation of the family is highly pious, religious and follows *Sanatan Dharm.*

Research work leading to M.A, M.Phil., and Ph.D. have been done in different Universities in Hindi, Urdu and Persian on Rai Narhari Pershad, Raja Girdhari Pershad 'Baqi', Raja Narsing Raj 'Aali' and Dr Sheela Raj.

Gold medals have been instituted in different Universities of India in memory of Rai Narhari Pershad, Raja Narsing Raj 'Aali', Narhar Raj Dr Bhasker Raj Saxena and Dr Sheela Raj. A fellowship has also been instituted in memory of Dr Sheela Raj. An annual memorial lecture is organised in memory of Dr Sheela Raj by H.E.H. The Nizam's Jubilee Pavilion Trust, Hyderabad, every year on 17th July.

Chapter – Two

Raja Ram Pershad

The history of the family of Raja Ram Pershad goes back to the period when the head of the family migrated to Hyderabad. Rai Daulat Rai son of Shitab Rai a kayasth Saxena belonging to Chabramau, Dist. Farukhabad in Uttar Pradesh accompanied Nizam-ul-Mulk Asaf Jah-I to Hyderabad. Daulat Rai had a brother Naubat Rai. Shitab Rai was a religious person and spent most of his time in meditation, religious activities and visiting pilgrimage centres. One day, he decided to detach himself from the worldly affairs. While he was in Jwalamukhi, he proceeded to the Himalayas, never to return to his home. He intimated his son Daulat Rai about his decision through a letter.

Daulat Rai was a *Musharif-i-Deodi* (a senior official in the palace of the Nizam) and in 1782, he laid the siege of Jagtial with his army. He was in-charge of the army. According to Dr Susheela Vyapari, Daulat Rai was a scholar of Persian and Hindi but due to non-availability of the document, it cannot be substantiated further. Dr Laeeq Salah, in her article 'Girdhari Pershad Mahbubnawazvant 'Baqi' wrote that Daulat Rai came along with Asaf Jah-I and was holding high position in the Government. Daulat Rai was appointed Superintendent of His Highness household and continued in his post till his death.

Daulat Rai had two sons namely, Narsing Bhan and Raja Ram. The former was in military and latter in the administration of the Nizam.

Raja Ram was a distinguished administrator in the Nizams Government. It is a fact that he was a trusted employee of the Nizam. This can be substantiated by the fact that Raja Ram was in-charge of thirty six departments of the Nizams Government including that of Kitchen. After the death of his father, Raja Ram was given the post of Superintendent of His Highness household by Nawab Nizam Ali Khan and like his father he continued in this post till his death. As a result of this, successive generations gained generosity and patronage of the Asaf Jahi rulers.

Raja Ram's original name was Ram Pershad, however, when he was awarded the title of 'Raja' he started writing his name as Raja Ram. He was also a '*Mustaufi*' or a Chief Collector.

As mentioned earlier this family of Daulat Rai played an important role in contributing to literature especially in Persian, Urdu and Hindi languages.

According to Prem Chand, noted Urdu fiction writer, literature is like a torch which takes society and its development towards the future.

According to Ram Vilas Sharma, the history of literature is a medium of expression preserving the achievements. Literature is the medium of expression and creativity of the best talent of society.

In fact, literature is nothing but a mixer of emotional sentiment and sensorial experience which takes the shape of creation by its lingual and its artistic creativity.

According to Acharya Ramchandra Shukla, the literature of every country is a compiled reflection of people's mentality. Mentality keeps on changing. It mostly depends upon the political, social, communal and religious circumstances.

Kayasths were the scholars in Urdu, Hindi and Persian literatures. Some of them, wrote their compositions in Hindi and triggered Hindi literature to new heights. Out of these families, Rai Daulat Rai's family served Hindi literature for five generations.

Raja Ram's '*Chitragupt Mahatm*' is a unique composition. On going through this poem, one realises that Raja Ram was influenced by the poetic composition of Tulsi Das and Surdas. '*Chitragupt Mahatm*' is in Braj Bhasha and this style is similar to '*Ram Charitra Manas*'- one couplet after every eight quatrains. The sweetness of Braj Bhasha made this poem easy and excellent.

The poet himself has praised Braj Bhasha in the following words:

मन में बहुत लालसा आई, बृजभाषा त्रिभुवन सुखदाई
इच्छा करत सारदामाई, भाषा रस रसना उपजाई।।

This composition written in Braj Bhasha can be included among the other creations of Bhaktikal. The pattern, creative-style, and the language of Chitragupt kavya is very close to the works of Bhaktikal, which used to have the description of Gods and Goddesses. It can be said with certainty that Hyderabad which is a famous city of South India and which is far away from the Hindi speaking belt, adopted Braj Bhasha *Doha* of Tulsidas and quatrains speak of the simplicity and excellence of his creativity.

It appears that Raja Ram was very much inspired by the poets of Bhaktikal and therefore, in the same sequence he wrote '*Chitragupt Mahatm*'.

He started the poetry with the praise of Gods and Godessess and of *Guru*.

सुमिरैं आदि अलख अबिनासी, जो परिपूर्ण हि घटघटवासी।
जोती रूप सब माहि बिराजै, पूर्ण जु षोडश कला समाजैं।
तुम्हारो अगम पंथ को पावे, कहा शक्ति रसना गुण गावै।
बहुरि गणेश सरस्वती धयाऊँ, जिन प्रसाद वे कुल जस गाऊँ।
पुनि सुमिरौं श्री आदि भवानी, माया परा अजा जग ठानी।
निज सद्गुरू शरणागत आऊँ, बार-बार चरण नवलि जाऊँ।
जिन प्रताप रसना गुण गावैं, मन इच्छित पूर्ण हि फल पावै।
जबलौं गुरु कृपा नहि करि हैं, जग के काज कौन विधि सरि हैं।

Further, the poet writes:

करुणा सिंधु कृपा करौं राज रहत नहि ओर।
मो समपति तौं पंगु कौं, तुम बिन नाहीं ठौर।।

Chitraguptji is the main deity of Kayasth clan. How and why he was born? The story is very interesting. Once when Brahmaji was in deep meditation, suddenly a person appeared from his body with a lot of paintings and colours on the body. He was holding a pen and an ink pot. As he was born out of Brahma's *Kaya* (body), he is called a 'Kayasth' and his name is Chitraguptji. On appearance, Chitraguptji asks Brahmaji about his duties. Brahmaji again went into *Dhyan* (meditation). When he came out of *Dhyan*, he told Chitraguptji to go to *Yamalok* and prepare in *Yamalok* accounts of the man's *pap and punya* (sins and virtues). Since that time onwards Chitraguptji is said to be busy in enumerating *Pap and Punya* in *Yamalok*. Chitraguptji had two wives. He was blessed with twelve sons – Saxena, Mathur, Asthana, Gaur, Srivastav, Bhatnagar etc. *Garuda Puran* describes the presence of *Chitralok* near *Yamalok*. *Yam* is worshipped on *Shukla dweetya kartik mas*. So, it is called as *Yamdweetya* too. The cursed King Sudas performed his puja on the same *Thithi* and went to heaven. Bheeshma Pitamah too said to have had the boon on *Itcha Mrityu* by the grace of Yamraj only. According to some other views, Chitraguptji's father was a Kayasth and he was named as *Mit*. His sister's name was Chitra. After father's death, he went to *Prabhas Kshetra* (east) for penance, and as a result acquired *Gyanoplabdhi*. Yamraj gave him the course of writer in his Court. From that time onwards, he is known as Chitraguptji. Yamraj explained him the secret of *Dharma*.

Chitraguptji is said to have constructed a very huge *Bhavan* with the help of his sister and decorated it so beautifully that even Dev Shilpi Vishwakarma started competing with him. According to this story, the Kayasth clan is said to be the descendant of Chitraguptji only.

Raja Ram wrote the following lines about the origin of the Kayasth legacy:

कायथ बंस जगत कहि लावै। कौन देवतें उत्पति पावै।।
जे जग के कारज सब करि हैं। राजनीति रीति मन धरि है।।
जिहिबिधि इनकी उत्पत्ति होई। कहौं प्रगट पूछत हौं सौई।।
रिषि वसिष्ट सुनिके यह बोले। अधरमधुर मधुबानी खोले।

Chitraguptji ask Brahmaji

मैं हूँ कौन-कहाँते आयो। किहि कारण मोकौ उपजायो
उत्पन्न करन हार मम को है। हौं जानौं नाहि प्रभुजो है।।

Brahmaji said

चार वरन प्रगटै मो तन सौ। मुख बाहू अरू जांघ चरण सौ।।
अंग-अंग सौ उत्पत्ति जौई। भिन्न-भिन्न कहि दीने सोई।।

तूं प्रगटयौ सब सैं मेरे अंग प्रसंग।
ताकारण कायस्थ है, तेरे बरण निसंग।।

ब्रह्मा यह गति देखि विचारौ। निजमन चिंता सोच निहारे।।
ऐसो पुरुष चाहियत कोई। लेखो जगको राखै जोई।।
भलो बुरो कारन जग माही। जे जन करैं तिन्हैं भय नाही।।
शुभ करनी करि शुभ फल पावैं। अशुभ कर्म कौ डंड दिखावै।।

भलो बुरो कारण जग माही। जे जन करैं तिन्हैं भय नाही।।
नयन खोलि सन्मुख जो देखे। एक पुरुष इस्थित अवरेखे।।
श्याम स्वरूप कमल दल लोचन। चन्द्रवदन सुंदर दुःख मोचन।।
कमल दवात हाथ के माहीं। लखि विरंच काया की छाहीं।।
करजोरे ठाडो दरसावै। नमस्कार करि विनय सुनावै।।

Poet Raja Ram has described Chitraguptji katha in detail in *Doha-Chaupai* style. This composition of Raja Ram is a biographical poem (*Charitra Kavya*). It has both the qualities-*Charitra and Kavya.* The main character of this poem is Chitraguptji who is the Lord of Kayasth community. He has been created by Brahma. This poem is written in Braj Bhasha in *Doha and Chaupai* style, some other *Chhands* are also used in between. Poet has described about the birth of Chitraguptji, the cause of birth, the main job of Chitraguptji, his marriage, the birth of his sons, their names, significance of Durga Puja in Kayasth community etc.

Chaupai

बारह पुत्र भये सुखदाई। एक-एक ते जस अधिकाई।।
सुता मनोहर राजा जोई। श्रेष्ट आत्मज रवि को सोई।।

Doha

निहितै चारो सुत भये। एक-एक प्रवीन।।
तिनके नाम विचारकरि। भिन्न-भिन्न धरि दीन।।

Mathur, Bhatnagar, Srivastav, Saxena etc. are the names (surnames) of Kayasth clan who are the decendents of Chitraguptji.

Describing about the glory of God, the poet has clearly explained that every creature, beasts, birds, human, the entire account of this world, since-virtues, good and bad deeds are the results of *Shubh-Ashub Karmas* which have to be experienced after death, to produce the entire statement before Yamraj is the duty/responsibility of Chitraguptji.

In all, 53 couplets have been composed in the poem. These couplets are in self-surrendering (*Atma Nivedan*), the reflection of politeness, humbleness, ignorance, apology are clearly visible in these *Dohas* similar to *Vinay Patrika*. Some of the compositions during the Nizam's period were written in Persian because at that time, Persian was the official language, obviously no wonder that the impact of Persian might have seen in the poet's composition. Hence, while requesting, the poet says thus:

लिखें यवन अक्षर लखे तासौं हरि मन आनि।
अक्षर की परिशुद्धता यासौं होय न जानि।।
बालबोध अक्षर लिखैं छंद भंग नहि हो।।
पढ़न समय निरदोष ह्वै पुरूषन कविता जोय।।
हरि कृपा पूर्ण हि भई सौं दिन करौं बखान।।
कार्तिक बदी एकादशी वारशुक्र सुख खान।।
हौं अज्ञानी हीनमति ढीटढिटाई जान।।
क्षमाबड़नकौ है उचित लखि निजबाल अज्ञान।।
रे मन धरि हरि ध्यान होय मनोरथ सब सफल।।
लाज रखत भगवान राजाराम भक्तन दासं लखि।।

While composing this poem, if I have been rude anywhere, then Oh! my God, please forgive me considering it as an ignorance of a small child, "because it is a known fact that the younger ones always commit mistakes but elders always forgives them". How humble, polite and simple the poet is!

This is the quality of the great person. A few lines of Tulsi Das can be quoted here - "You are merciful, you have been a donor and myself a beggar". According to the old tradition of literary practice, the poets appreciated the City, State and the administration of that time. The poet had adopted Braj Bhasha, the language of his deities native Vihar's language, easy, sweet, full of melody, the language which was used by Sur Das who gave it a form of literary pattern with his unique talent.

Before Sur Das, no composition was written in Braj Bhasha. For the first time, Sur Das only used it for composing poetry and gave it a literary form. He decorated the simple *Jana Bhasha* (public language) with various *Sanskars* and established it as a literary, language.

Though Raja Ram Pershad was living in Hyderabad where Persian was the official language, still he created *Chitragupt Mahatm* in Braj Bhasha. While clarifying this, the poet said:

भागनगर बड़ भागी आति नाम हैदराबाद।
आसफ् की सरकार जो रहे सदा आबाद।।
चित्रगुप्त महिमा कथा निजआजाकृतपाय।।
बृजभाषा हरिभाषा लाखि यौं मन आयो चाय।।

Raja Ram Pershad was commanding high position in the Government of Nizam as well as in the Royal Palace. He was not only a good administrator but also a good literary figure. He was a scholar of Hindi and Persian languages. He is said to have translated books from Persian into Hindi but these documents are not available as it is over two hundred years since he passed away.

His book *'Chitragupt Mahatm'* has been published under the title *'Sri Chitragupt Ki Katha'* by Narhari Pershad Charitable Trust, Hyderabad-India in the year 2015.

After leading a successful and illustrious life Raja Ram passed away in 1782.

RAI SWAMI PERSHAD

Chapter – Three

Rai Swami Pershad

Raja Ram left behind the only son Swami Pershad. Swami Pershad was brought up by his maternal grandfather, Rai Chimna Lal Munshi, a Scholar of repute of his time. Swami Pershad married the daughter of Kumari Lal, Peshkar of Muslim Noble Himmat Yar Khan.

Swami Pershad was awarded the title of 'Rai' and the Mansab of 500 rupees per month. Later, Swami Pershad inherited the Peshkari of Asaf Garh Fort. After the death of Raja Ram, Nawab Sikandar Jah, Nizam-III, appointed Swami Pershad as Superintendent of the Royal Household. He had three sons, out of them, two sons, Narsing Pershad and Narayan Pershad died at the young age. Narhari Pershad, the second son survived, who was born in the year 1810 AD.

In his book *Sahu-O-Suragh*, Kalidas Gupta, a renowned Urdu scholar and writer wrote that non-de-plume (*Takhallus,* meaning the short name the poets assume) of Swami Pershad was *'Asghar'*. The tutor of Swami Pershad was Nawab Badruddin Khan, Amir-ud-Dowla *'Laiq'* who was in the employment of Nawab Sikandar Jah, Nizam-III. Swami Pershad was a Poet of Persian, Urdu and Hindi languages. His collection of Urdu *Gazals* in the form of manuscript is available.

Another famous Urdu scholar and writer, Naseeruddin Hashmi, in his book entitled *'Deccani Hindu Aur Urdu'* published in the year 1958 mentioned that the Persian and Urdu collection of poems of Swami Pershad is available at the Asafia Library, Hyderabad.

However, presently this manuscript is available under the reference *'Dawaween-501' Dakhala No.10677* at Government Oriental Manuscripts Library and Research Institute, Osmania University Campus, Hyderabad, India. This *Majmuvae Asghar* contains *Ghazals, Rektha, Rubai and Geet.* This is written in the year 1239 H (1822 A.D.).

The specimen pages of the Manuscript of Urdu book *Majmuvae Asghar* are given below:

هو الكريم

بسم الله الرحمن الرحيم

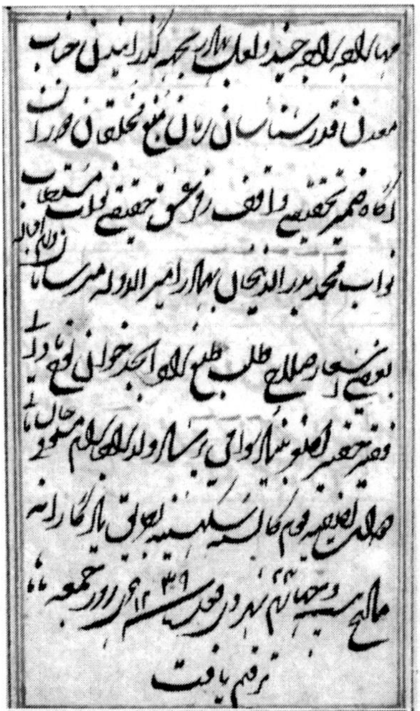

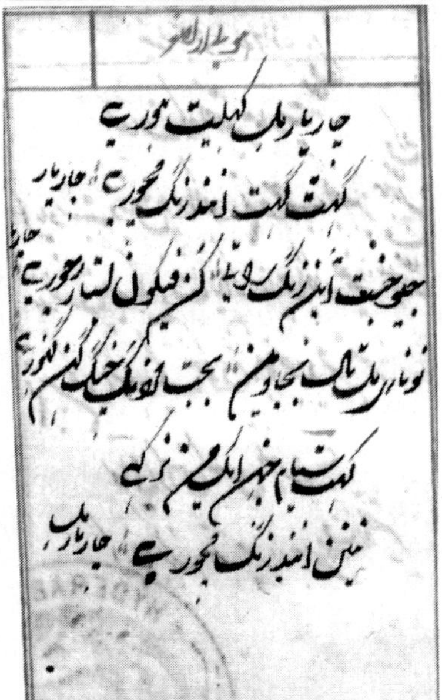

It may be noted that Rai Swami Pershad a staunch follower of *Sanathan Dharm* has started his book with *"Huwal Kareem" and "Bismillah-Hir-Rahman-Nirraheem"* (In the name of Allah, the most beneficient and merciful). The question therefore arises as to why he did so; it can be said with certainty that in those days there was no discrimination of caste and religion. Everyone respected each others' religion. The people were broadminded and civilised.

However, in these days there are some groups who do not have respect for other religions. There is certainly a discrimination of caste and religion. These people are narrow minded, uncivilised and fanatics. As a result, they refuse to say *'Vande Matram'*. If any Muslim says 'Jai Sri Ram' a 'Fatwa' is issued against him. This speaks volumes about mindset of the present day society specially the radical groups in our country. In other parts of the world these groups do not hesitate for a minute to destroy their own mosque. It is radicalism and nothing else. Such groups are trying to divide the country for their own benefit, if they succeed, it will have disastrous effect. Such groups should be denounced in the strongest words and crushed.

Dr Sheela Raj a noted historian wrote in her book *'Portrait of an Era'* that the collection of Urdu and Persian *Ghazaliyats* of Swami Pershad was compiled and also mentioned that a Marsia (Elegy) is found at Page-653 written by Swami Pershad in *Deccani Mukhtutat* in British Library, London.

Rai Swami Pershad wrote in Hindi under the non-de-plume 'Swami'.

Rai Swami Pershad was a great scholar of Hindi and had written in this language as well. His few stanzas of Hindi poem are given below:

जहाँ पायो तू पायोरे मन।। जहं।।

अंड पिंड ब्रह्मांड सकल तू।।

त्रिभुवन तू दरसायो।।

जल चर थल चर नभ चर तू ही।

तू ही तू तन भायो।।

निरगुण माया सहित सगुन है।

तू बैराट लखायो।

दृग दृष्टि दृष्टा दृपू साछी।

रूप जगत बनि आयो।

नर तूं हरि तूं तूं मन

'स्वामी' चेतन जडै रमायो।।

His other work in Hindi is *'Mann Updesh'*. In this composition, Swami Pershad addressed himself into *'Mann'* and stated – You have to keep total control, because, lust, anger, attachment, greed, jealousy and envy are main disorders and one has to be cautious about these. All the Saints and Mahatmas whoever controlled their minds (*Mann*) have conquered the world and worked for his welfare.

Human life is full of sorrows. To get rid of this life *(Moksha),* one has to keep aside his / her ego, be polite and take shelter under the seat of the *'Guru'*. Only after conquering his ego, one can obtain knowledge (*Gyan*). Even pilgrimage is a waste, without *Guru's Kripa* (Blessing). All these facts have been enlightened in the poem *Mann Updesh*.

In fact, Swami Pershad addressed his mind, the mental disturbances, pleasures, sorrows, sins, virtues, glory of *Guru* (Preacher) etc. in detail.

The *Mann* through which the process of churning (*Manthan)* takes place is called *'Mann'* (Mind). Mind instigates the indriyas to take the worldly luxury. Hence, it has to be controlled. One who conquers his mind becomes *Jitendriya.* But, it is unstable in nature. It is not easy to have control on it just as we can't control wind.

For obtaining mental purity or ***Chittashuddi,*** we have to be cautious about lust, anger, attachment, hope, luxuries, jealousy-envy etc. Therefore, all the great saints controlled their minds strongly and strived hard for the welfare of mankind.

The mind of a common man is deviated in many sides, even after experiencing all the luxuries, it never gets satisfied and becomes restless. Thus, it destroys precious human life.

The mind of an ordinary person, deviates in all directions, it remains dissatisfied even after enjoying all the comforts, it always gets agonised due to the bindings of society, thus it destroys life. Human mind accumulates carnal desires. This happens due to lack of sense of repression. There are two ways of sense of repression, *Abhyas* (Practice) and *Vairagya* (Detachment). Even impossible could be achieved by practice. The compulsions of sense – repression is admitted / accepted in parts of life – *Gyan Bhakti and Yoga.*

The poet addresses his mind and says – Oh mind! (*Mann*) please don't hope for wealth and women, it develops ego, and ego destroys the human body. The human body is acquired after wandering 84 lakh births. It is priceless which is not obtained repeatedly. One gets salvation only when he is free from all the desires.

Human life is sorrowful (Tragic) and not comfortable. There are more sorrows than pleasures. One has to be humble, abandon his ego and should take shelter at the feet of *Guru* (Preacher), to get rid of this world. Like other saints, even Swami Pershad acepted the theory of *"Guru Bin Gyan Na Hoye"* (No knowledge without Guru).

Oh mind! Don't feel proud for this mortal body, you always prefer money, prosperity and woman; you can conquer all these temptations with the help of *Guru* only. Otherwise, desires of Guru will always remain dissatisfied.

The person can be knowledgeable, suppressing his ego. Devotion, pilgrimages etc. are of no use. If there is no *Kripa* (Blessings) of *Guru* (Preacher), salvation is impossible. Hence, the poet is preaching the mind to surrender before *Guru*. The *Guru* is the same for a King or a Beggar. He provides the wisdom of *Nishkam* (Desire) *Karma*, who is worshipped by *Kalyug*, you take the shelter of such a Guru.

Rai Swami Pershad feels that this mind is tragic. There is more sorrow than pleasure, one has to be humble and should be above his ego and take shelter of the *Guru* to get rid of the world.

He used 4 *Krits,* 20 *pads,* 2 couplets and one *ashtapadi.* Its language is Braj Bhasha. This composition is still unpublished.

Swami Pershad wrote some *Skands of Sri Bhagwat Puran* which is written in Persian / Sanskrit / Braj Basha. The writers of this *Bhagwat Puran* are Lala Hukumat Rai, Swami Pershad and his son Narhari Pershad. Swami Pershad has affixed his seal at the end of each *Skand* he wrote to establish its authenticity.

This *Bhagwat Puran* which is about 600 pages remained unpublished. It is available at the Salar Jung Museum Library, Hyderabad, India, in the family collection of Raja Narsing Raj.

Swami Pershad visited Nasik, Tirambakeshwar. He passed away in the year 1822.

RAI NARHARI PERSHAD

Chapter – Four

Rai Narhari Pershad

As mentioned in the earlier chapter, Rai Swami Pershad had three sons– Narayan Pershad, Narhari Pershad and Narsing Pershad. Narayan Pershad and Narsing Pershad passed away at an early age. Narhari Pershad was the only surviving second son of Rai Swami Pershad.

After the death of Rai Swami Pershad, responsibility of the household affairs fell on the shoulders of Narhari Pershad. He was born in 1810 and he was 11 years old at the time of the death of his father. In 1822, Sikandar Jah, Nizam-III made Narhari Pershad, Incharge of Royal Kitchen and *Mashaal Khana.* Soon after the dismissal of Raja Balmukund, Narhari Pershad was found capable to be made *Sarrishtedar* of the *Sarf-I-Khas* Army, in 1846. Raja Balmukund was the head of the Customs Department, he was replaced by Raja Nanak Baksh of Peshkar Family in 1853. Raja Balmukund passed away on 17th April 1854.

Narhari Pershad was entrusted with the formidable task of organising the army in the capacity of *Sarrishtedar,* during the reign of Nawab Nasir-ud-Daula, Nizam-IV, to succeed his father. He awarded him *Jewels, Khillat* etc.

In the year 1858, the title 'Rai' was conferred on Narhari Pershad by Afzal-ud-Daula, Nizam-V on the occasion of Birth Day *Darbar* and a *Mansab* of 500 rupees per month.

Rai Narhari Pershad was a renowned scholar of Hindi and Sanskrit languages. He could converse in both the languages fluently. He wrote a number of books on different topics, such as, *'Narhari Gyan Updesh', 'Narhari Mal'* and *'Nahari Prakash'*, which were his scholarly works. 'Narhari Prakash' is the translation of *'Yog Vashisht'* into Hindi from Sanskrit language. It is said that it took almost 10 years to complete the translation of *'Yog Vashisht'*. (*'Yog Vashisht'* is a Hindu mythological book. The author of this book is generally believed to be Valmiki, the author of the Sanskrit epic *Ramayana*. In *'Yog Vashisht'* Valmiki narrates in detail the spiritual teaching of *Guru* Vashisht to Lord Rama, and it is a very lengthy description).

Rai Narhari Pershad worked in different capacities during the reign of three successive Nizams. Sikandar Jah, Nizam-III (1803–1829), Nasir-ud-Daula, Nizam-IV (1829-1957), and Afzal-ud-Daula, Nizam-V, (1857-1869). It is a known fact that Narhari Pershad saw many political disturbances in the State and the efforts of Sir Salar Jung, the then *Diwan*, to resolve normalcy and to reorganise State administration.

Narhari Pershad was also the witness to the establishment of the British Residency in Hyderabad and the British interference in day-to-day administration of the State. Narhari Pershad was also witness to the disturbances in the country during the Mutiny of 1857.

Narhari Pershad was not only elevated the status of the family but also established himself as a renowned and distinguished scholar. He was a great person, a true devotee, faithful employee and patriot; the symbol of Indian cultural tradition, an excellent person and a multilingual scholar. The rise of his literary accomplishment could be seen in '*Narhari Prakash'*. It is an outstanding gift to mankind. He was aware of the fact that *'Yog Vashisht'* was not translated into Hindi earlier. He, therefore, took up the task.

He had true love for his mother tongue, he therefore, wrote poems in Hindi. He had a command over languages and as well as in poetry. He expressed his emotions for Braj Basha in the following manner:

भाषा ब्रजभाषा जु है, बृजभूषण भगवान।

तिन चखन सुमिरण भजन वर्णन किया पुराण।

ज्ञान ध्यान सागर भरयो सो लहरें लहराय।

नरहरि दासानुदास रज ब्रजभाषा गुण गाय।।

Narhari Pershad considered himself enlightened and had divine love for the Supreme. He was especially interested in meditation and *Manan*. He used to address his deity Ram, Govind, Hari Jagannath, Vasudev and Krishna etc. The self enlightened Narhari Pershad never considered human life separately from God. He wrote:

नंद जसोयति जू के बालक। गोपाल गोविंद नायक।।

दुष्ट दलन सुधर्म स्थापना। गिरधारी धारे गोवर्धन।

जगन्नाथ जगदीश हरि। कलियुग मध्य सुजान

बुद्ध धरयों प्रभु रूप निज। भक्तन हित भगवान

विश्व पूर्ण प्रभु जीव लखाने, बिंब वही प्रतिबिंब सुहावै

एक रूप व्यापक जग माहि, ज्यौ बिछाह पर दिक माही।

As mentioned earlier, Narhari Pershad was a patriotic literary figure. He expressed his sentiments about his country (*Bharat*) in the following lines:

यह जो सप्तद्वीप कहिलावै। तामैं जंबूद्वीप सुहावै।।

तिहि में है नवखंड सुधामा। भरत खंड जिहि अविराम।

वही खंड माही तुम जाओ। वहाँ बसौ हरि के गुण गाओ

जनपद नगर देश तहे सोहैं। ग्राम सु भग जन मन कौ मोहैं

Swami Pershad died in 1822, Narhari Pershad was in his childhood days at that time. He was just 11 years old. Narhari Pershad described this incidence in his biography in the following lines.

माता-पिता यह दास के बाल अवस्था माहिं।

सुरपुर के वासी भये, रहयो छत्र नाहि छां है।

पिता दास के जानिए स्वामी प्रसाद कहाय।

जवै काल को काल लखि ध्यान धरे रघुराय।।

तिहि समय सेवक जु बय ग्यारा वर्ष लखाय।

मातु पिता ममता जु व्है सो बर्नी नहिं जाय।

अंत समय यह दास कौं पिता निकट बैठाय

जो कछु मन उपदेश हो सो बनै समुझाय।।

गुरु कारण आज्ञा दई हम गुरु द्वारे मांहि।

राधावल्लभ लाल-बिन दूजों कीऊँ नांहि।

मातु पक्ष गुरु द्वार जो तिहि शरणगत होय।

जिन नाना सौं मंत्र लै कीजै काज ही सोय।।

तात वचन गुरु जाति मन बड़ भागी निज पाय।

श्री सदगुरु चरणन शरण त्रिभुवन सुख दरसाय।।

In all, Narhari Pershad wrote five books which are *'Narhari Gyan Updesh'*, *'Narhari Maal'*, *'Narhari Prakash'*, *'Shree Bhagwat Puran'* and *'Narhari Pershad Kritik Awadhi Bhagwat'*.

Narhari Gyan Updesh:

It is composed by Narhari Pershad in Braj Bhasha. This is a dialogue between Uma and Maheshwar. This work is written in couplets, quatrain, *Sortha and Chhand*. It begins with the *Vandana* of the Almighty God. *Brahma* is an eternal force. The *Nirgun* described in *Ved Vedanta* is only *Brahma.* There are three elements of this *Parabrahmana – Sath* (Truth), *Chit and Anand* (Pleasure), *Sachchidanand* is also called *Sadanand,* the natural qualities *(Dharma).* The Brahma is called *Nirgun.* Similarly, when it is full of divine pleasure, virtue is called *Sagun.*

Surdas had clearly mentioned that the *'Almighty'* who is all over and present everywhere, cannot be expressed and it is very difficult to understand Him, know Him. Hence, it is very easy to worship *Sagun* form of God. The soul is ignorant; it gets trapped in the illusions of this mortal world and forgets itself. Only Guru can clear this ignorance. Due to ignorance and misconception, the soul undergoes many difficulties and tortures. The difference of knowledge *(Vidya)* and ignorance arises due to illusion *(Maaya).* It forgets itself and it gets deviated. Hence, the well-being of human life is hidden in *Bhagwad Bhajan.* We need the blessings and knowledge of *Satguru* to acquire *Bhagwad Gyan.*

In his composition, Poet, Narhari Pershad elaborated the creation made of *Panch Mahabhutas,* life, creatures, movables and immovables etc. Human body is considered as the best among 84 lakh births. But the humans (birth) love for their purpose and forget that, their soul is a part of *Paramatma.* This ocean like world can be crossed with the help of knowledge and we need a *Guru* to give us this knowledge.

In this poem, *Guru Gyan,* Narhari Pershad had analysed, the main spiritual substance of the world through Shiva and Parvathi. The creation made of *Panch Mahabhutas* where the God *Shagun* and *Nirgun* (visible and invisible), dual and non-dual, has *Satva, Raj* and term qualities. This world has many impurities like lust, anger, fascination etc. The world is mortal, one has to practise, *Pranayam, Yogsadhana, hathyog, Somyan – Sadhana* to acquire freedom for devotion.

The ignorance of the person can be evacuated only by Guru. Guru is greater than Govind. We can understand Govind through Guru only. Our doubt can be cleared by Guru only. It is fortunate to regret by *Satgurus*. The glory of Guru has been described by Lord Shiva himself before Parvathi in *Narhari Gyan*.

Narhari Pershad was associated with the *Darbar* of Nizam of Hyderabad. He, therefore, according to the old tradition, started the poem with *Ganesh Vandana, Satguru Vandana* etc. At some places, ruler has been praised. Through this poem, he tried to explain *Atmagyan* and the importance of *Guru*.

बहुरौ गणपति सीस नवाऊँ। मंगलदायक कृपालु पाऊँ।।

तासौ सतगुरु चरण निहारौ, परस प्रेमरस पाय परवारौ।।

This poem consists of Shiva Parvathi dialogue. Couplets, quatrains *Sorthas* and *Chhand* have been used in it. The format is similar to *Ram Charithra Manas* and *Kavitha Bali* of Tulasi Das.

In *Mangala Charan* poet says that Brahma is integrated, non-dual and *Anadi*. The *Nirgun* who is described in *Vedas* etc. is only *Prabrahma*. It has three fonts – *Sat, Chit* and *Anand–Satchidanand*. He is also called *Sadanand*. The same Brahma is called as *'Nirguna'* in the absence of natural *Dharmas*. He is also known as *'Shaguna'* because of having ecstatic qualities. Actually, *Nirgun* only converts into *Shagun*. All Saints agreed with this element.

Surdasji had clearly mentioned that God is everywhere and He is inspirable and it is very difficult to understand and know Him. So, the worship of this *Shagun* form is simple and easy. The creature is ignorant, world is temporary, creature gets trapped in the worldly luxuries and relations and forgets its own existence. This ignorance can be clear through *Guru* only. The glory of *Guru* has been described by all the Saints and *Mahatmas*. 'No knowledge without *Guru* is a fact'.

After describing the glory of *Shiva-Parvathi*, the poet has emphasised the self enlightenment. Narhari Pershad has tried to explain through Shiva-Parvathi dialogue. *Guru* acquired the very high position in the realm of knowledge. *Guru* is treated superior to God. Therefore, all the Saints have stressed the importance of *Guru*.

In *Narhari Gyan,* poet has described about *Guru* and his knowledge through *Pratyaksh Shiva*.

Doha:

गुरु कीजिये जानि कै, निज मन समुझि विचार।

पूरन चेतन ब्रह्मगुरु, जाहि मिलै सोपार।।

The poet has successfully tried to explain such a deep thought in easy and simple Braj Bhasha through *Dohas, Chaupai* and *Chhand.*

The book *Narhari Gyan* is available at Salar Jung Museum Library, Hyderabad, India, under the family collection of Raja Narsing Raj.

Narhari Maal

In *Narhari Maal,* the poet has described Indian culture. He had narrated Indian festivals, functions, ceremonies and expressed his views to the people. He has also described about the activities which take place during the above celebrations. He conveys that the present generation is forgetting Indian culture, so the poet has tried to pursue the ancient culture, the significance of which is slowly disappearing. But in certain odd situation this composition is helpful to revive the feelings of humanity among the young generation. Indian culture is sketched through Bhajans in *Narhari Maal.*

त्रिभुवन रास रचाओ मोहन, रूप अनूप सहायो मो,

आद मुरलिया नाद मनोहर चेतन जडै रिका यो

गोकुल तन बन माहि गोपिन दैर सरुचि यो मोहन

चौदह मंडल रास रचाओ जुगल मध्य एक पाओ

खिआनंद समाज बेदमुख नेतनीतिगा-यो

राधे कृष्ण विलास निहारित नरहरि आनंद छायो।

धमा राग-छायानट

आज हरि होरी मचायो ब्रजनारी के संग

कहु फुहार रंग प्रेम भिजावत कहुं कुछ

लाल गुलाल बंदन कुच मंडित लहरत का मतरंग

राधे कृष्णा बिहार निहारत नरह,

मल्हार

सरवीरी यह सावन की डुरिया सखी

धन गरजत चमकत अति बिजुरी बरसत मोतिन लरिया

जानत हौं पिय बिन नहि भावत, जूलन अरियांबरि

ताही छिन पाती पियपा ई बाँहससी गहि अरियाँ

This book is available at Salar Jung Museum Library, Hyderabad, India, under the family collection of Raja Narsing Raj.

Narhari Prakash

Narhari Prakash written by Narhari Pershad is the first Hindi verse translation of '*Yog Vashisht*'. It was transformed in the year 1856.

'*Yog Vashisht*' is the poetic spiritual composition written in *Sanskirt*. It is also known as '*Maha Ramayan*', '*Argh Ramayan*', '*Vashisht Ramayan*', '*Gyan Vashisht Ramayan*'. It is said that it had 32,000 *Sholakas*, but in the edition published in 1918 by Nirnaya Sagar Press, Bombay, there are only 27,687 *Sholakas*. Sometime back, in '*Achyut Granth Mala*', the entire composition with its Hindi translation was published by '*Gowri Shankar Goenka Samarpit Nidhi*'. In 1837, English translation was published from Calcutta which is more popular than *'Sampoorn Yog Vashisht'*. It is known as *'Laghu Yog Vashisht'*. It was written by a Kashmiri Pandit and Pandit Abhinanda Gaud in the ninth century. This was translated into Persian by *Dara Shikoh*. The hand written copies are available in many museums.

'Yog Vashisht' is wonderful and great spiritual composition in which knowledge and accomplishment both have been analysed elementally. It is stated in 'Yog Vashisht' that by reading this *'Shastra'* repeatedly and by using the principles formulated in this composition, a person acquires great virtues. Just by listening to this composition only supreme knowledge can be obtained and the soul starts experiencing salvation.

Indian Saint, Swamy Ramteerth had even told that, *'Yogvashisht'* is one of the best and unique books of the world. It is impossible that someone who reads this book and doesn't aquire *'Brahma Bhavna'*.

There are seven chapters in *Yog Vashisht – Narhari Prakash*

(1) *Vairagya,* (2) *Mumuksha,* (3) *Utpatti,* (4) *Sthiti,* (5) *Upasham,* (6) *Nirvan Poorvardh* and (7) *Nirvan Uttavardh.*

In the **first chapter**, the poet has emphasised that the person has to be always curious about the creation *(Srishti)* to obtain self-knowledge *(Atmagyan)* and he has to make efforts. The endeavour of Shukdev is an ideal example of the curiosity of human beings and he tried to solve the doubts raised about the *Srishti*, successful.

In the **second chapter**, *"Mumuksh"* he has tried to explain the different ways of getting salvation through Rishi Vashishta.

In the **third chapter,** the author has tried to highlight the importance of the unlimited power of human body and the slogan of *'Atma-so-Parmatma'*, which means that 'Soul' is part of *'Parmatma'*.

The **fourth chapter** is *"Sthiti Prakaran"*, in which, the poet has tried to explain to *'Janta Janardan'* that how mankind is under the grip of this illusive world, and is committing mistakes of ruining his own existence. He has explained it by citing the example of the story of Shukracharya. Again his father Bhagu tries to explain him about reality. It proves that, even the Saints *(Rishimuni)* get attached towards this illusive world.

The **fifth chapter,** *"Upasham"– 'Upa'* means near and Sham means solution. Man is the slave of *indriyas.* The verbal meaning of *'Upasham'* is control on these desires. How a person can be detached from worldly affairs, is described here. In this chapter, the poet has formulated the forms of *'nirguna'* and *'sagun brahma'* and discussed about their alternatives.

Through the **sixth chapter** *'Nirvan'* the poet has formulated the importance of *Karmayoga* on the basis of *sat, Raj* and *tamo guna. Nirvan* chapter is the extract of this poem.

The research on the unlimited capacity of *Chittavrithi* and mind is possible in the contemporary period. A person can understand, through a particular science that he can overcome many difficulties of life, such as, the importance and the dignity of women.

The **seventh chapter** *"Narhari Geeta"* is an independent chapter, which comprises *'Geeta Upadesh'.*

In fact, *'Yog Vashisht'* is the Ganges of non-dual *Vedantha,* which is driven from the Himalaya. There is a wonderful *Sangam* (junction) of philosophical Yamuna and statistical Saraswati. Person acquires knowledge and *Purusharth* develops by studying this Triveni and one can become a world level successful citizen.

Vashisht has advised everybody to develop their *Purusharth* and to make their own fortune.

नरहरी परशाद रचित 'नरहरी प्रकाश' की कुछ पंक्तियाँ द्रष्टव्य है-

योगवशिष्ठ इच्छा मन भाई। सोतो सागर सम दरसाई।

ता में कुदिप रयो एक बारा। तुंम बिन कौन करे अब पारा।।

जो तुप कृपा दृष्टि है जावै। छिन में बेड़ा पार लखावै।

जिमि हनुमंत नाम आधार। सागर फाँदि गयो इक बारा

यह तर सौ वह तरै लंघाई। प्रभु कटाक्ष दृष्टि जब पाई।।

रघुबर नाम प्रताप सहाई। भवसागर सौ पार व्है जाई।।

मैं कवि जनम नाम जो लीन्हयो। यह सागर पर नमन दीन्हयो।

दास जानि बिनती सुनि लीजै। जहाँ अशुद्ध शुद्ध तहं करितै।।

A seminar was organised in Kashi to discuss about and evaluate *'Narhari Prakash'*. The copies of *'Narhari Prakash'* were distributed among the scholars and pundits. More than 500 scholars had assembled and participated in the discussion. After the discussion, scholars declared that *'Narhari Prakash'* is a true and correct translation of *'Yog Vashisht'* and a high literary achievement. Nahari Pershad was honoured with citation.

Unfortunately, the writer of *'Narhari Prakash'* though a renowned Hindi writer, had never been appreciated because he belonged to the southern part of India. Somehow, with his own efforts, he was able to get his composition recognised (attested) by the Kashi Scholars. Unfortunately, this remained out of the sight of historians of Hindi literature. Thus, a 'unique' work of a renowned poet remained unknown in the literary world.

'Narhari Prakash' is not only a significant composition but it is the first and last work consisting the *Triveni* of devotion, knowledge and salvation. The poet spent about 10 years in translating 'Narhari Prakash' from Sanskrit into Hindi.

This composition though the translation of '*Yog Vashisht*' but the poet has written it in the contemporary Braj Bhasha. The deep *Shlokas* quoted in '*Yog Vashisht*', reflect the secretive *Soothras* and meaning, therefore, the poet has not only translated them but he has transformed them independently which need the indepth knowledge and poetic ability. Narhari Pershad was well known and a learned person. He was in the official service of the Nizam of Hyderabad.

One more speciality of this composition is that it is written in the narrator and listener style, similar to '*Ramcharita Manas*' of Tulsidas, the way Tulsidas started his epic with *Mangalacharan,* the same tradition has been followed in this work. It is a fact that *Ramayan* by Tulsidas is a legendary work accepted by various *Puranas* as a self-ecstatic and ideal for human life. Similarly, '*Narhari Prahash*' is work of self-ecstasy for its poet i.e. style and at the same time the listener too takes a dip in self-satisfaction. The mysticism (*Rahasyavad*) of *Advait* (non-duality) *matt*, has been reflected in this work and the poet seems to be compatible with Kabir's '*Yog Sadhana*' *Surati* and *Sahaj Marg*. By describing about the *Anhad* and seven *Chakras* located in our body, the poet has sketched a live picture for his readers.

Thus, the '*Mumuksh Prakaran*', enlightens Lord Ram by '*Vashisht*' to acquire the ability of '*Nijaswaroop Sakshatkar*'.

Narhari Prakash comprises the story derived from various stories. The poet has narrated the secret of this creation. Vashisht explains Shri Ram about the unlimited strength / power of human body. He establishes the theory of '*Atma–Paramatma*' through different stories.

The '*Mann*' (Mind) of the devotee always blossoms like a golden lotus. Pleasure and sorrow, day and night are the same for him. Therefore, one is *Sthit Pragya* (stable) and is regretted in his *Jeevanmukth* (Life).

Similarly, in *Sthiti Prakaran*, Narhari Pershad has highlighted the condition of this world.

Narhari Prakash is the *'Upasham'* which analyses how one can remain indifferent to this *Sansar* (world). The word *'Upasham'* means 'up' *'Sham'* means solution. A human being is a slave of five senses. *(Panch Indriyas).* Thus, the verbal meaning of *Upasham* is prevention or control over the desires related to five senses.

Very few poets of Hindi literature have described *Yoga Sadhana* in such an exact and effective manner, as Narhari Pershad did.

The poet has also described about *'Nirgun'* and *'Shagun'* the two forms of God. The *'Nirgun'* element is acquired through *'Gyan Sadhana'* whereas a *'Shagun'* form of devotion is obtained through *'Sahaj Yoga Bhakti'*. The objective is the same but, according to convenience and interest, the devotee may adopt either of the two faiths.

It is a very difficult task for a person to keep away from these worldly affairs *(Maaya).* Any one can accumulate the materialistic wealth but very few persons can conquer their anger, madness, attachment etc. Undoubtedly, the way poet, with the help of his talent and imaginary vision, has described *'Mukti Marg'*, *'Brahma Sadhana'* and devotion in *Yog Vashishst* can really help guide a person to understand the correlation between his real existence and supreme substance of this creation and can become competent enough to do something for his society.

Narhari Pershad has also highlighted the significance of *'Sat'*, *'Raj'* and *'Karmayog'*. *'Nirvan Prakaran'* is the extract of this composition. Through the following lines, the poet has tried to clarify this fact:

हे रघुवर ब्रह्मज्ञान जो वेदांत कहात है।
करो प्रवेश सुजान मन निश्चय सत सत्य धरि।।
वचन गुरु को श्रवणकरि ताकौ मनहिविचारि।
सौ पावै तत सार कौ, आत्मस्वरूप निहारि।।

तीनि शब्द वेदांत के गुण रूपी कहिलाय।
सतगुण रजगुण और तम कारण जगत लखाय।।
दश प्रकार सौ जानिये इन सबके बिस्तार।
सो बनौ श्रवणन सुनौ एकन एक सार।।

Now the question arises as to why Narhari Pershad had chosen *'Yog Vashisht'* for translation. Probably none of the scholar has tried to transform this *'Vedgranth'* before him. In fact, *'Yog Vashishst'* is the Ganges of non-dual *'Vedanta'* which is drived from the Himalaya of *Upanishad*. When *Yamuna* of philosophy and *Saraswathi* of *'Sakhya Shestra'* come and meet the Ganges then it becomes *Triveni* of Indian philosophy.

The main objective of this composition is that human beings themselves are responsible for the success and failure of their lives. Life is another name of struggle. No eternal force is helpful in the struggle of life but the person only can make his life successful or destroy it too.

'Yog Vashishst' is a unique *'Granth'* (Composition) of *'Vedant Darshan'*. Narhari Pershad has shown his interest to translate it because he felt that it is the most suitable *'Granth'* for the world. The facts which can contribute to the welfare of mankind are certified and relevant and even they are non-suspicious. Presently, though the circumstances are changed still discrepancies and inequalities are the same. Their forms have changed. Such compositions can play key role to make the human lives more meaningful, there is no doubt about it. It is an outstanding gift to the mankind.

As mentioned earlier, *Narhari Prakash* was published in the year 1856. However, the new edition of *Narhari Prakash* was published in the year 2005 at Hyderabad.

The original manuscript *Narhari Prakash* is available in Salar Jung Museum Library, Hyderabad, India, under the collection of the family of Raja Narsing Raj.

Shree Bhagwat Puran

Shree Bhagwat Puran written by Lala Hukumat Rai, Rai Swami Pershad and Narhari Pershad. This *Shree Bhagwat Puran* is written in Urdu script, using Persian, Sanskrit and Braj Bhasha. As mentioned earlier, Rai Swami Pershad wrote some of the *Skands* and after his demise, Narhari Pershad wrote the remaining *Skands* and completed *Bhagwat Puran*. This *Bhagwat Puran* is about 600 pages. *Bhagwat Puran* needs no introduction, hence the details are not provided here.

It is in the form of a manuscript. It is available at Salar Jung Museum Library, Hyderabad, India, under the family collection of Raja Narsing Raj.

Narhari Pershad Kritik Awadhi Bhagwat

Narhari Pershad wrote Bhagwat in Awadhi language consisting of about 1000 pages. This Bhagwat was published in the year 2014 till such time it was in the form of a manuscript preserved by the family.

The copies of *Narhari Pershad Kritik Awadhi Bhagwat* are available at the Lok Sabha Secretariat Library, New Delhi, Sahitya Akadami, New Delhi, Raza Library, Rampur, Khuda Baksh Library, Patna, Swami Vivekananda Library, Hyderabad. This is probably the only Bhagwat written in Awadhi language.

A research dissertation leading to M.Phil. in Hindi has been done on Narhari Pershad in the year 2008 at Maulana Azad National Urdu University, Hyderabad, India. The topic of this dissertation was '*Narhari Pershad Ki Rachanaon Ka Mulyankan*'. It was written by Umesh Kumar Sharma.

In memory of Rai Narhari Pershad, a Gold Medal has been instituted for the student who tops M.Phil. in Hindi at Maulana Azad National Urdu University, Hyderabad, India.

A Charitable Trust has been created in the year 2001 in the memory of Rai Narhari Pershad known as ***'Narhari Pershad Charitable Trust'***, in Hyderabad.

Views of different scholars and writers about Rai Narhari Pershad:

— Gafoor Ahmed in his article on Raja Mahbub Nawazwant *'Baqi'* in *'Murraq-E-Sukhan'* published in the year 1935 wrote that the father of *'Baqi'* (Narhari Pershad) was a renowned scholar of Sanskrit and author of several books.

— Dr Syed Mohiuddin Qadri *'Zore'* in his book entitled *'Dastan-E-Adab-E-Hyderabad'* published in 1951 wrote that Narhari Pershad was a great scholar of Sanskrit and author of several books.

— Professor Mughni Tabassum wrote in *'Deewan-E-Mahboob'* that Narhari Pershad was a dignified person who held high positions.

RAJA GIRDHARI PERSHAD alias Bansi Raja

Chapter – Five

Raja Girdhari Pershad Mahbub Nawazwant 'Baqi' *Alias* Bansi Raja

A number of examples can be cited of the mutual confidence between Mir Mahbub Ali Khan Nizam-VI and his subjects, but impartial historians will agree that the relations between Bansi Raja and Nizam-VI were closely knit. There was no equal to Bansi Raja for his sincerity, faithfulness, loyalty, affection to his sovereign, a rare example which undoubtedly finds a place in the pages of history of the Asaf Jahi dynasty.

The details of the early education of Bansi Raja are not available but it is said that he learnt Persian from his tutors Hazrath Mohammed Ali and Urdu from Hazrath Hafiz Mohammed Shamsuddin 'Faiz'. 'Faiz' was a renowned Urdu poet. Bansi Raja was considered to be a brilliant student and completed his education at a very early age. He was closely associated with the learned scholars and developed the taste of poetry right from his childhood. Dwarka Pershad 'Ufaq' of Lucknow mentioned that the name 'Bansi Raja' was given by Nizam-VI and his pen name was 'Baqi'. During his childhood Bansi Raja spent most of his time in reading and writing.

Bansi Raja had only two surviving children from the first wife; a son, Keshav Pershad who was the Assistant Accountant

General in the Government of Nizam, and a daughter, Silo Rani, who married Rai Ram Pershad. Bansi Raja's first wife passed away in the year 1874 after a brief illness.

On the insistence of Rairayan Raja Maharaja Narender Pershad, the then Peshkar, and Sir Salar Jung-I, Bansi Raja married for the second time the daughter of Rai Bansidhar, son of Rai Alamchand, who was the Secretary to the then Peshkar. In fact, Bansi Raja was very much aggrieved and upset on the death of his first wife. He was not at all interested in marrying the second time.

The engagement ceremony took place at Keshavgiri, where Raja Narender Pershad, the Peshkar graced the occasion personally. The Prime Minister, Sir Salar Jung, along with his two sons, also attended the ceremony.

In 1851, Shambu Pershad was deposed and the services of Bansi Raja were utilised for settling the salaries of the army. He amicably did the settlement and as a result Shah-Yar-Mulk was very much pleased and personally called on Rai Narhari Pershad, the father of Bansi Raja and expressed his happiness over the ability of his son Girdhari Pershad. He expressed his desire to appoint him as a *Sarishtedar* of his army. Bansi Raja was young at that time; therefore, Shah-Yar-Mulk assured his father that he would take the entire responsibility of training Bansi Raja as *Sarishtedar*.

When Bansi Raja established himself as *Sarishtedar* of the army of Shah-yar-Mulk, thereafter, Bansi Raja had to join the services of the Nizam at the instance of his father to continue to assume the ancestral responsibility. His father had decided to retire from service due to his old age. Sir Salar Jung-I, the then Prime Minister and an able administrator, found Bansi Raja the most capable person. As a result, Bansi Raja became his most trusted man. Salar Jung-I entrusted him with the responsibility of organising Regular Forces of the Nizam. Bansi Raja accepted the responsibility with self-determination, diligence and hard work. In the year 1862, the Regular Troops were organised. As a result, Bansi

Raja was made the *Sarishtedar* of Regular Troops. The formation of Regular Troops and *Nazm-i-Jamiat* was a notable contribution of Bansi Raja.

Bansi Raja had the monopoly of offering ***itr*** and ***pan*** during the Moghlai and English *Darbar* and on the occasions of *Darbars*, held outside Hyderabad.

He was a fair complexioned, beardless person of medium height and very active. He was always present in the Nizam's Palace in the traditional dress of '*Dastar*', '*Jama*' and '*Neema*' or '*Dagla*' with his family headgear and '*Patka*' round the waist. Bansi Raja was assigned many more duties.

Sir Salar Jung assigned Bansi Raja a typical and a very delicate task of acting as a mediator between himself and Shams-ul-Umra, Amir-i-Kabir. Bansi Raja handled this delicate task successfully. Both the parties expressed satisfaction and confidence over the selection of Bansi Raja as a mediator. It is a fact that Bansi Raja had good relations with the families of Sir Salar Jung, and *Paigah*. All of them felt that Bansi Raj would surely handle situation delicately without damaging any one's sentiment whatsoever. In fact, Bansi Raja handled it as per their expectations.

Raja Girdhari Pershad was nominated on different committees by the Government of Hyderabad, such as, those for the famine relief, matters related to the public controversy, communal harmony and scholarships.

It is a fact of the history that Bansi Raja had the honour of becoming the tutor of the young Nizam, Mir Mahbub Ali Khan. In fact, Mahbub Ali Khan recognised his services during his young age and when he took the reign of the government in 1884, after the death of Sir Salar Jung-I, he was interested in having a trusted person like Bansi Raja.

In 1884, Bansi Raja was honoured with '*Naubat*', '*Roushan Chowki*' and '*Ambari*' at his palace by Mir Mahbub Ali Khan, Nizam-VI. These honours were the crowning symbols of the degrees of the success of Bansi Raja. He was also granted a '*Mansab*' of Rs 1,500 and the title of 'Raja Bahadur'.

It was a very special and unforgettable day in the life of Raja Girdhari Pershad when on the occasion of the Birth Day *Darbar* in 1894 the Nizam of Hyderabad, Mir Mahbub Ali Khan conferred on him a unique title 'Mahbub Nawazwant' a *'Mansab'* of Rs 3,000, a band of 2,000 *'Sawars'*, *'Alam'* and *'Naqara'*. This was a rare gesture from Nizam-VI which Bansi Raja rightly deserved. This title was obviously a belated acknowledgement of the services which Bansi Raja had rendered to the Government of Nizam. It is pertinent to mention that the name 'Mahbub' was bestowed as the title to this fortunate man in 1894. This rare gesture was in recognition of the fact that Nizam had great attachment and appreciation for the services of Bansi Raja. This distinction remained a symbol of honour, dignity and pride for the future generation of the family.

One of the responsibilities of Bansi Raja was to organise and make all arrangements for the *Darbars,* both Mughlai and English. He had the distinction of offering *'Itr'* and *'Pan'* at the conclusion of *Darbar*. This was not only the honour to Bansi Raja but to his entire family. After the death of Bansi Raja the responsibility to offer *'itr'* and *'pan'* on the occasion of *Darbars* was entrusted to his son, Raja Narsing Raj.

It was customary that Nizam would bestow jewels on the appointment of *Diwan* and *Peshkar* and other nobles on the occasion of their marriages. The responsibility of recommending the jewels to be bestowed to the nobles rested with Bansi Raja.

Raja Shivraj Dharamwant of the Malwala Palace had the privilege of recommending the 'titles' to the Nizam, he being the head of the office of *Manasib-O-Khitabat*.

In 1894, the Nizam enquired from Bansi Raja, the procedure followed in the past for bestowing jewels and robes of honour to be presented to Viqar-ul-Umra on his appointment as the *Diwan* or the Prime Minister. As usual, Bansi Raja made all the arrangements for the *Darbar* organised at *Khilwat* adhering to the Asaf Jahi tradition. In the very same *Darbar*, Bansi Raja was awarded the title of 'Mahbub Nawazwant'.

It may be mentioned here that the *Darbars* were not only the backbone of the Nizams Court but they were the specimen of pomp and splendour. These *Darbars* were usually held late in the evenings. The *Darbar* hall was brilliantly illuminated with beautiful crystal chandeliers. The musicians with their musical instruments in the traditional fashion used to perform on such occasions. The glamour of the *Darbar* dazzled the eyes of the spectators.

The *Darbars* were generally organised on the occasion of the visits of Governor General or the British Residents. They were referred to as English *Darbars*.

The Mughlai *Darbars* were organised on the occasions of *Eid*, *Dussehra*, *Diwali, Holi* and *Nouroz* etc. The Mughlai *Darbars* were also organised on the occasions of the appointments of *'Diwan'* and *'Peshkar'*.

The differences between the Arabs and the Rohillas were common in Hyderabad. It was generally accepted that even Arabs and Rohillas who were known for the turbulence had great respect for Bansi Raja. In view of this fact, he resolved the disputes between the two classes and the government, amicably.

In the year 1884, there was a turbulence in Hyderabad city. As a result of this, the peaceful atmosphere of the city was disturbed. In order to bring the situation under control and restore peace and normality the regular forces have to be deployed by placing a gun on the roof top of Mecca Masjid.

On the 10th *Moharram* 1302 Hijri (30th October 1884), there was some dispute between the children belonging to Sultan Nawaz Jung, an Arab, *Jamedar* and the Police, which resulted in the massacre of the policemen. The disturbances spread all over the city which resulted in the closure of shops.

Salar Jung-II, the then Prime Minister reported the matter to the Nizam and requested to depute Afsar Jung, the then Commander-in-Chief.

Afsar Jung treating the situation serious suggested to the Nizam that it was not the appropriate time for the deployment of the army. In order to bring normalcy, Afsar Jung sought Nizam's permission to meet Sultan Nawaz Jung who was the Arab *Jamedar* of *Nazm-i-Jamiat.* It was later decided that Akbar Jung, the then *Kotwal* to take over all police stations and law and order to maintain peace. However, Akbar Jung was hesitant to take the charge of such a tense situation. As a result, Golconda Brigade took over the charge.

Later, Mir Mahbub Ali Khan, Nizam-VI, appointed a commission. After thorough investigation, the commission came to the conclusion that Sultan Nawaz Jung and his troops were at fault, and that they should be fined an amount of Rs one lakh and sent out of the Hyderabad State. This recommendation was brought to the notice of Nizam and Salar Jung-II. However, the news also reached Sultan Nawaz Jung. He started planning for more disturbances and to have a confrontation with the government.

Afsar Jung was ordered by Nizam to control the situation. It was decided that the gun should be placed on Mecca Masjid facing towards the palace of Sultan Nawaz Jung in such a direction that if it was fired, it should directly hit the bedroom of Sultan Nawaz Jung. It was impossible for Sultan Nawaz Jung to escape the attack. The planning was perfect.

Later, Salar Jung-II handed over the '*Chobdar*' the order of the Nizam, ordering Sultan Nawaz Jung to leave Hyderabad immediately. The *Chobdar* was instructed to accompany Bansi Raja. Raja Girdhari Pershad was selected by the Nizam as he has full trust in him to handle this delicate mission.

Afsar Jung briefed Raja Girdhari Pershad that before handing over the orders, Sultan Nawaz Jung should be informed that the army has been deployed and surrounded his palace and as well as Mecca Majid. The army and the gun placed on Mecca Masjid would destroy his palace, if Sultan Nawaz Jung hesitated to obey Nizam's order.

Sultan Nawaz Jung had prior information about the army deployment before Girdhari Pershad reached his palace. On arrival, Bansi Raja was received at the main gate of the palace by Sultan Nawaz Jung. Under these circumstances, Sultan Nawaz Jung had no alternative left but to surrender. He requested Raja Girdhari Pershad that Nizam should permit him eight days time to leave Hyderabad.

Raja Girdhari Pershad returned and informed Salar Jung-II. His Highness granted eight days permission to Sultan Nawaz Jung. Later, Mir Mahbub Ali Khan, Nizam-VI, pardoned him on 20th April 1886 and permitted Sultan Nawaz Jung to enter into the city.

Mir Mahbub Ali Khan, made use of sacred place like Mecca Masjid for maintaining peace and utilised the services of a Hindu at that critical juncture.

It can therefore be concluded that Nizam and the government did not have any hesitation in using the sacred place like Mecca Masjid for maintaining law and order, to avoid bloodshed of the innocent people, unlike these days some Radical group are using sacred places to create disturbances, murders and taking life of the innocent people. These Radical groups and fanatic are not only making use of sacred Masjid, for creating disturbances but damaging the holy places. They have no respect for their own religion.

Erstwhile Hyderabad State was one of the few places in India where the Hindu-Muslim harmony existed. Nizam maintained perfect harmony between various classes. He himself was a man who believed in unity between the classes.

The present day politicians should take the lesson from this historical fact. But it is unfortunate that the politicians themselves are indulging and responsible for communal disturbances in India.

Hyderabad State was not an exception and was prone to periodical famines of more or less severe nature. The government constituted a Famine Committee during 1876-1877. Bansi Raja was one of the members of the Famine Committee. The Committee had to ascertain the condition of the peasants of various famine stricken areas.

Lord Rippon, the British Viceroy, visited Hyderabad in 1884 to attend the Installation Ceremony of Mir Mahbub Ali Khan, Nizam-VI. Bansi Raja was one of the members of the Managing and Reception Committee for making all necessary arrangements.

In 1885, it so happened that the festival of *Dassehra* coincided with *Moharram*. In the past, in the years 1852, 1854 and 1855 *Dassehra* festival coincided with *Moharram*. During that time, it was decided that *Dassehra* festival should be celebrated in houses and the band should not be taken out.

However, during 1885, it was decided by the government to consult Hindu nobles on the matter. A Committee was constituted for the purpose. This Committee was consisted of Raja Shivraj, the then Head of Malwala Family; Bansi Raja; Raghunath Rao from the Estate of Rai Rayan and Rasool Yar Khan. After long discussions, the committee submitted its recommendations to the government. The government issued order based on the recommendations of the committee. The Hindus were permitted to celebrate *Dassehra* and they were allowed to visit temples and use of band. However, the use of band was prohibited in public places, but permitted inside the temple.

A committee was constituted which included two Hindu nobles, Bansi Raja and Raja Shivraj to ensure that Hindus also get scholarship for going abroad for higher studies.

The government made an attempt in 1892 to negotiate with the *'Jagirdars'* and appointed a commission under the chairmanship of Nawab Viqar-ul-Umara. Raja Murali Manohar was appointed Secretary of the commission. The commission consisted of notable nobles and *jagirdars*. Raja Girdhari Pershad was appointed as one of the members of the commission. The main aim of the commission was to negotiate to abolish all the *Abkari* rights of the *jagirdars* by giving them compensation.

Bansi Raja's counsel was frequently sought by Mir Mahbub Ali Khan and his opinion was never disregarded. He was consulted in routine and also in confidential matters. It so happened that during the time of the marriage of Najeebunnisa Begum the sister of Nizam-VI, Bansi Raja came out with a valuable suggestion. For this marriage, Bansi Raja was instructed to take the money from *Diwani* to meet the expenses of the marriage. He advised Nizam and requested him to reconsider his decision. In other words, he indirectly advised Nizam not to use this money to meet the expenses of the marriage of his sister which was a personal matter and the funds of the *Diwani* were of the State.

In the year 1884, Mir Mahbub Ali Khan decided that his sisters marriages should be arranged with Salar Jung-II and his brother Saadat Ali Khan. The Nizams were the Sunnis and the Salar Jungs were Shias. The marriages between these two communities were not permitted. Raja Girdhari Pershad received secret orders from Nizam to arrange engagement ceremony. The order was in writing and signed by Mir Mahbub Ali Khan, Nizam-VI, himself. Further, Bansi Raja was asked to enter the order in *'Siyaha'*. Bansi Raja withheld the order until he ascertained the wishes of the senior Begums.

Bansi Raja suggested to Nizam that though he had full liberty to take decision, the ceremony cannot be performed without the consent of his grandmother, Dilawarunnisa Begum, and mother, Allah Rakhi Begum. Both the Begums were against the marriage since the Nizams were the Sunnis and the Salar Jungs were the Shias. Moreover, both the Begums were unhappy with the proposal.

Though it is a matter connected with a royal family, Bansi Raja was taken into confidence since he had the courage to advise Nizam independently in the matters of such nature. This was possible because of his close association with Nizam and his involvement with the palace affairs.

As mentioned above, Bansi Raja organised various religious and social ceremonies and rituals connected with the royal palace. It may be mentioned here that, Bansi Raja had the privilege to organise marriages of the Nizam's sisters. While organising these marriages Bansi Raja not only had to consult Nizam and report day-to-day progress but had to take the consent of the Begums of the palace. Bansi Raja also had the opportunity to make arrangements for the marriages of three successive members of the *Paigah* family who had matrimonial alliances with Nizam's family.

In 1872, when the marriage of Jahandar Unnissa Begum sister of Mir Mahbub Ali Khan, Nizam-VI was arranged with Iqbal-ud-Daula of *Paigah* family who was the son of Nawab Rasheed Uddin Khan, Amir-i-Kabir-III, Bansi Raja made arrangements from both the sides as desired by the ruling family and the family of *Paigah*. It may be mentioned here that Nawab Rasheed Uddin Khan, Amir-i-Kabir, later became the Prime Minister in 1893. All the arrangements of the marriage, such as, costly clothes, jewellery, food, *thora* or distribution of food, *Alams*, fireworks etc. and the other ceremonies connected with marriage, were the responsibility of Bansi Raja. The marriage was performed on a grand scale. Bansi Raja was in the palace right from the commencement of various ceremonies of marriages until its completion.

Similarly, Bansi Raja made all the arrangements for the marriage of Siraj Unnisa Begum, daughter of Afzal-ud-Daula with Asaf Yawar-ul-Mulk, great grandson of Sikandar Jah, Nizam-III during 1879. During this marriage as well, Bansi Raja made the arrangements at the palace as well as on behalf of the groom.

Bansi Raja made the entire arrangements for the marriage of Parvarish Unnisa Begum, daughter of Afzal-ud-Daula, Nizam-V at the royal palace during the year 1889. Parvarish Unnisa Begum was married to Nawab Basheer-ud-

Daula, Asman Jah of the *Paigah* family. Later, Asman Jah became the Prime Minister of Hyderabad in 1887. The marriage was performed on a very grand scale, as the families of the Nizam and *Paigah* were equally matched.

In fact, according to the rank and status, the *Paigah* family was next to the Nizam's family and had the privilege of matrimonial alliances. It was customary in those days that during such marriages, large sums of money and food used to be distributed as charity and the attendants were given expensive clothes.

Bansi Raja served Hyderabad State with the rare distinction of working under three Nizams and five Prime Ministers. His father Narhari Pershad had also served three successive Nizams. Raja Girdhari Pershad started his career under Salar Jung's guidance. It is a known fact that Salar Jung-I had an enlightened mind with the comprehensive grasp of things. Salar Jung's ability to judge correctly and to decide wisely is a notable feature. It was a wise decision of Salar Jung to select Bansi Raja for the formation of Regular, Irregular Troops, and subsequently Nazm-i-Jamiat-Mahbub. In fact, during this period, Bansi Raja came close to Salar Jung which was further strengthened the relationships during 30 years of his tenure. Bansi Raja mentioned in his various poems that he owed to Salar Jung a lot. History is witness to the fact that during the life of Salar Jung, Bansi Raja climbed the social ladder and reached greater heights.

Imad-us-Sultanat followed the footsteps of his father and he too had confidence in Bansi Raja. He had high regard for Bansi Raja. It was on the suggestion of Salar Jung-II, Nizam bestowed on Bansi Raja, the '*Naubat*' and '*Roushan Chowki*'.

To act in an advisory capacity and as a mediator, it is necessary for a person to have the foresight, wisdom, calmness in the decision-making and to act with firmness. Bansi Raja possessed all these qualities which made him the advisor and a good mediator. It is pertinent to mention here that in all the matters related to royal household, Mir Mahbub Ali Khan,

Nizam-VI always consulted him. As mentioned earlier, Bansi Raja acted as a mediator between Salar Jung-I and Amir-i-Kabir.

All the nobles considered Bansi Raja as a man to be trusted. The members of the *Paigah* family acknowledged the capability of Bansi Raja. Amir-i-Kabir Rasheed Uddin Khan, Asman-Jah and Viqar-ul-Umra had very good and cordial relations with Bansi Raja. No doubt, there were differences of opinion between the Regent and Co-Regent during the young age of Mir Mahbub Ali Khan, Nizam-VI, it was Bansi Raja who acted as a mediator between them on the advice of Sir Salar Jung-I. Initially, Bansi Raja was reluctant to accept the proposal of Sir Salar Jung-I but both the sides insisted him to be the mediator which he later accepted. He proved himself an impartial, loyal, confidant and trusted mediator.

Besides close relationship with Sir Salar Jung's family and *Paigah* nobles, Bansi Raja had close relations with the families of *Peshkars*.

When Maharaja Narender *'Peshkar'* passed away in the year 1889, after a brief illness, his enemies with the support of some influential persons, tried to prevent Maharaja Kishan Pershad from performing the last rites. Raja Narender had no sons and Maharaja Kishan Pershad was his grandson (son of the daughter).

Bansi Raja played a major role. He convinced the Nizam that Maharaja Kishan Pershad should perform the last rites of Maharaja Narender. Maharaja Kishan Pershad performed the last rites. As a result of this; Maharaja Kishan Pershad became a legal heir according to the Hindu customs. This made Kishan Pershad become the *Peshkar* after a lapse of four years. Maharaja Kishan Pershad always acknowledged the important role Bansi Raja played and had great regard for him for his gesture. This incident resulted in close intimacy between the families of *Peshkar* and Bansi Raja which continued even after the death of Bansi Raja. Raja Narsing

Raj, son of Bansi Raja was also closely associated with Maharaja Kishan Pershad.

Sir Salar Jung considered Bansi Raja to be the suitable person to work on the settlement of the personal account of Raja Murali Manohar, who was the younger brother of Raja Shivraj Dharamwant of Malwalas. Bansi Raja completed the assignment in two years. Bansi Raja made it clear that he had nothing to do with the accounts of *'Daftar-i-Maal'* which was under Raja Shivraj Dharamwant.

It was a known fact that Bansi Raja was closely associated with the family of Malwalas from the time of Raja Inderjeet, the father of Raja Shivraj.

As mentioned earlier, Afsar Jung, the Commander-in-Chief of the Nizam's army had great regard for Bansi Raja and his contribution during the critical juncture when Sultan Nawaz Jung was asked by the Nizam to leave Hyderabad. Bansi Raja was also very closely associated with *Sarwar-ul-Mulk*, the Tutor of Nizam-VI. *'Sarwar-ul-Mulk'* in his autobiography praised and mentioned Bansi Raja at several places. He described his relationship with Bansi Raja in these words. "He had a special regard for me and during his spare time, he whiled away reciting Persian Poems".

Bansi Raja not only had cordial relations with the above mentioned families but he also had intimate relations with almost all the nobles of Hyderabad, such as, Rajas of *'Samasthans'* and a number of literary figures of Hyderabad and northern India.

Bansi Raja was a man of unique capabilities and capacities which raised him gradually to this status and position. He was modest, courteous and a sympathetic person with an open heart and a open mind. Pride was miles away from him. He always fought for the good cause. He was very capable in discharging his duties and responsibilities.

After due analysis of this multi-faceted personality, the role of Bansi Raja in all his activities reflects his greatness, foresightedness and depths of thoughts. He had a fine tactics to settle disputes. In this process, he never displeased anyone. As a result of these qualities, Bansi Raja became a trustworthy person of Nizam, the nobles and the people in general. He served his ruler whole-heartedly without any aspirations, whatsoever.

The British in order to prove supremacy concluded many treaties with all the native princes. The Asaf Jahi rulers were no exception. By entering into treaties with the British, the Indian rulers and the princes had become the instruments of convenient rule and had to depend on the British for their maintenance from time to time.

It is a fact that the British promised to provide security to the rulers and the States against the external aggressions but they did not fulfill their promise in the real sense. The States were only dependent on the British Raj. By these treaties the British tried to maintain their supremacy and got de facto sovereignty of the rich Indian States. The British had selfish motives in the matters of such nature.

Raja Girdhari Pershad wrote in his diary that prior to 1862, the Nizam's State had no regular army of its own and the Prime Minister had to depend on the British contingent under the Resident as and when required. For Hyderabad State, being one of the largest States in India, it was considered to be an insult to depend on the British. Therefore, the Government of Nizam decided to have its own regular troops. Qum Qam-ud-Daula, Ghalib Jung an Arab Jamedar was first instructed to form a Platoon.

In 1862, Sir Salar Jung entrusted the formidable task of organising Regular Troops to Bansi Raja who was a person of proven competence and ability. Sir Salar Jung was very well aware of this fact that Bansi Raja had successfully managed and settled the dispute in the army of Raunaq Ali Khan, Shah-yar-Mulk and brought the unruly troops under control. This was a new and challengeable assignment for Bansi Raja. He organised the entire Regular Forces in an orderly manner and he was made the Head *'Sarrishtedar'* of the Regular Forces.

The formation of the Regular Forces was based not only on perfect planning but Bansi Raja established a gunpowder factory in 1864 and an arms and ammunition and gun factory in 1868. All the requirements of the Regular Forces were met from these factories. He did not end his planning. He also set up a buff and leather factory to supply necessary buff and leather goods to Regular Forces. He further thought that his responsibility did not end here and requested the government to allot him a grass plot for the supply of grass to cavalry as well as grain and gram. It may be mentioned here that the Reformed Troops were set up on the sound footing at the initiative of Bansi Raja. Bansi Raja had mentioned that the government approved two million rupees for the annual military expenditure and it was made necessary that he should maintain the records of annual expenditure and the disbursement of monthly salaries to the armed forces.

As a result of all this planning and its implementation, Sir Salar Jung achieved his main objective of setting up of an army for the Nizam's Government with the help of Bansi Raja. It was a matter of great satisfaction and joy for Sir Salar Jung and Bansi Raja.

Jamiat-i-Nizam-i-Mahbub or *'Myseram Regiment'*, consisted of two battalions of infantry, one stationed at *Keshavgiri* and the other at *Myseram*. This consisted of Arabs and Rohillas, the formation of this Regiment was in fact, the brainchild of Bansi Raja. Sir Salar Jung had a earnest desire to get rid of large proportion of these turbulent Arabs, Sikhs and Rohillas.

It was unfortunate that during the year 1850, many districts of Hyderabad were under the control of Arab Chiefs, such as, Abdullah-Bin-Ali, Mudabbir Jung, Saif-ud-Daula, Omar-Bin-Ouz, Janbaaz Jung and many others.

These people were only *Jamedars* but became *Talukdars* and were holding the area of land mortgaged by the government. They were lending money to the government. They also held the power of life and death over their men. The recruitment of soldiers was shown many times on paper but actually, less number of persons were recruited. These *Jamedars* opposed the move of taking over the districts and the revenue by the government.

Sir Salar Jung entrusted the responsibility of organising *Nazm*-i-*Jamiat* to Bansi Raja who was the key figure in military transactions. Bansi Raja was successful in tactfully taking over the districts from these *Jamedars* and placed them under the government. The system of recruitment on paper was discontinued.

The payment of salaries was restricted to the actual amount based on the number actually recruited in service. These measures were of great help to the government as there was financial saving to it and number of people were also reduced. The Arab *Jamedars* were brought under the control of the government and the arrears of the Arabs and Rohillas were paid.

Bansi Raja succeeded in settling the competitive issue by persuading Arabs and Rohillas to join Irregular Troops.

Even the first Assistant Resident of the British Government, Euan Smith commended the services of Bansi Raja and wrote:

> **"When the Arabs were to a great extent deprived of their Jagirs and enrolled into *Jamiat-i-Mahbub*, Sir Salar Jung entrusted the whole conduct of this delicate affair to Bansi Raja and he carried it through to a successful conclusion".**

Bansi Raja was appointed the Head '*Sarrishtedar*' of the Regular and Irregular Troops. He had the honour to lead the famous langar procession on 10th *Moharram* with the Regular and Irregular Troops.

The role of Bansi Raja in the reorganisation of Reformed Troops and *Jamiat-i-Mahbub* was of great significance not only to the State but to Sir Salar Jung as well. It was not an easy task especially when the Arabs and the Rohillas were turbulent they had the power of life and death. His foresight, perfect planning, calm and perfect judgement, soft attitude and nature during the entire transaction made him an efficient organiser and a great administrator as well as the mentor. It is said that Bansi Raja gained immense respect from these classes and became the key figure in the military transactions of Nizam's State.

At the beginning of the Nineteenth Century, Hyderabad was a feudal morass, the rising power of the British, the weaknesses of the State Administration, intrigues and political maneuverings, treaties with the British, handing over the most fertile districts of Berar, were some of the main causes for the poor economic growth of the State. The economic condition of the Hyderabad State was on the verge of collapse during the nineteenth century. The main reason being the handing over of Berar the most fertile District of Hyderabad, to the British.

It is a fact that Hyderabad was famous for its cottage and small scale industries. Its products captured the market. By the middle of the nineteenth century, the *'Himru' 'Mashru', 'Kamkhawb', 'Sela', 'Carpet', 'Bidriwares', 'silverwares'* specially the *filigri* work of Karimnagar, handmade papers, sarees, leather, oil pressing and different types of arsenals were manufactured all over Hyderabad State.

Bansi Raja played a very important role in establishing some of the industries in and around Hyderabad. His arms and ammunition factory was the great cause for the anxiety of the British Raj. It had shaken the high officials of the Government of India and the British. His arms and ammunition factory, gun power factory, leather factory, paper factory and workshop for clothing, made on machine are worth mentioning.

The arms and ammunition factory started by Bansi Raja in the year 1868. This was situated in the heart of the city.

Bansi Raja wrote in his book, *'Kalam-i-Mutafarikhat'* that he started this factory and other factories at the insistence of Sir Salar Jung.

Mr. C.B. Saunders, the then Resident of Hyderabad sent a confidential note to Sir Salar Jung-I, during the month of August 1875, enquiring about the details of the military force known as his Highness the Nizam's Reforms Troops and the State arms and ammunition. The question of guns and other arms procurements was also raised by the British.

During August 1876 the Secretary of State for India in London sent a telegram to Viceroy of India, stating that the personal information has reached them in London, revealed that an arsenal factory had been established in Hyderabad. If it is true, some legal action becomes necessary for making such proceedings penal for the Queen's subjects.

During this period, Sir Richard Meade sent an interim report telegraphically to the Foreign Secretary, Government of India at Simla. In fact, he had expressed his desire to see Bansi Raja's arsenal, but failed to obtain access to it.

In the year 1872, another British officer also expressed his desire to visit the arsenal but it was never included in his programme.

On receipt of telegram from Sir Richard, dated 7th August 1876, a search was made in the Foreign Office for previous information relating to the arsenal. It was found in Hyderabad confidential report of 1875, where it was mentioned that the Muskets and the Rifles can now be manufactured in Hyderabad. It also mentioned that gunpowder, ammunition, swords and lancers can be turned out by numerous artificers in the service of the government and the private persons.

Sir Richard Meade arranged for the inspection of the arms factory of Bansi Raja by Major Euan Smith, the then First Resident of Hyderabad. Meanwhile, many queries were made on the subject by the then Secretary, Government of India, Military Department.

Major Euan Smith visited the arms and ammunition factory of Bansi Raja on 9th August 1876. He mentioned in his report that he was received by Bansi Raja whom he described as 'a most talkative and courteous Kayasth Hindu who expressed willingness to show him everything. He further wrote, 'I saw no signs whatsoever of any apparatus for casting guns'. Bansi Raja complained very strongly to Smith of the opposition he had met in carrying out the manufacture of both at the hands of Major Neville and Mr. Graham. He further said that Major Neville wished the factory to abolish and that all the arms for the Hyderabad contingent should be procured from Europe. Bansi Raja further complained to Smith that the government had done nothing to encourage him to overcome these difficulties. He had no assistance from the government.

Major Smith described Bansi Raja in these words:

"He is in many ways, I am told, a remarkable man, and has been often made use of by the minister to carry through many delicate and confidential transactions. One of these occurred some two years ago, when the Arabs were to be a great extent deprived of their Jagirs and enrolled into '*Jamiat-i-Mahbub*'. Sir Salar Jung entrusted the conduct of this delicate affair to Bansi Raja and he carried it through to a successful conclusion. It also said and believed that to his initiative is due to the establishment of the Reformed Troops in their present footings".

Major Smith further states in his report:

Bansi Raja has monopoly of all the supplies for the army including Reformed Troops and the Police. He supplies all their accoutrements and has a large buff and leather manufactory in another part of the city. He supplies grass and grains to cavalry. He has the monopoly of supplying powder and ammunition, and is also employed in many offices

about the Nizams palace and has the monopoly of supplying *Itr and Pan at the Darbars* and is always present at the palace on the occasion of the visit of the Resident.

While concluding the memorandum, Major Smith wrote:

'I may add that I was received with the greatest civility and shown the greatest attention by all employed in the so called manufactory'.

The report of Smith was forwarded to the Foreign Secretary, Govt. of India. Later, the Viceroy decided that any further extension of the arms should be prevented and no employment should be given to the European without the prior and special sanction of the Govt. of India.

The British had great confidence in Sir Salar Jung which was shaken by the military situation of Hyderabad and as well as the arsenals. They formed an opinion that it was not safe to trust Salar Jung anymore. The arms and ammunition factory of Bansi Raja was a great cause of anxiety to the British. They were not even satisfied with the report of Smith, but report also reached the Resident from various independent and unofficial sources.

Colonel Fraser also visited the arms and ammunition factory of Bansi Raja, during the year 1877. Fraser did not add much about the factory as Major Smith had fully reported this, but he did add that 200 workmen were employed that too after the reduction, according to Bansi Raja. He also mentioned that there was a Boring Machine which was imported from England. Bansi Raja informed Fraser that he usually makes three Muskets a day. He also informed Fraser that he supplied 10,000 Muskets to the Police, 10,000 to Mysram Troops and 2,000 for the Reformed Troops.

The enquiry and the investigation of the arms and ammunition factory of Bansi Raja did not end with the visit of Smith and Fraser. Resident subsequently, in his letter dated 4th October 1877 forwarded the details of the arms and ammunition factory of Bansi Raja to the Govt. of India. Informal reports also reached the Resident that about 30 workmen were employed under the supervision of Graham who was a British. Mr. Graham stated that 3,000 stands of arms per month could be turned out and the informant believed that these might be breech-loading and rifled.

Sir Richard Meade admitted, 'there is no doubt Sir Salar Jung entertained ambitious projects'. Sir Salar Jung was of the view that there was no need for him to obtain prior sanction of the British Government. It was not necessary for him to inform British Government of the existence of Arsenals in Hyderabad. The main objective of the British was to put pressure on Sir Salar Jung and the State not to encourage such projects which in the long run will create serious problems for the British Raj.

The British succeeded to a great extent in inducing Sir Salar Jung to keep in abeyance all these reformatory measures. However, they did this at the cost of hampering the industrial growth of Hyderabad State. They also deprived jobs to the people of Hyderabad State. This decision of the British led to serious consequences. The machinery imported from London by Bansi Raja for his ambitious projects remained unutilised. His further development plans were hampered which resulted in the serious financial losses.

In the same factory, 87 tonnes of iron was cast monthly beside arsenals, articles like iron pillars, lanterns etc. Bansi Raja faced too many problems, such as, lack of govt. assistance, lack of demand and non-availability of skilled labours.

In one of the suburbs of Hyderabad, Balapur, near Chandrayangutta, Bansi Raja established an industrial unit for the manufacture of paper by steam machine, in 1877. The British also ensured that this factory of Bansi Raja is closed. Their aim was to ruin local industries and to make available imported goods from Britain. The progress of these workshops began to decline when its production was affected by the imported cheap foreign paper which was sold at a lower price to capture the market. As a result, the paper manufactured at his workshop remained unsold and finally, Bansi Raja had to close down his factory in the year 1881.

The services rendered by Bansi Raja for the development of industries needs appreciation and cannot be ignored by the Hyderabadis. Amongst the deteriorating situation of law and order and bankruptcy, he stood firm and proved to be a pioneer in the field. He struggled hard right from the beginning in establishing these industries and later for their survival. He faced many problems.

It is a fact of the history that the selfish policies of the British Raj were the most cruel. It was an attempt to make a nation over a nation. As Lord McCauley has rightly said "of all forms of tyranny, the worst is that of a nation over nation, heaviest of all yokes is the yoke of a stranger".

The efforts of Bansi Raja to establish different industries were in vain, with a view to generating income to the State and employment to the people and to achieve self sufficiency in material requirement, less dependence on the import and the British Raj, went futile.

It is a fact that Bansi Raja was able to establish many industries due to the support and favour of the Nizam and Sir Salar Jung. He further proved that he was a very efficient and capable industrialist and manages industries professionally against many odds especially the British policies.

Bansi Raja proved beyond doubt that Hyderabad State had all the capabilities of manufacturing arms and ammunition, paper, leather etc. of good quality which is comparable to that manufactured in Britain. He also proved that he could manufacture gun comparable to Henry Martini in Hyderabad. This fact was acknowledged and accepted when the gun manufactured in the factory of Bansi Raja was taken to England for demonstration by Sir Salar Jung-I and was acclaimed by the British. The selfish motives of the British ruined many industries in Hyderabad due to their selfish policies.

As has already been mentioned above not only the Asaf Jahi rulers but the nobility encouraged the development of industries in rural and urban areas of the State. No doubt, the process of development was slow compared to that of the present day development due to lack of facilities and technology. The products of cottage industry were no doubt superior in quality and had their own antiquity. These policies had disastrous effect on the growth of Hyderabad State. The Britishers cannot be excused at any cost for their selfish motives in hampering the growth of Hyderabad State.

The sagacity of Sir Salar Jung's foresightedness, devotion and Statesmanship not only brought changes in the mediaeval stagnation but his progressive policies led to the creation of a richer and healthier Hyderabad State. It was unfortunate that the Hyderabad State lost a statesman like Sir Salar Jung. However, after his demise in 1883 Mir Mahbub Ali Khan, Nizam-VI, a progressive ruler and subsequently Maharaja Sir Kishan Pershad, the then Prime Minister from 1901-1911 were the two towering personalities who not only contributed to the state but transformed the State from the antiquated feudal structure into a modernised one. This was possible due to administrative reforms implemented by these masterminded personalities; the State underwent cultural, administrative, social and economic developments on unprecedented lines.

It may be mentioned that the history of Hyderabad from the time of the establishment of the Asaf Jahi rule witness many ups and downs throughout the eighteenth and the first half of nineteenth century. The socio-economic life of the people was far from satisfactory. They led a very unhappy and discontented life. The treasury of Hyderabad was almost empty and the economic instability and the bankruptcy were the main causes. These deteriorating conditions had far reaching effects on the socio-economic life of the people.

It may be mentioned here that the most noticeable feature of the late nineteenth century was the development of heterogeneous society by different communities, castes and classes. As mentioned earlier, Bansi Raja had won the heart of the turbulent class of Arabs who advanced money to the government and the State. It was Bansi Raja who settled the dispute between the Arabs and the Government of Nizam for the repayment of loans. He later enrolled them into Regular and Irregular Troops and *Jamiat-i-Mahbub*.

As stated earlier, the social and official life of Hyderabad was a pleasing spectacle of Hindu-Muslim unity in the real sense. It was often difficult to make out whether a person was a Hindu or a Muslim as they dressed alike, food habits were similar, marriages and death ceremonies had similarities and Urdu was their common language. In fact, the second half of the nineteenth century of the Hyderabad was the wonderful State.

Bansi Raja maintained the customs and traditions of the Asaf Jahi rulers like other nobles and *jagirdars*. The common dress of the Hindus and Muslims was *Nima, Jama, Angarkha* with their respective headgear. Bansi Raja's dress was Daghla (a quilted long garment upto the ankle), like *Angarkha* particularly used during the winter by nobles and high dignitaries. This dress once prompted the Resident to ask Bansi Raja humorously why he preferred the dress of the English women. Bansi Raja retorted immediately 'it is not a dress of the English women, but of an English Priest and it should be given due respect at all the times'.

Bansi Raja participated in all functions connected with *Moharram*, at his palace in Hussaini Alam and *Ashoor Khana* from 1st to 10th *Moharram*. This is a fine example of Hindu-Muslim unity and respect for other religion. His family members arranged annual *'Nyas'* at Hussaini Alam. During the *Moharram*, Bansi Raja used to wear green clothes and distributed green clothes to the poor. A procession was taken out from Hussaini Alam to Purana Pul on the 5th day of *Moharram*. Bansi Raja as a Head *Sarrishtedar* of the Regular and Irregular Troops, used to lead the procession seated on the elephant. Every year, Bansi Raja used to organise an *'Iftaar'* Party during the month of *'Ramazan'* for those who observed fast in this Holy Month.

Raja Girdhari Pershad held the hereditary post of being incharge of the Royal kitchen, of the Nizam's Palace, during the reign of Mir Mahbub Ali Khan, Nizam-VI. He maintained the splendour of the Royal kitchen and used to arrange the parties. Hospitality was his second nature.

Bansi Raja was very much depressed and upset by the premature death of most of his children. He took his two surviving sons, Raja Narsing Raj and Mahbub Raj on a pilgrimage to Puri and Benaras to obtain the blessings for their survival and long life. During the visit to Benaras, he met his Guru Swami Bhaskaranand Saraswati. The Swami assured Bansi Raja that the responsibility of the welfare and prosperity of these children rested with him. On the advice of his Guru, Bansi Raja performed *Pati* ceremony and later arranged the marriage of his elder son Narsing Raj at Benaras with a girl belonging to Saxena family of Bhopal in the year 1896.

Being a generous, benevolent and kind hearted person, Bansi Raja arranged the marriages and rites at his own expenses for the other castes also. Charity was the daily routine in his life. As has rightly been said by his son Raja Narsing Raj, 'Most of these charitable works remain *'Baqi'* to this day and would remain till the word *'Baqi'* remains (The word *'Baqi'* means lasting).

The temple of Keshavgiri dedicated to Shri Keshav Swamy Maharaj is situated on the hill at Keshavgiri in the suburbs of Hyderabad. The then Asaf Jahi rulers stationed a Police guard for the protection of the temple and its property. At that time, the temple was under the management of the pujaris.

Bansi Raja was a pious and religious person. One day, he dreamt that the temple on a small hill at *'Chennarayani Gutta'* was in a precarious condition and it needed to be rehabilitated. The Lord entrusted this task to Bansi Raja. When Bansi Raja visited the place, he found exactly what he had dreamt. The *'Pujari'* of the temple was in distress and fearful since he had to live alone on a deserted hillock.

Bansi Raja narrated the whole details to the then Nizam Afzal-ud-Daula, Nizam-V. This happened in the year 1859. Later, Bansi Raja submitted a Petition to the Nizam to grant him the land around the temple for its rehabilitation. Probably, this was done with an intention that if the areas around the temple were populated, then the temple would become more popular as a public place.

In the year 1860, Bansi Raja was granted 15 *bigas* of land for the rehabilitation of the temple by the then Nizam Afzal-ud-Daula, Nizam-V. This grant was given under the seal of *'Ikhtedar-ul-Mulk'* (Salar Jung Mukhtar-ul-Mulk), on a lease basis. In addition to this, an amount of Rs 15 was fixed towards the *Pan* (land tax) of the land given. The management of the said temple was also entrusted to Bansi Raja in accordance with the request of the pujaris. Bansi Raja has described this gesture of Nizam and wrote that Afzal-ud-Daula is the 'Ocean of Charity'. Subsequently, additional land was also granted measuring about 25 *'bigas'* to Bansi Raja by Mir Mahbub Ali Khan, Nizam-VI on the lease basis under the seal and signature of Nawab Viquar-ul-Umra at Rs 60 per annum towards *'Pan Maqtha'*. Thus, the total land donated to Bansi Raja was 40 *bigas* (30 Acres).

Bansi Raja was able to rehabilitate it slowly and by 1883 the entire area was populated. The locality around *Chennarayani Gutta* acquired the name of the Deity of the Temple, Keshavpet or Keshavgiri. A huge gateway was constructed to give access to the enclosed area from outside which inscribed the name of the temple.

Bansi Raja wrote in one of his diaries that he then spent Rs 1,00,000 on the renovation of the temple. Four gates and ramparts were constructed to protect the temple from robbers.

He constructed gardens also. Bansi Raja also constructed a building called *Darshan* Bungalow and *Mandapam* in front of it.

Bansi Raja also constructed the temples of Goddess Durga, Jagannath and Manik Prabhu. A *Rathshala, Gowshala* and many other buildings were also constructed for the purpose of rehabilitation of the place. Besides the construction and rehabilitation, with the efforts of Bansi Raja, grants were obtained from the nobles and other dignitaries of Hyderabad for the temple.

Raja Narender Pershad (1882 – 1889), the then *Peshkar* issued grants to the temple from one of his *Maqtas*. Raja Inderjeet of the Malwala family granted *Yomia* (Daily maintenance) to the temple. This was later continued by his son Raja Shivraj Dharamwanth (1848 – 1925). Beside these, the temple also received grants from Raja Rameshwar Rao of Wanaparthy Samasthan, Rai Keval Kishan, son of Raja Bhavani Das of *'Dafter-i-Maal'* and Nawab Asker Jung, son of Abbas Ali Khan. The Abkari (Excise) revenue of the Chennarayani Gutta was directed to be paid to the temple by the orders of *'Madar-ul-Maham'* in 1880.

Bansi Raja constructed houses for the *Pujaris* and their monthly salaries were also restored. In fact, it will not be wrong to say that Bansi Raja put in heart and soul into the rehabilitation and restoration of the temple. He himself donated thousands of rupees to this temple.

The annual *Jatara* of *Keshavgiri* temple used to be organised on a grand scale. Besides the local inhabitants, distinguish personalities like the nobles and the Prime Minister of Hyderabad used to attend the *Jatara*. Raja Shivraj Dharamwant of Malwala Palace and Maharaja Kishen Pershad, the then Prime Minister of Hyderabad, were the regular visitors during the *Jatara*.

After the death of Bansi Raja, his son, Raja Narsing Raj and his heirs continued the traditional rituals and annual *jatara* on a grand scale.

Raja Girdhari Pershad rehabilitated another deserted temple at Damagundam near Vikharabad, presently in Ranga Reddy District of Telangana. Bansi Raja wrote in his diary of 1894 that the Temple at Damagundam is an old temple of Lord Shiva and its history dates back to the time of Lord Rama who laid the *Shivling* during his exile. Since Lord Rama laid the *Shivling,* the place was earlier known as Ramagundam. Thereafter, it became popular as Damagundam. Bansi Raja further wrote that there is a mention about this temple in *Puranas.* The earlier Kings issued cash grants to the temple. However, during the Asaf Jahi period, the grants were discontinued and as a result of which the temple was neglected and deserted.

It so happened that Bansi Raja visited the temple of Damagundam in 1870 and on his return, he requested Sir Salar Jung to issue a grant in order to resume daily *pujas* and *jataras* which was discontinued earlier. Sir Salar Jung acceded to the request, and later Bansi Raja renovated the temple. Bansi Raja got made a wooden chariot and arranged *Palki, Ban, Nishan, Chanwar* and *Chathur, Nawbat Tamboor* (A Drum) and *Dhol.*

The annual *Jatara* of the temple was started by Bansi Raja. It was organised after the 10th day of *Holi* Festival. During the *jatara* a large number of pilgrims mostly peasants and villagers used to gather to celebrate *jatara.*

In 1890, Bansi Raja visited the temple of *Phatakshila* at Anagondi. He was fortunate enough to take the responsibility of rehabilitation of this place also. He renovated the temple and arranged for the daily *puja* and annual *jatara.*

Bansi Raja realised the difficulties faced by the public during the rainy and summer season and constructed a pavilion type structure in memory of his father in 1880, at *Purana Pul,* which is a Hindu crematorium in Hyderabad. He also constructed a ghat in memory of his son, Keshav Pershad known as Keshsav Ghat at Mirzapur in 1886.

On the eastern side of Hyderabad, there is a village known as Jadkal. This village is about eight miles from Warangal and 90 miles from Jangaon. A temple is situated in this village and every year, thousands of pilgrims assemble there and take a bath. Bansi Raja erected an arch in front of the temple and on the top of this arch, *Naubat Khana* was built. Nizam-VI not only awarded the *Naubat* but sanctioned a grant of Rs 600. Besides this, 24 *pujaris* of this temple were sanctioned daily allowance.

Bansi Raja constructed a dam and a canal at Hanamkonda, in 1885, as a result of which a deserted land turned into a fertile land for cultivation. The farmers of Hanamkonda were delighted since the water of the dam and the canal were utilised for irrigation purposes. He also spent a substantial amount for repairing the old tank of Redepalli now in Medak District, in 1895.

Bansi Raja had the heart that cared for the others. Whenever he found anyone in trouble, he readily solved his problems and helped the needy. Looking back on the life of this noble personality, one may conclude that his enormous public works and the variety of his experience, marks him out as **'A man among men'.**

Bansi Raja travelled extensively throughout India from 1850 to 1896. He recorded his 12 travels systematically in Persian language. While giving the detailed accounts of his travels, he recorded historical background of the places he visited, social and economic life of the people, their customs and traditions and architecture. No doubt, he was a perfect narrator and he had mastery over his pen. His lofty thoughts and minute observations provide interesting material for the readers in the travels he recorded. He offered *pujas*, clothes, jewellery and money and the *'Brahmbhoj'* (Food for the priest). Bansi Raja had liberty to perform such acts of reverence on behalf of the Nizams as well. Similarly, the offerings and *Nyas* were also arranged at the Muslim shrines and *Dargahs*.

Bansi Raja undertook his first travel during the year 1850 at the request of Raunaq Ali Khan Shah-Yar-ul-Mulk, son of Mustafa Ali Khan. Bansi Raja used to accompany him for the inspection of his *jagirs* at Alpur earlier known as Alampur. While visiting Alpur, he got an opportunity to visit the temple of Brahmeshwar, which is situated at the bank of the river Tungabhadra. Bansi Raja requested Shah-yar-ul-Mulk to sanction a grant for this temple which he accepted.

Bansi Raja, thereafter, visited Mallikarjun and Pataal Ganga at Srisailam, Ambika Devi and Mahanandi on the occasion of *Mahashivratri*, Baiganpally, the *Jagir* of Nawab Muzaffar-ul-Mulk, the nephew of Shah-yar-ul-Mulk. They stayed there for one month; Bansi Raja spent most of his time in hunting around with Shah-Yar-ul-Mulk.

Raja Girdhari Pershad was depressed and upset due to the premature death of most of his children. To overcome his grief and to divert his mind, he decided to visit holy places, such as, Khanapur, Tuljapur and Pandharpur, during the year 1860, which he recorded as his second visit. On the way he visited Manikpur to meet Saint Manik Prabhu. His disciples were both the Hindu and the Muslim and that too in large numbers. It is interesting to mention here that the Hindus were allowed to perform *puja* of Shri Ram or Shri Krishna in front of his seat, and the Muslims had the privilege of offering *'Niyaz'* of Mahbub Subhani. His doors were open for the *'Bhoj'* irrespective of caste, class and distinction, where elite and the poor had food from his kitchen together.

After visiting Manik Prabhu, Bansi Raja proceeded to Khandoba Temple in Khanapur and the famous temple of Tuljapur.

After completing the successful task of re-organising the Regular Troops, Bansi Raja had proceeded to Makhtal, Raichur, Sholapur and Lingsugur Cantonments, where Major Henry Rock of the Regular Troops was to visit. It was the seat of Raja of Anagondi, who was a lineal descendant of the King of Vijayanagar. It so happened that when Bansi Raja reached the place it happened to be the annual *jatara* of Pampapati Mahadeo. During this period, he met the Raja of Anagondi, Raja Dharmavtar, known for his refined manners. Bansi Raja requested him to sanction a grant to the temple of Phataksila in the territory for the continuation of daily *puja*. The Raja accepted the proposal of Bansi Raja and sanctioned the grant. As a result of this meeting, a cordial relationship developed between the Raja of Anagondi and Bansi Raja.

In 1874, soon after the death of his first wife, Bansi Raja decided to visit the famous temple of Lord Venkateshwara at Tirupati.

Bansi Raja also went to the temple of Srirangam near Madras and wrote in his travel that the temple has seven enclosures. Three enclosures are meant for the Brahmins, and fourth and seventh were meant for the stay of prosperous people. He also went to Kanchipuram and paid a visit to the temple of Kamakshidevi at Shivkanchy.

During the year 1875, Bansi Raja visited Aurangabad, Nasik, Trimbakeshwar. While narrating the history of Ellora, he narrated that a Raja known as Ell fell in love with one *Apsara* and he constructed some of the temples, caves at Ellora in her memory.

Bansi Raja also visited the Holy Shrine of Hazarat Zarzari Baksh, Burhanuddin Janam and offered *Fateha* in Aurangabad. He also visited the tombs of Aurangazeb Alamgir, Nizam-ul-Mulk Asaf Jah-I and Nasir Jung at Khuldabad. He concluded his pilgrimage with the visit of Nasik and Trimbakeshwar.

As has already been mentioned earlier, Rai Narhari Pershad, the father of Bansi Raja translated *Yog Vashisht* into Hindi under the title of ***'Narhari Prakash'***. Learned *Sanskrit* scholars reviewed the book at Banaras about five hundred people daily visited the palace of Hari Narayan where the book was being reviewed. The learned *Pandits*, discussed and the discussions continued for four months. After a long and due deliberations *'Narhari Prakash'* was released at Banaras and the copies were distributed free of cost to the learned scholars.

When Bansi Raja visited the pilgrim centre of Kashi, Benaras and Gaya, he described not only the historical background of these places but also the art and architecture, the surroundings, the customs and traditions of performing *puja.*

Soon after the Mutiny of 1857, East India Company was abolished introducing a direct link with the British Crown. The Queen of England assumed the title of *Kaiser-i-Hind* or the Empress of India. In 1877, a grand *Darbar* was organised by the then Governor General of India. All the kings, *Rajas and Nawabs* of different states in India were invited for the celebrations. Nawab Mir Mahbub Ali Khan, Nizam-VI was also invited to attend the *Darbar*. All the *nobles* of Hyderabad including Sir Salar Jung, Amir-i-Kabir, Maharaja Narender Pershad, the *Peshkar*, accompanied Nizam-VI, who was in his teen age. Bansi Raja was also ordered to accompany Nizam and was assigned the responsibility of making necessary arrangements during the visit of Nizam.

Bansi Raja was against the British rule in India. He composed a poem in Persian and had five hundred copies printed in Delhi. The copies of the poem were distributed among the dignitaries who attended the Delhi *Darbar*. The free translation of the Persian Poem is as given below:

> **"The Queen has become 'Empress', a fact which my heart doesn't accept. It is difficult for her to become the 'Empress of Europe'. If she claims that she has become the 'Empress of India, it has no sense because there is no King in India. Under these circumstances the declaration that the Queen has assumed the title of 'Empress' is surprising. The once prosperous Delhi lost its splendour and became deserted. Madras has no life and has lost its glory. The State of Oudh is divided into pieces, like its own name (in Urdu there are four separate letters**

in the word Oudh), and the King has met his end. Nothing is left in Gujarat, Lahore and Multan; these States have no rulers and monarchs. The Raja of Nagpur met with a sorrowful end. Mysore is ruined. The wailings of Holkar rise to such an extent that the ears of the sky became deaf. What should I say about the Marathas? Their name is destroyed. Rana became helpless. The Dominion of Indore lost its glory since there is no prosperity, peace and tranquillity. Baroda is frigid (the ruler of Baroda was ruthlessly brought to submission). Many parts of the Nizam's Dominion are usurped. The remaining rulers of the states are being paid stipends for their services. It suits well if an 'Empress' bestows a crown and throne to the rulers, because she accepts tribute from them. If the 'Empress' or the British desire justice, they should grant the Dominions to the heirs of the Kings. It is an accepted fact that monarchy brings prosperity to a country, otherwise it leads to anarchy. The destiny of anarchy in the world is ungracious. Keeping in view the destiny of the world, there should always be justice, only then, would the title of 'Empress' become famous, otherwise it will remain meaningless".

All the dignitaries' who attended the Delhi *Darbar* of 1877 appreciated the poem of Bansi Raja. He was probably the only person, who had the courage to express his anti-British feelings and that too on the occasion of the Imperial *Darbar*. The fact should not be forgotten that it was the time when the British had already established their rule on Indian soil. The poem created quite an impression amongst the then ruling class.

Nawab Afzal-ud-Daula, Nizam-V died in 1869. It was decided that a co-regency be formed with Amir-i-Kabir Rasheed Uddin Khan who was appointed the Co-Regent and Sir Salar Jung was appointed as Regent, since Mir Mahbub Ali Khan was a young boy of about two years. This was done with a view to carrying out on the administration of the state smoothly. Subsequently, differences arose between Sir Salar Jung, the Regent and the Co-Regent. As a result, the administration of the State suffered and with the consent of both the Regent and the Co-Regent, Bansi Raja was appointed as the mediator on the suggestion of Rasheed Uddin Khan to settle the differences between him and Sir Salar Jung. It is a fact that Bansi Raja was closely associated with the *Paigah* family for decades, so also with Sir Salar Jung.

After obtaining the permission from Sir Salar Jung, Bansi Raja left for Allahabad with his son, Keshav Pershad to attend the '*Kumbh Mela*'. He gave the details of the *Kumbh Mela* and mentioned that millions of people gathered at *Kumbh* amongst them some noted Rajas and Maharajas of different States also attended with their family. After performing the rituals at *Kumbh,* Bansi Raja met heir apparent of Kashi Naresh Raja Isri Pershad at Allahabad with a view to maintaining cordial relations with the Raja and his family.

Nizam left for Sholapur on his way to Aurangabad where he offered rich tributes to the Hindu Saint Sadguru Mallappa Maharaj. According to the custom and traditions of the Asaf Jahi *Darbar*, a *Dastar, Shawl* and food items were offered to the Saint through Bansi Raja. The Nizam then left for Aurangabad. Bansi Raja accompanied the Nizam during his visit to Aurangabad. Describing the visit of the Nizam, Bansi Raja narrated the historical background of the place. He mentioned that the Aurangabad was the old capital of Nizam-ul-Mulk Asaf Jah-I who left some of his Begums at *Naukhanda* Palace to look after the affairs of the old capital which indicates that Nizam-ul-Mulk wanted Aurangabad to remain as a capital, eventhough, he had made Hyderabad a permanent capital. The Nizam granted these Begums stamped ***'Sanads'***. In the event of the death of a Begum, her daughter was made the successor. A grant was fixed for them on the occasion of *Eid, Talukdar* of Aurangabad offered ***'Nazar'*** at the Palace.

This tradition continued until the reign of Nasir-ud-Daula Nizam-IV.

All arrangements were made by Bansi Raja at Naukhanda Palace to welcome Nizam. *'Nazars'* were offered by the nobles accompanying Nizam. As per the tradition of the Palace *'Naubat'* was played and the ceremony of presentation of sweets and gold was performed. The *'Nazars'* were offered to Nizam. The people of Aurangabad prayed for the long life of Nizam.

Nizam left by special train, accompanied by Raja Narender, Khursheed Jah, Laiq Ali Khan, Muneer-ud-Daula, Saadat Ali Khan, Shuja-ud-Daula, Zafar Jung, Bansi Raja and other nobles and dignitaries to Calcutta. When the train reached Benaras on the 3rd Day, the British officials were present at the Station to receive and welcome Nizam. Bansi Raja has recorded a very interesting incident about the journey. He wrote that when Nizam reached Benaras Station, Raja Isri Pershad, the Kashi Naresh was not present at the station to welcome Nizam instead, he had sent his representatives. This was not liked by the Nobles of Hyderabad who had accompanied the Nizam. Raja Narender and Khursheed Jah were unhappy. They decided to refuse the hospitality of the Maharaja of Benaras. Bansi Raja intervened in the matter and suggested that it would not be advisable to refuse the hospitality of Maharaja.

The next day, Maharaja arrived and was received by Raja Narender, Khursheed Jah, Muneer-ud-Daula. The Nizam himself went up to the gate to receive Maharaja. Maharaja expressed his apologies for not being present at the station to welcome Nizam because of his old age and poor eye sight and that the Crown Prince could not make it as his uncle was seriously ill. He humbly stated that he committed a sin and deserved punishment. The nobles of Hyderabad were very much impressed with the etiquette and manners of Maharaja. Later, it was decided that some nobles should pay a return visit to Maharaja at his Ram Nagar Palace. After due discussions and suggestions from different nobles and Bansi Raja, Nizam then decided to visit Ramnagar Palace to meet Maharaja of Benaras. Bansi Raja's foresight, tact and maturity had helped avert a misunderstanding which could have led to serious complications at the highest level.

Nizam left for Calcutta from Benaras. There was an exchange of visits between Nizam and the Governor General. Nizam visited the exhibition and other places in the city. Prince Wajid Ali Shah of Lucknow and other nobles, *Maulavis*, and Holy persons called on Nizam and thanked him for the visit. Nizam discussed with the Governor General, the problem faced by Hyderabad State.

Bansi Raja then visited the famous Kaali Temple and offered prayers. With the permission of Nizam, he offered brocade canopy and distributed 500 rupees to the *pujaris* of the temple. On his way back to Hyderabad, Bansi Raja visited Jwalamukhi, Jahar Khand Baijnath temple, Kanpur, Amritsar and Pushkar Raj. He regretted that he could not visit '*Ajmer*' as he was ordered by Nizam through a telegram to return to Hyderabad immediately.

Mir Mahbub Ali Khan was not only had faith and confidence in Bansi Raja but had given him full liberty to make offerings at sacred places on behalf of the Government and Nizam, this indicates that Mir Mahbub Ali Khan believed in religious tolerance and multi-cultured harmony.

Among many distinguished families of Hyderabad, Saxena family of the Kayasths was famous. Its members were in the army and administration of the State. This family produced many poets and scholars of different languages. They were men of literary taste. The family of Rai Daulat Rai, subsequently produced the great Persian scholar, statesman and poet, Raja Girdhari Pershad 'Baqi' alias Bansi Raja (1828 - 1896).

With the advent of the Turko-Afghans and the Persians, Persian became the language of administration in the Mediaeval India. It also served as a link between the Hindus and the Muslims. The contribution and development of Persian language and literature by Muslims and the Hindus was notable feature of the Mediaeval Indian history. It is also a fact that during the Mughal period, Persian literature rose to its glory. Noted Muslims who contributed to the development of Persian were Amir Khusro, Faizi, Abul Fazal, Mulla Masih, the historian Abdul Quader Badauni and host of others. It should not be forgotten that the Hindus also whole-heartedly developed Persian language and literature along with the Muslims. To name a few, Anand Ram Mukhlis, Harcharan, Madhavram, Jethmal, Munshi Ramsingh, Bheemsen Saxena etc. were famous.

During the reign of Mir Mahbub Ali Khan, Nizam-VI, Raja Girdhari Pershad 'Baqi' occupied a prominent place in the literary field and was considered as one of the best Persian poet, Hyderabad had ever produced. 'Baqi' showed early signs of intelligence and great poetic capabilities. As a young man, he was passionately fond of associating with the learned scholars of that period. He had exhibited his great poetical gift and love for reading and writing, right from his childhood. Later, he made himself one of the most distinguished poets and writers of his age. 'Baqi' was not only a great Persian and Urdu scholar but had considerable proficiency in Sanskrit. His book 'Keshav Puran' is the Hindi translation from Sanskrit which is a testimony to this fact. He had also a fair knowledge of Arabic. His tutor of Persian was Hazrath Mohammed Ali, whose pen name was *'Ashiq'*. He learned Urdu from Hazrath Hafiz Mohammed Shamsuddin 'Faiz'. 'Baqi' had high regard for his Persian and Urdu tutors.

It will not be out of place to mention that 'Baqi' was appointed as a tutor to the young Mir Mahbub Ali Khan, Nizam-VI by Sir Salar Jung. As a result, Nizam developed a great regard for 'Baqi' and always appreciated his poetry.

As Ben Johnson rightly said "Poets are rare births than kings". 'Baqi' composed all major genres of verse recognised in Persian, such as, *Ghazal, Qasida, Masnavi, Salaam, Hamd,*

Naath, Qata, Rubai. He was also known for composing chronograms.

'Baqi' had written seven stanzas *(Haftband)* on Prophet Mohammed. This is a *'Naath'* in which, at the end of each stanza, he offered hundred salutations to the Prophet.

Bar rawanat sad darud o sad salam
Hum bar al pak o ishah-i-Karam

"I offer hundreds of Salutations
to the holy Prophet and to my friends."

He published four hundred copies of this *Haftband* and distributed most of them in Bhopal and Lucknow. 'Baqi' received praise from the literary personalities like Raja Durga Pershad of Sandela, Kamta Pershad, Magistrate of Benaras, brother of Raja of Sandela and Safi-ud-Daula, Hisamul-Mulk. Mohammed Ali of Bhopal wrote that *Haftband* of 'Baqi' was incomparable for its use of appropriate words and that the subject 'Baqi' had selected was very apt.

'Baqi' also composed *Salams*. In *Salam* each verse differs from the other and new topics are not obligatory. 'Baqi' wrote Salaams in his *Diwan 'Baqa-i-Baqi'*. They were considered excellent in all respects. He used appropriate words and maintained elegance and introduced varieties.

'Baqi' was also known for his *Ghazals* in Persian and Urdu. His Persian *Ghazals* are smooth flowing and spontaneous. His diction is very elegant. In his verses, he has expressed the views which are considered and judged as embodying religious tolerance of *Sufi* doctrine. He led the exemplary life of a true dervish. He wrote....

Dariya Se Mouj, Mouj Se Dariya Nahin Alag
Ham Se Juda Nahin Hai Khuda Aur Khuda Se Hum.

"Neither is the river apart from waves nor
the waves from the river.
So also God is not aloof from us nor we from God."

The compositions of 'Baqi' had their own style. His *Ghazals* are of high standard, thoughts are noble and emotions refined. In fact, 'Baqi' was proud of his individuality and style. He was one of the shining stars of the school of 'Shamsuddin Faiz'. 'Baqi's *Ghazals* are simple in language. The phrases used in daily conversation find place in his poetry. The usage is excellent. He wrote....

Aap Ne luft se Anso Jo Na Ponchhe Hote
Dekhte, Phir Yeh Mera Didaye Tar Kya Hota

"Had you not wiped off my tears with love and kindness,
you would have seen my eyes full of tears"

'Baqi' also composed a number of *Qasidas. Qasidas* may be didactic or instructive, philosophical or religious, consisting of twenty five to hundred and seventy couplets. In his *Qasidas* 'Baqi' used dignified, learned and elevated language. The uses of high sounding phrases are another highlight of his *Qasidas*.

'Baqi' wrote *Qasida* in Persian in praise of Nizam, Sir Salar Jung-I, and his father Rai Narhari Pershad. He also wrote *Qasidas* on famine in 1877, buildings, River Musi etc. The *Qasidas* of 'Baqi' in Persian are the master pieces of literary skill.

Another favourite composition of Baqi was *'Masnavi'*. The rules of *Masnavi* are similar to Prosody. *Masnavis,* are narrative poems considered to be the subordinate form of poetry. The appropriate use of words, eloquent, flowery language for the narration is similar to the string of pearls.

'Baqi' was an expert in composition of rhetoric. The *'Masnavi' 'Sanae Badae'* is the first specimen of Persian literary merit of 'Baqi'. The exploitation of figures of speech is superb in his *'Masnavi'*. He had proved that he was the master in the art of the literary expression.

'Baqi' like other great poets, had not only composed *Rubaiyat* but had also translated them from Persian into Urdu. *Rubai* consists of two couplets of which the first, second and the fourth rhymes in one particular metre. Baqi translated the Persian *Rubaiyat* of Khaja Mir 'Dard' (1720-1784) into Urdu. Khaja Mir 'Dard' is ranked as one of the greatest poets Urdu literature has ever produced. He had no parallel in India as a *Sufi* poet. 'Baqi had maintained the beauty of his style, while translating these *Rubaiyat*. The elegance and command of diction, technique, loftiness of thoughts, and delicacy of sentiment are superb. These *Rubaiyats* are extremely elegant and are ranked as the best *Rubaiyats*.

Eventhough, 'Baqi's favourite language was Persian, he translated these *Rubaiyats* into Urdu. In fact, the *Rubaiyats* of 'Dard' are full of compassion and Sufistic doctrine. The book entitled *'Dard-i-Baqi-o-Durd-i-Saqi'* consists of translations of Mir Dard's *Rubaiyats* compiled by Raja Narsing Raj 'Aali', the son of 'Baqi' who published it.

Besides the translation of *Rubaiyats* of Khaja Mir 'Dard', 'Baqi' had written *Munajat-i-Baraan-i-Rahmat* and *Rubaiyat-i-Babarkat*. The study of *Rubaiyat-i-Babarkat* indicates that 'Baqi' was fascinated by Islam. He not only made a thorough study of it but had its vast knowledge. His book *'Rubaiyat-i-Babarkat'* is the rarest of the rare books ever written. These *Rubaiyats* contain 99 names of *'Allah'*, the 'Creator'. This Book was published in Delhi in the year 1892. When it was presented to Mir Mahbub Ali Khan, Nizam-VI and Viqar-ul-Umra, they commended it very much even Maharaja Kishan Pershad the then *Peshkar,* a poet and scholar of repute was pleased to review this book. Maharaja Kishan Pershad appreciated the wonderful composition. Nizam not only expressed happiness over its publication but awarded the Robes of Honour to the publisher of the book. 'Baqi' received letters of appreciation from all corners of the world as this book was widely circulated in and outside India. This book was republished twice as it was in demand.

This was again published by the Iran Culture House, New Delhi, India. This book is available at Khuda Bakhsh Library, Patna and Rampur Raza Library, Rampur.

'Baqi' specialised in another form of words which is *'Tarikh'* or composing chronograms. He wrote chronograms on different occasions, such as, marriages, birth of a son, mutiny, formation of regular forces, famines, festivals, *Darbars*, ceremonies for the award of titles, awards.

He composed seven different chronographic verses on the award of two pieces of brocade to him by Nizam in the year 1310 A.H. :

Rana Kamkhwab Besh Baha 1310 (1892)
Khilat Abro 1310 (1892)
Zaib Dah Iftakhar 1310 (1892)

His book 'Kunuz-ul-Tawarikh' is the collection of his chronographic writings.

'Baqi' wrote Persian prosody. Prosody can also be called a science of verification or the study of speech rhythm. The prosody of Urdu is the prosody of Persian which is also the prosody of Arabic. In prosody the rhyme *(Qafia)* and the double rhyme *(Radif)* are of great significance, especially, in Urdu poetry.

Baqi also composed one *'Mukhammas'* which is found in his *Deewan*. *'Mukhammas'* is a kind of verse containing five lines or five rhyming hemistichs instead of four. It contains verses only about love.

'Baqi' was a habitual writer and that too in poetry. He used to submit petitions to Nizam in the form of poems suggesting necessary action and remedial measures. In 1893, he submitted a petition to Nizam urging him to have a *'Tuladan'* in order to eradicate zodiacal influence which would cast bad effect. He composed a poem consisting of 58 verses, describing the entire ceremony and the different items in which Nizam was weighed as suggested by the Brahmins. *'Tuladan'* is the ceremony which even the Mughal rulers used to perform on various occasions. 'Baqi' wrote...

Mubarak Jashn Wazn Shah Aamad
Bajae Kufa Mehr Aur Mah Aamad

"The auspicious occasion of the weighing ceremony
of the king came, the Sun and Moon also
arrived, in place of the scale.'

'Baqi' as a poet and scholar was ranked high among the North-Indian Scholars and centres of Urdu journalism. He was in close contact with the Nawab of Bhopal, Raja of Sandela, Maulana Rafath Abbas, Raja Jugal Kishore of Bhopal, Dwaraka Pershad 'Ufaq' of Lucknow and Naubat Rai *'Nazr'*, the journalist from Lucknow, Khanulal 'Taib' of Lucknow, Rai Ram Sahe 'Tamanna', Kanta Pershad, Editor of Kayesths Hitkari, Jay Prakash Lal, K.C.I.E., *Deewan* of Dharmavaram State, the Raja of Wanaparthy and other nobles and scholars.

'Baqi's correspondence was mostly in Persian verses with Hindu and Muslim scholars in Lucknow, Bhopal, Gwalior and other places. He was in close contacts with the Saxenas in Lucknow. Whenever, he travelled to the North, he ensured that he meets the local Saxena members.

Mushairas are very common among the literary circles. In fact, it is a arena of literary activities wherein the poets on a set topic recite their poems. These gatherings were arranged in Hyderabad during the reigns of Maharaja Chandulal 'Shadan' and Maharaja Kishen Pershad 'Shad'. The eminent poets like Shustri, Baqi, Khuram, Urshi and others were invited for *Mushairas*.

He also composed poems in the form of riddles or puzzles *(Cheestaan)* in Persian. On one occasion, when he found Nizam very upset and anxious to divert his mind from anxiety, he submitted *'Cheestaan Fikr'* or riddle of anxiety. He wrote ....

Ye Bala hai ya fikr insan ko
Khwar karti hai jism ko jan ko

"Anxiety is an evil which affects the thought of the man
Which damages his body and life"

He had a fine sense of humour. When there was a difference between Sir Salar Jung and Amir-i-Kabir, he used to mediate between them. He composed a humorous poem entitled "Salt and Sugar". In this poem, he compared Amir-i-Kabir with sugar and Sir Salar Jung with Salt. Sugar and salt have different properties so also were Salar Jung and Amir-i-Kabir of different temperaments. 'Baqi' wrote....

Hast misl shaker Amir-i-Kabir
Ke ba khalfish ba khulq nist nazir
Hast Mukhtar-ul-Mulk misl namak
Shor awaz zamin sat ta ba falak

In his poem, 'Baqi' wrote that Amir-i-kabir was a treasure of sweetness. He possessed status and wealth and was a religious man. In view of his great qualities of heart, he endeared himself to the people. Mukhtar-ul-Mulk, Salar Jung was like a salt. Salt is an absolute king, no food is worth eating without salt.

'Baqi' was not only a poet of repute but he was equally known for his writings in prose. His style was excellent in prose writing. He used to compose speeches in Persian for Sir Salar Jung-I. Inspite of his busy schedule, the fact is that 'Baqi' devoted most of his time for his literary activities. He left behind voluminous and precious literary works. He had written more than 30 books. Out of them, 23 books are in his favourite language, Persian, of which 20 books are in Persian verse and three in prose. He wrote five books in Urdu and four in Hindi. His books were not only circulated in different parts of India and abroad but were popular and always in demand, especially in Persia (now Iran).

He wrote the following books in Persian verse:

1. *Masnavi Bahar-i-Aam* 1873

   In this Masnavi, 'Baqi' described the arrangement and the lighting of different types of fireworks at the banquet arranged in honour of His Excellency Lord Peneer of Macdolla. Dining tables were arranged with beautiful glassware, chinese cutlery, a variety of food dishes including fish, chicken, *kabab, pulav,* different types of desserts, fruit juices and fruits. A beautifully decorated house was arranged for his residence.

This *Masnavi* is a fascinating combination of words. With a few strokes of his pen, he made readers imagine as if they themselves were the participants at the banquet.

2. *Prince Nama* – 1875

   In 1875, the Prince of Wales, the Crown Prince of the Empress of India, visited India. 'Baqi' wrote a detailed account of Prince of Wales and the purpose of his visit. Prince Nama is in the form of a *Masnavi*. The following couplet is sufficient for praising this *Masnavi*.

   Aabdar aisi masnavi likhi ke Baqi jo sunen
   Phenk den apna qalam ahal sukhan pani men.

   'Baqi', you have composed a brilliant and sparkling Masnavi, such that other poets, whoever hears this, will throw away their compositions in water."

3. *Masnavi Sanae Badae* – 1876

   It is the best example of the art of literary expression. It was an accepted fact that 'Baqi' was one of the best poets for eloquence in Persian verse Hyderabad had ever produced. In this *masnavi* 'Baqi' described figures of speech.

4. *Kuliyat Yadgar-i-Baqi* – 1882

   Kuliyat comprises his Persian *Ghazals*, which show his mastery over the Persian language. Choice of idioms, apt construction, lofty thoughts, beauty and eloquence have given life to his *Ghazals*. His *Ghazals* bear testimony to his excellent knowledge of Persian. 'Baqi' wrote about his *Ghazals*.

   Sani Tumhara Koi Baqi Nanin Deccan Men

5. *Qasaid-i-Baqi* – 1882

   'Baqi' wrote *qasidas* in Persian language in praise of

God, Mir Mahbub Ali Khan, Nizam-VI, Sir Salar Jung-I, his father Rai Narhari Pershad, and also the River Musi and natural topics. He had great regard for the Nizam and Sir Salar Jung-I and was very sincere to them. He was their genuine well-wisher. These *Qasidas* are full of chastened emotions, delicacy of ideas, and refined diction.

6. *Kunuz-ul-Tawarikh* – 1884

   It is a collection of historical events in the form of chronograms. A chronogram, records graphically the moment or duration of an event. 'Baqi' composed chronograms on different occasions. It is divided into four parts. The volume of work itself shows that these chronogrammatic verses evince considerable literary merit.

7. *Munshiat-i-Baqi* – 1884

   Munshiat-i-Baqi is a composition comprising many figures of speech.

8. *Zarb-ul-Amasal* – 1885

   'Baqi' composed poems from popularly known proverbs. The subjects, which he has chosen are very considerable and thoughtful. These verses are judged as an excellent works.

9. *Pairaya-i-Uroz* – 1887

   A Persian prosody used in poetry. It can also be called a science of versification of speech rhythm. It was written keeping in view its usefulness to modern poets. Its lesser-known Arabic rhythms are used commonly in Persian. Pairaya-i-Uroz dealt with the methodology used in Persian prosody.

10. *Kalam-i-Mutafarikhat* – 1887

    A collection of miscellaneous petitions in poetry addressed to Nizam, Salar Jung-II, Moulana Rafat Abbas, Gen. Council Balus of Iran and others. Besides these, it contains his *Qasidas* and *Ghazals*.

11. *Bhagwat Sharif* – 1889

    In 1894 'Baqi' sent twenty copies of '*Bhagwat Sharif*' through Pandit Gokul Pershad for its distribution in the literary circles of North India. *Bhagwat Sharif* is the translation of *Bhagwat into Persian language.* It is the sacred book of the Hindus.

12. *Rubaiyat-i-Babarkat* – 1892

    'Baqi' composed these Rubaiyat on the ninety nine names of ***'Allah'***. The book also contains one *Qasida, Haftband* and a *Marsia* (elegy) on Hazrat Imam Hussain. These Rubaiyat show that 'Baqi' was deeply influenced by Sufi thoughts.

13. *Masnavi Shama Munwar* – 1894

    'Baqi' was the follower of Bhaskaranand Swami, a saint from Benares. Most of his children died at a very young age. Due to this loss, he was very depressed. When his son, Narsing Raj fell sick at the age of five, he went to Benares along with his son and met swami, who consoled 'Baqi' and assured him of the speedy recovery of his son. Thereafter, 'Baqi' became the follower of Bhaskaranand Swami. *Masnavi* Shama Munawar is the biography of this saint written in Persian verse.

14. *Masnavi Bagh-i-Razakh* – 1894

    This *Masnavi* is in Persian. It is an eloquent literary work of 'Baqi'. The eloquent and rhetorical descriptions in this *masnavi* are just like a combination of sugar and milk.

    On the advice of Nizam, 'Baqi' studied in detail, the medicinal properties, benefits and ill-effects of all the food items, such as, vegetables, pulses, grains, fruits, flesh of animals and birds, juices and beverages, Bagh-i-Razakh is composed in alphabetical order of these items.

    Subsequently, Bagh-i-Razakh was translated into Urdu by Abid Ansari in 1983 and published by Rai Narhar Raj 'Saqi'.

15. *Keshavnama*

    Keshavnama is written in praise of Ad-Keshav. Besides this, 'Baqi' compiled the ancestral history and the history of the rehabilitation of the deserted place of Chennarayani Gutta at Keshavgiri in the same book.

16. *Tambihat-i-Baqi*

    'Baqi' had written *Tambihat* or admonitions in the form of *masnavi*. In the beginning, he composed a *Hamd*. A very good example of such an admonition is:

    Ghadiyal jo takh se nahin hat ti hai
    Kante ki zuban se bas yahi ratti hai
    Badhta hai na din na raat badhti hai dekh
    Her aan teri umer kis khader ghati hai

    The clock which is permanently hanging on the wall and its hands in the form of tongue goes on reminding us that neighther day nor night increases but it is man's life which decreases every second."

17. *Maktoobat-i-Manzooma*

    A collection of letters addressed to different personalities by 'Baqi' are composed in poetical form. Besides this, he has described the visits of Nizam to various places, his birthday celebrations, and the ceremony of Salar Jung-II assuming the charge of Diwan.

18. *Zamzame-Baqi*

    Persian songs based on the metres of *Kabat* or Hindi verses were the main features of *Zamzame* 'Baqi'. The governor of Iran, when invited by 'Baqi' to his residence, enjoyed these songs sung by expert *Qhawwals,* and was surprised at the perfect composition. The governor named it as *Tohfa-i-Hind !* (Gift of Hindustan)

19. *Rubaiyat Munajat-e-Baraane-Rahmat*

    In 1877, Hyderabad was affected badly by famine due to scanty rainfall. In the city, prayers for rain were held in mosques and temples. Anxiety and worry were drawn upon the faces of the Hyderabadis. Like other citizens of Hyderabad, 'Baqi' too was worried. He composed *Rubaiyat* for the prayers of rain and named it as *'Munajat Baraane-Rahmat'*. He presented his composition to Salar Jung-II. It is said that Salar Jung daily recited these *Rubaiyat* during the famine. When it started raining, he was delighted at what he perceived as the effect of his recitation of these *Rubaiyat*.

20. *Baqi Nama* (Details of this book are not available)

    The list of poetry books shows that Baqi was more interested in poetry than prose. There are only three books available in Persian prose.

21. *Afzal-ul-Tasih*

    A lexicon in Persian language.

22. *Tosha-i-Akhebat* (Provision for the last journey)

    'Baqi' travelled throughout India extensively, and visited religious and sacred places of both the Hindus and the Muslims. By visiting these holy places, he not only had the chance to have the darshan of God at various places and sought blessings, but also by the grace of God he prepared himself for the last journey and believed that he had ensured good in the life to come. *'Tosha-i-Akhebat'* is the collection of his travels in Persian.

23. *Mahabharat*

    Out of eighteen chapters, 'Baqi' could translate only two. The translation of *'Mahabharat'* remained incomplete due to the death of Baqi in 1896.

24. *Teerath Mal*

    Teerath Mal is the collection of *Bhajans*, which he composed during his travels to the holy places.

25. *Keshav Puran*- 1884

    Keshav Puran is composed in the Hindi language. It was published in 1884. It is a translation from

Sanskrit. 'Baqi' had described the greatness and glory of Keshav.

At the end of the book he wrote that this book was written in 1884, when the Asaf Jahi ruler Mir Mahbub Ali Khan was the ruling King and Laiq Ali Khan was *Diwan.*

26. *Bhagwatsaar* – 1890

'Baqi' had attempted the impossible and proved that he could condense a subject into a few words. *'Bhagwat'*, the sacred book of the Hindus, is a voluminous work about the glory of Lord Krishna. 'Baqi' summarised it and published it in 1890, comprising only ten pages. This book is useful for the followers of Lord Krishna for daily recitation.

After completing the book, he handed over the manuscript to Pandit Munnalal of Kashi for necessary correction before its publication.

27. *Shambo Puran*

Katha, Doha, Chaupai, Ram Charitra Manas.

This is a *Katha* of Shri Mahadev in poetry which contains 149 *Dohas* and 1192 *Chaupai*. In fact it is on line with Ramcharitra Manas.

'Baqi' also has Urdu publications to his credit. The following are his Urdu books.

28. *Tahqheeqhat Siyaq-i-Baqi* – 1887

He started this book with a *'Hamd'* (Praise of God). He was not only a scholar, philosopher and poet, but also a mathematician. This book contains arithmetical calculations, both in prose and poetry. He has shown simple ways of making calculations.

29. *Baqa-i-Baqi* – 1890

A *diwan* or collection of Urdu *Ghazals*. It contains simple language and apt idioms which are the essence of his Urdu *Ghazals*. He had composed *Ghazals* in small metres.

30. *Dard-i-Baqi-o-Durd-i-Saqi-* 1891 (Published in 1922)

    'Baqi' translated Persian Rubaiyat of Khwajah Mir Dard into Urdu, eventhough his favourite language was Persian. Mir Dard was the most conspicuous Sufi poet. His *Rubaiyat* are replete with sufi verses. 'Baqi' was probably influenced by his sufi doctrines. As a result, he decided to translate them into Urdu. He composed a chronogram at the end of the book and mentioned that "even though he was not very proficient in Urdu, he ventured to translate it into Urdu from Persian".

    Unki jo rubaiyat Farsi mein thein
    Urdu men Kiya Jo na thi mashaqi

    The translations of *Rubaiyat* of Khaja Mir 'Dard' are neat, eloquent and can be ranked among the best. The translation is excellent.

    These *Rubaiyats* were translated in the year 1892, but 'Baqi' could not publish them during his life time. His son, Raja Narsing Raj 'Aali' got them published in the year 1922.

31. *Shiv Puran* – 1890

    'Baqi' wrote in 1890 *Shiv Puran* in Urdu verse using mainly the words of Braj / Awadi Bhasha. It remained unpublished. *Shiv Puran* is transliterated from Urdu script to Hindi. It is published in the year 2017.

32. *Sudhamaan Nama* (Persian)

    This is an unpublished manuscript written during 1307 A.H. (1889 A.D.). It contains brief description of Bahmani period. It gives a message of tranquility and also contains proverbs.

33. *Khulasa Karistan Bukaram* (Persian)

    This is an unpublished manuscript written in the year 1313 A.H. (1895 A.D.). This book contains different types of prayers of God.

Most of the above books are available at Salar Jung Museum Library, under the family collection of Raja Narsing Raj.

The voluminous publications of 'Baqi' in Persian prose and poetry are the testimony to the fact that he was well versed with Persian. Besides these, 'Baqi' maintained daily diaries in Persian language. These diaries are important sources of reference of historical value. These diaries also provide the present day scholars the glimpses of the events in the royal palace. These diaries are excellent source of information on social, religious and cultural ceremonies connected with the Nizams Palace in chronological order. Besides these, diaries also present the events, such as, visit of the Royal dignitaries, *Darbars* and other important events in Nizam's Palace.

'Baqi' encouraged others in their literary activities. He published two manuscripts – one, *Inshai Chimnalal*, which is about his maternal grandfather and *Ramayan Masiha* in 1890. At the request of Raja Girdhari Pershad, in 1894 *'Yaticharitra'* a short biography of Swami Bhaskaranand Sarswati, written by Babu Gopalchand Chatterjee in English, was translated into Urdu.

No doubt, the study of the voluminous works of 'Baqi' shows that he had authority over Persian language. He was a genius of many facets. He had close contacts with literary figures of Northern India who always acknowledges the genius and profound knowledge of 'Baqi'.

As mentioned earlier 'Baqi' was a Urdu poet of repute as well. When his Urdu *'Deewan'* was published, Munshi Dwaraka Pershad *'Ufaq'*, Munshi Ram Sahai *'Tamanna'*, Mata Pershad *'Nisan'* and Dhanpat Rai wrote chronograms in appreciation of his *'Diwan'*.

It can be concluded that 'Baqi' was a prolific writer in Persian. His writings were not only on Sufism, which were predominant, but he was the master of sentiments, philosophy and naturalism. He had written on a variety of subjects. It can be said that he widened the field of human society, customs, manners, and festivals observed during the period. No doubt, he was a gifted poet and the genius in his own way. His chronograms are considered to be best and invaluable contribution to the history of Hyderabad.

In her book entitled Hafiz 'Mir Mohammed Shamsuddin Faiz : Life and Works', Dr Laeeq Salaah wrote that 'Baqi's book entitled *'Shajaratul Ansaab'* which is available at Osmania University Library. Its manuscript number is 923/1 it is an unpublished manuscript. 'Baqi' completed this in 1309 A.H. (1891A.D.). In one of his *Qataa*, he explained importance of *Shajara* (Family Tree) and from the second *Qataa*, the year of its calligraphy could derive.

The book begins with *'Hamd'* (Praise of God) and the family tree of Prophet Mohammed (P.B.U.H.). The date of death etc. have been derived from the couplets and *Misras* (single line of a couplet). One of them is under the period 103:

"Az Mohammed Zamana Khaali Shawad (11, H)

Beside the family tree of Prophet Mohammed, the family tree of 12 *Imaams* of the Muslim, rulers of the Asaf Jahi dynasty, Anwaruddin Khan, ruler of Arcott, Amir-i-Kabir, Abul Fateh Khan and Salar Jung are given.

It is a fact that 'Baqi' occupied a prominent place among the literary figures of India. He was a man of merit and the master of his craft, a distinguished poet and a philosopher of repute.

Besides Persian and Urdu, 'Baqi' wrote poetry in Hindi language also. He wrote *Bhajans* in Urdu whenever he visited the religious places in India; he has described the importance of God and Goddesses in his *Bhajans*. These *Bhajans* are available in his book *'Tosh-i-Akhibat'*.

'Baqi' was a very good calligrapher and known for his calligraphy. He was also a *Zoodnavees* a fast writer.

It was a red letter day in the life of Raja Girdhari Pershad, when Mir Mahbub Ali Khan paid visit to Bansi Raja at his palace during 1895. Bansi Raja could not visit Nizam for a month due to his ill health. As a result, Nizam decided to visit Bansi Raja without prior intimation. Bansi Raja was caught unaware.

It was a honour not only to Bansi Raja but the entire family. The joy came out of the heart of Bansi Raja in the form of verses. 'Baqi' wrote poems, *Rubai* and *Qatats* in Persian and distributed among the relatives, close associates and friends. He wrote:

Ba, Qasr-I Past Baqi Qaiser-i-Ali Muqam Aamad

Zahe Izzat Afzai Pushtaini Ghulam Amad

It was a great pleasure and honour for 'Baqi' when the exalted King visited the humble palace of his old servant.

In one of his poem, he expressed his joy in the following stanza:

Nazr Dil Dar Dad O Dar Pesh Us Aqidat Amada

The visit of Nizam to my palace is great honour for me. On this occasion, I offer *Nazr* and my heart to the King with devotion and firm belief.

After leading a pious and benevolent life, Bansi Raja closed his eyes on 24 July 1896. It is said that when Mir Mahbub Ali Khan 'Asif' was informed about Bansi Raja's passing away, tears rolled out of his eyes. The grief and sorrow of Mir Mahbub Ali Khan cannot be described in words, but '*Tears of Asif*' were rich tribute to the departed soul.

It was customary during those days that the funerals of the nobles had to be arranged only after the permission of the Nizam. Accordingly, after obtaining the Nizam's permission the funeral of Raja Girdhari Pershad alias 'Bansi Raja' was arranged with state honours. People of different communities accompanied the funeral procession.

A number of poets of Hyderabad and outside paid their tributes to Bansi Raja by writing chronograms on his death. Maharaja Sir Kishan Pershad, the then *Peshkar* wrote

Bansi Raja chu Raft uz alam
Shair-i-Khush tabiyat o khushkho

Saal tarikh-i-fout o ae shad
Baqi khush mizaj mard bagu

1314 A.H. (1896)

Bansi Raja went away from this world. He was a poet of good temperament and good manners. O' Shad -! tell the year of death of 'Baqi' good natured.

The tutor of Nizam-VI and the famous Urdu poet '*Fasih-ul-Mulk'*, Nawab Mirza 'Dagh' expressed his grief in these words....

Baikunth ko jab sidhare Raja nagaah
Kya sadma o gham dil ko hua jankaah
Likh 'Dagh' ye saal swargbashi ka tu
Karta rahe Baqi aur Fani ae ah

"When Bansi Raja suddenly left for heavenly abode,
It was a moment of shock, grief and distress.
O 'Dagh', write the chronogram for the departed soul,
'Baqi' is no more."
Continue to say 'Baqi' (immortal) and say mortal.

Munshi Khanulal 'Talib', a poet of Lucknow expressed his feelings in these following verses:

Raja Baqi ka sunkar dar-i-fani se safar
Ahel-i-duniya surat-i-ainah shashdar ho gaye
Uth gayi duniya se rasm-i-khalq o hamdardi quam
Faiz men ye abre nisan ke baraber ho gaye
Qadrdani khatam thi is zat par har ilm ki
Fun-i-nazm o nasar men Saadi ke ham asar ho gaye
Farsi men is khadar hai apka shaya kalam
Dekh kar jisko tahaiyur men sukhanwar ho gye.

After hearing the journey of Raja 'Baqi' from this mortal world, people of the world were shocked like a mirror. The tradition of benevolence for mankind from the world. In generosity, he turned like a spring cloud. The appreciation of every knowledge ended with this personality. His contribution in the art of composing prose and poetry made him the contemporary of the Persian Poet *'Saadi'*. His contribution in Persian is so much published that by seeing it many poets got astonished.

The name 'Bansi Raja' will remain immortal. His son, Raja Narsing Raj 'Aali' while paying rich tributes to his father rightly wrote ...

Aali Na Mitega Kabhi Nam-i-Baqi

'Aali, the name 'Baqi' will never be erased'.

No history of the erstwhile State of Hyderabad would be complete unless sufficient prominence is given to the contribution made by him.

Different research scholars have done research on 'Baqi's contribution to Urdu and Persian literature.

Ms. Najeeba Begum wrote a dissertation entitled *'Raja Girdhari Pershad 'Baqi' 'Shaqsiyat Aur Urdu Shayeri'* for her M.A. Degree in Urdu to Osmania University, Hyderabad, in the year 1967.

In the year 1976, an M.Phil. dissertation in Urdu was submitted to Osmania University by Ms. Pavan Kumari under the title *"Raja Girdhari Pershad 'Baqi' Aur inke Khandan Ki Urdu Adabi Khidmat"*. She published it in the year 2009.

A Ph.D. Theses entitled *'A Critical Study of the Persian Poetry of Raja Girdhari Pershad 'Baqi' alias Bansi Raja'* was submitted in Maulana Azad National Urdu University, Hyderabad, India, by a Research Scholar Mohammed Quader Mohiuddin Siddiqui.

The letters addressed to Bansi Raja by Mir Mahbub Ali Khan, Nizam-VI, Salar Jung, Amir-i-Kabir, a renowned Urdu poet, nobles, dignitaries, Dagh Dehlvi, scholars from the Northern India, are available at the Salar Jung Museum Library, Hyderabad, India, under the family collection of Raja Narsing Raj 'Aali'.

Views of different scholars and writers about Raja Girdhari Pershad 'Baqi':

— Writing about Masnavi Sanae-Badae, Sarfaraz Ali 'Wasafi' wrote that 'Baqi' is an incomparable master of the time. His *Masnavi* is pleasing, eloquent and chaste.

— Maulana Syed Shushtari 'Tuba' wrote a review in Arabic for Baqi's book 'Rubaiyat-e-Babarkat'.

— Mirza Abbas Khan Sherwani, Mohd. Abdul Majeed, Yousuf Hussain 'Raza', Kifayat Ullah 'Baig' and many others including Kayasth Saxena from Northern India praised Baqi's literary contribution. They have written *Qasidas, Chro*nogram, Verses and Reviews.

— In 1892, Kamta Pershad, *Sarishtedar* of Gwalior, wrote to 'Baqi' that the verses from *'Kuliyat'* made him delirious and that he had never read before such a high hyperbole. He considered 'Baqi's verses superior to the poets of Iran.

— Ram Babu Saxena in his book *'History of Urdu Literature'* wrote that Dagh Dehlvi sought introduction to Nizam Mir Mahbub Ali Khan through Bansi Raja. Later, Dagh Dehlvi became the tutor of Nizam for Urdu poetry.

— While writing about 'Baqi', Dr Syed Mohiuddin Qadri Zore, in his book *'Muraqqa-e-Sukhan'* Volume-I (1935) wrote that in Urdu *Ghazals*, the influence of later poets of Lucknow is predominant. More emphasis is laid on the appearance of couplets, correct usage of Urdu, their structure, relevance and language.

— In his article 'Few Kayasths, Urdu Poets of Deccan' in *'Subras' (*January 1940). Professor Mahender Raj

Saxena wrote that the poetry of 'Baqi' is very simple, although, he laid stress on paronomasia which was the prominent feature of the literary taste of that period. Describing four examples or more in a couplet, far-off words construction, ambiguity, verbosity were the main literary trends of that age, 'Baqi' also could not prevent himself from this trend.

— Dr Laeeq Salaah in her book Hafiz Mir Mohammed Shamsuddin Faiz: Life and Works (1980) wrote that 'Baqi' translated Khaja Mir Dard's Persian quatrains so nicely that they have the beauty of preservation.

She further wrote that an unpublished quatrain (*Qasida*) is preserved in Salar Jung Museum, Hyderabad, India, which he had written to analogize Nawab Salar Jung. She also wrote that 'Baqi' illuminated the lamp of the School of Shamsuddin 'Faiz'. Idiomatic expressions, views of colloquial language and beautiful way of expression makes his couplets attractive.

She also wrote that Munshi Dwaraka Pershad of Lucknow praised the poetry of 'Baqi'. *Ufaq* in his *Qataat* wrote that 'Baqi' was on par with *Khusro, Saadi, Firdousi, Mir, Sauda and the great Urdu poet Ghalib.*

— In the article 'Girdhari Pershad Mahbub Nawazwant 'Baqi' by Dr Syed Mohiuddin Qadri Zore referred in *'Ifaadaat-e-Zore'* Volume-IV compiled by Syed Rafiuddin Qadri, it is mentioned that Girdhari Pershad Mahbub Nawazwant is known as Bansi Raja. His palace is still there at Hussaini Alam. It is a centre of various literary activities.

— In the article 'Girdhari Pershad Mahbub Nawazwant 'Baqi' – a review' published in *'Etemaad'* Urdu daily on 30th April 2017, Dr Mohsin Jalgaonvi wrote that in 'Baqi' we find scholarly maturity and grip of language. We also find admonition, advice, anxiety and about doomsday, remembrance of God and the poems on Sufism. In addition to these qualities, construction of thought, relevance, suitability, ambiguity and colloquialism are found.

RAJA NARSING RAJ

Chapter – Six

Raja Narsing Raj 'Aali'

In the realm of Urdu literature and poetry, the personality of Raja Narsing Raj 'Aali' needs no introduction among the prudent, eloquent and intelligent circles of Urdu poets. He was the son of Hyderabad's renowned personality, Raja Girdhari Pershad, Mahbub Nawazwant, 'Baqi'. He was born in November, 1889. With the blessings of God-loving veteran, Swami Bhaskaranand Maharaj of Benaras, he came out of the clutches of death and cured. After recovering from ailment, he engaged himself in the worldly affairs and other struggles of life.

Bhaskaranand Swami desired that Raja Girdhari Pershad alias 'Bansi Raja' should perform the marriage ceremony of Raja Narsing Raj at Benaras. Matrimonial alliance was finalised in the Kayasth family of Bhopal. Swamiji himself performed the wedding of Raja Narsing Raj. The father of the girl was Rai Kanhaiah Lal. In 1896, the wedding ceremony of Raja Narsing Raj was performed with great pomp and glory in Bhopal. Kashi Naresh had made all the arrangements of marriage under his personal supervision. The marriage was attended besides Kashi Naresh, Rani of Damaron and Raja of Sandela. Noted respectable persons were invited from Itarsi and Bhopal. Kashi Naresh presented him a Diamond *Jigah*. During this period, Nawab Mir Mahboob Ali Khan, Nizam-VI was the ruler of Hyderabad. Raja Girdhari Pershad was not only the *'Sarishtedar'* but he was also incharge of all the Royal Palaces beside Royal kitchen.

At the instance of the King, a warm welcome was given to Raja Saheb, bride and other guests at the railway station when he returned from Bhopal after the marriage on 19th February 1896.

To his surprise, he found elephants and *Amari,* two *Palkies,* troops of *Sarf-e-Khas*, Arabs of his *Sharishta*, and cavalry of Sultan Nawaz Jung. Bansi Raja was on the *Palki* and the bride and groom were seated on the *Chandole*. The nephew of Bansi Raja, Sri Pershad, led the procession in the *Ambari*. All the other relatives accompanied the procession. A*'Taifa'* performed the dance from Station to Bansi Raja's Palace at Hussaini Alam.

It was customary in those days that in marriages, functions and on auspicious occasions, *Taifa*, *Mujra* and *Qawwali* were the entertainments to the nobles, aristocrats and other dignitaries. There was a separate department known as *Daftar-i-Tarab-O-Nishat* which was created for the need of women. They were paid monthly salary to enable them to lead a decent life. These women were respected and given jewellery, clothes etc. on different occasions.

A few days after the marriage of Raja Narsing Raj, Raja Girdhari Pershad passed away. At the young age of Narsing Raj, his father's demise put him in the difficult situation. It is said that on hearing the demise of Bansi Raja, tears rolled out of the eyes of Nawab Mir Mahbub Ali Khan, Nizam-VI. Expressing his grief, the king, sent a white Shawl on this occasion. Since both the sons of Bansi Raja were very young, his estate was given under the control of Court of Wards, *Sarf-e-Khas* estate. This status was revoked by the King later.

Raja Narsing Raj 'Aali' received his early education in Hindi, Marathi and Persian at home. Later, he was admitted into *Madrasa-i-'Aaliya*, where he studied upto matriculation. His classmates were Turab Yar Jung 'Sayeed', Raja Pertap Girji, Syed Ali Akbar, later he became the Principal of the Nizam College, Professor Hasan Khan Sherwani and many others.

On the occasion of 40th anniversary of Nawab Mir Mahbub Ali Khan, in 1905, Raja Narsing Raj 'Aali' was awarded the title of "Raja Bahadur". After the death of his father, both the brothers, Raja Narsing Raj and Mahbub Raj were nurtured under the guardianship of their mother. This affection of their mother was consoling to both the brothers. 'Aali' wrote about his mother.

Rishte 'Aali' Bahut Hain Duniya Mein
Madiri Meher Kis Se Mumkin Hai

(There are many relations in this world, but who can give the kind of affection, the mother gives.)

Raja Narsing Raj 'Aali' performed the wedding ceremony of his younger brother, Rai Mahbub Raj under the benevolence of the mother with the daughter of Rai Thakur Pershad in 1911. He never made his younger brother Mahboob Raj felt the absence of his father.

He was habituated to bear the grief and sorrow right from the young age. In 1922, his wife passed away after a brief illness. He thought that instead of becoming the target of mourning and to receive condolences from the friends and relatives, it is fit to make best use of the available time. He, therefore, took out the manuscript of Bansi Raja which was a translation of Persian quatrains *(Rubaiyat)* of Khwaja Mir Dard into Urdu.

Raja Narsing Raj 'Aali' writes that the compilation of a perfect and God-fearing person (Mystic), in whatever language in which, it is written, its beauty and its interpretation, lofty thoughts and superb quality of its thought contents could only be enjoyed by a person who is an expert of that language. He alone can comprehend the thoughts of the poet.

Khwaja Mir Dard's poetry is very explicit, clean, commonly comprehensible and very effective immersed in the mystic colour. He, therefore, thought that it is his prime duty to get the Urdu translation of Khwaja Mir Dard's *Rubaiyat* published. He got this compilation published in 1922 under the title *'Dard-i-Baqi-o-Durd-i-Saqi'*.

Keeping in mind, the domestic responsibilities and better care of children, he refused to marry again. In Secretariat of

Government Army, Raja Narsing Raj 'Aali' was appointed as Honorary Assistant in 1916. As per the Royal Order, he was also made the member of the Commission for Celebrations. He held this position for one and half year. In 1919, he was appointed as the Superintendent of Saving Bank and Deputy Director of Posts. In addition, to these positions, he was selected for Railways Department also. In whatever Department, he was posted; Raja Narsing Raj earned a good name and fame.

Raja Narsing Raj had the honour of presenting *'Itr'* and *'Pan'* during the Mughlai and English *Darbar*. This was an hereditary honour.

After his father's death, his mother took care of both of her sons, Raja Narsing Raj 'Aali' and Mahbub Raj. She paid special attention on both these children. She imparted such a nice training to them that they had no parallel in morals and character. They were the complete embodiment of love, sincerity and kindness. They were compared by the members of the family as they refer to them with the smile, the pair of "Ram Lakshman". Not only their relatives but their friends recognised their good character.

Bahadur Yar Jung and Mandoor Khan were brothers. After the demise of their father, there was a dispute about the division of property. The case went to court. At that time, Maharaja Kishan Pershad intervened and appointed Raja Narsing Raj as an arbitrator and desired that he should guide both the brothers. Raja Narsing Raj settled this matter in an amicable way. Both the brothers accepted his verdict and evaded their differences. Both the brothers got very much impressed with the personality and advice of Raja Narsing Raj. They used to respect him and maintained brotherly relations with him.

Bahadur Yar Jung had hosted an "At Home" on the occasion of Mohammed Ali Jinnah's visit to Hyderabad in 1945. Raja Narsing Raj 'Aali' was also invited for this function. Introducing Raja Narsing Raj to Mr Mohammed Ali Jinnah, Nawab Bahadur Yar Jung told him that he had learnt the lesson of "Morals and Unity" from Raja Narsing Raj. It reveals that Raja Narsing Raj's personality, morals and manners had cast a deep impression on Nawab Bahadur Yar Jung.

Raja Narsing Raj was very orthodox. He strictly followed all the traditions of his family. He had imbibed the hereditary attribute of hospitality from his father. He was a man of pleasant etiquette and kindness. He used to meet everyone cheerfully. It was against his nature to hurt the feelings of others. He always used to be ready to help others. Whenever there was an opportunity to recommend, he never used to find pretexts. Earnestness, seriousness, tolerance and forbearance were the special characteristic features of his personality.

Raja Narsing Raj 'Aali' used to consider education as the necessity of life. Keeping in tune with the importance and demands of that time. He laid more emphasis on women's education. He, set up two schools, one for boys by name '*Kayasth Pathashala*' located within the premises of the Palace of Bansi Raja and a girls' school by name '*Shakti Kanya Pathashala*' at Hussaini Alam.

Like Raja Girdhari Pershad, he was interested in social reforms. He used to avoid large sums on the occasions of weddings and advised others to follow it. In olden days, the marriage functions used to be held for three days. He advised that it should be held for only one day. He raised his voice against bridal dowry. He himself practiced it and advised others also to follow.

He started a Co-operative Society of *Kayasth Mansabdars* and became its President.

Through his poetry, he raised his voice against the social evils. He made an attempt to create awareness about the evils of gambling and drinking wine. About the gamblers he writes:

Quatrain

Juwwe Mein Hai Qatl Aur Ladna Ziyada
(In gambling, there is more killing and quarrels)

Sambhalna Hai Kum Aur Ujadna Ziyada
(There is less sustainment and more ruination)

Kahein Aur Kya Mukhtasar Hai Yeh 'Aali'
(What should we say, this is summary of it)

Ke Banna Hai Kam Aur Bigadna Ziyada
(To become good is less and to destroy is more)

Har Ek Ghar Mein Hota Shivala Nahin Hai
(There is no Shiva's temple in every house)

Andhere Mein Hargiz Ujala Nahin Hai
(By no means there is sunshine in darkness)

Na Khele Juwwa Koi Hai Hukm-e-Mazhab
(No one should gamble, it is the tenet of the religion)

Diwali Hai Yeh Kuch Diwala Nahin Hai
(It is Diwali and not Diwala (Bankruptcy))

About drinking wine, his advice is:

Shaukh Mein May Ke Deke Zar Naqd Liya Hai Muft Dard-e-Sar
(In fondness for wine by giving money in cash invited headache)

Barah Mahine Raat Din Dekhiye Hai Woh Doctor Ka Ghar
(All the twelve months, day and night, he sees the doctor's house)

Ghar Ki Na Ho Fikr Us Ko Kya Bachon Ki Le Khabar
(One who does not bother about his house, how can he take care of his children)

Kahne Ka Kya Hai Asar Baqi Na Ho Jo Dil Jigar
(What is the effect of telling him if his heart and liver are damaged?)

Sheesha Wo Jaam Chorh do Chorh do Chorh Do Sharaab Chod Do
(Leave the bottle and cup, leave wine, leave wine)

Sharaab Peene Ko Khoon Samjho Na Dil Jalakar Kabab Kardo
(Think drinking wine as drinking blood, don't burn the heart to make kabab)

Yeh Ahle Dil Ki Naseehatein Hain Yeh Hukme
Sharaab Woh Kitab Bhi Hai
(It is the advice of the God-fearing people; it is also the
tenet of the jurisprudence and the book)

Jo Is Ko Chorho To Fayeda Hai Tamaam
Ghar Mein Rahegi Barkat
(Anyone who leaves it, it is completely benefited, there
would be grace in the entire house)

Azaab Se Najaat Hogi, Aur Is Se Haasil Sawaab Bhi Hai
(You will be relieved of punishment and it is also virtue)

Sheesha Wo Jaam Chorh Do Chorh Do Sharaab Chod Do
(Leave the bottle and cup, leave wine, leave wine)

Raja Narsing Raj 'Aali' was not only the protagonist of the Ganga-Jamuni civilisation of Hyderabad but he was also the supporter of patriotism, sincerity, unanimity, truthfulness, far-sightedness, human friendship and an embodiment of sacrifice. He was rightly proud of his native place, Hyderabad.

'Aali' Ko Baja Naaz Hai Is Mulk-e-Deccan Par
('Aali' is rightly proud of this province of Deccan)
Taqdeer Isi Aab Se Gil Se Lagi Hai
(My fate is associated with this water and soil)

Rahe Aabaad 'Aali' Hyderabad
Hamein Kya Haajat Iran Isfahaan Ki
(Let Hyderabad be inhabited. What is the need
of Iran and Isfahaan for us)

About the grandeur of India, he writes:

Hamara Hind Sub Se Ho Buland Aur Shaan Wala Ho
(Let our India be the highest of all and of grandeur)

Ke Duniya Ke Mumalik Se Badhe Aur Aan Waala Ho
(Let it progress than other countries and let it
hold dignity and self-respect)

On the occasion of the second anniversary of Indian Independence on 15th August 1949, 'Aali' wrote a long poem in *"Hind Naama"* in which the ancient and modern history of India is written in a very attractive way:

Tera Jalaal Aur Jamaal Hai Yeh
(It is your grandeur and prettiness)

Tujh Pe Marte Hain Sab Kamaal Hai Yeh
(Everybody longs for you, it is wonderful)

Donon Qaumoun Ki Tu Hi Maadar Hai
(You are the mother of both the communities)

Sab Pujari Hain Tu Hi Mandir Hai
(All are devotees, you are the temple)

Nazre Bad Kahin Na Lage Tujhe
(Let not evil eye cast on you)

Dushmanoun Ke Yeh Dastras Se Bache
(May it be saved from the access of the enemies)

Saari Duniya Mein Bol Baala Hai
(There is a fame in the entire world)

Har Taraf Roshni Ujala Hai
(Everywhere there is light, sunlight)

Ek Hi Tera Lakhlakha Rah Jaye
(Let only your memory remain)

Hindu Muslim Yahanka Sab Ko Bhaye
(Let it be liked by all the Hindus and the Muslims)

Tu Phale Phoole Tera Naam Rahe
(May you flourish, let your name remain)

Tere Bachchon Ko Tera Kaam Rahe
(Let your work remain for your children)

Dil Se Deta Hai Dua Yeh 'Aali'
('Aali' offers prayers from the heart)

Aur Ho Tera Martaba 'Aali'
(Let your status be elevated more 'Aali')

Along with patriotism, he advised his brethren to maintain brotherhood, unanimity and to lead the life of peace and tranquility since he was above the concept of narrow-mindedness and prejudice. For him, the Hindus and the Muslims were like brothers and both had intense relations. The following quatrains represent his passions and teachings.

Haq Walo Batao Dair Wo Haram Kahan
(O' people of God, show me where is temple and Kaaba)

Jab Ek Watan Mein Ho To Phir Bair Kahan
(When you are in the same homeland where is enemity)

Khaliq Donon Ka Jab Nahin Do 'Aali'
(When the Creator of both is one not two 'Aali')

Hindu Muslim Hain Ek Ghair Kahan
(The Hindus and the Muslims are one, not aliens)

Ahle Duniya Bigadte Jaate Hain
(The people of the world get enraged)

Hindu Muslim ke Gahre Nate Hain
(The Hindus and the Muslims have intense relations)

Sab Biradar Hain Ghair 'Aali' Kaun
(All are brethren, who are aliens)

Yeh Buzrugoun Se sunte Aye Hain
(We have been hearing it from the ancestors)

Taassub Se Khuda Mahfooz Rakhe
(May God protect from prejudice)

Hazaron Mar Chuke Hain is Waba Se
(Thousands have died from this epidemic)

In the beginning of the Twentieth Century, the conditions were peaceful. Everywhere there was peace and safety. The Hindus and the Muslims used to participate in the festivals of each other. They used to attend *'Jataras', 'Melas'* and *'Urs'* (Death Anniversary of Muslim Saint). The *'Moharram'* of Hyderabad is an exemplary example for national integration. Raja Narsing Raja 'Aali', used to celebrate the *'Jatara'* of the ancient temple of Keshavagiri every year on a grand scale. The invitees used to be from the relatives and friends. The good natured temperament and humility of Raja Saheb used to welcome everyone equally.

Raja Narsing Raj was a philanthropist. He used to perform the *Jatara* of the temple on a grand scale. He maintained temples. The *Jatara* of Keshava Swami temple used to be conducted on a grand scale wherein the then Prime Minister Maharaja Sir Kishan Pershad and other dignitaries used to attend.

He donated about 35 acres of prime land within Hyderabad City limits to a saint of Maharashtra for his *'Ashram'*.

Bansi Raja himself, his relatives and the younger generation kept the candle of knowledge and literature illuminated. They added to the treasure of literature with their valuable contributions and magnificent masterpieces, which is a valuable literary heritage. There is hardly any precedent of their literary contributions.

Raja Narsing Raj "Aali" wrote the following books:

'Dard-e-Baqi-o-Durd-e-Saqi':

"Aali" compiled this book which contains the translation of Persian *Rubaiyat* of Khaja Mir Dard into Urdu, which his father, Raja Girdhari Pershad 'Baqi' had translated from Persian into Urdu. He published in the year 1922.

'Armughaan-e-Mehbub':

'Aali' wrote this book in 1931 in the memory of his brother Mahbub Raj, who passed away after a brief illness. This book contains poems and chronograms compiled by his family members to pay tribute.

'Josh-e-Gham':

'Aali' lost his mother in the year 1939, which gave him a deep shock. He published a long poem in memory of his mother whom he considered supreme. She was compassionate by heart and used to get worried for him. He published this book in Hindi as well under the title ***"Shok Charitra"***.

'Gham-e-Ahbaab-e-Shaad':

This book was published in the year 1940 on the demise of Maharaja Kishan Pershad 'Shad'. It is in the form of *'Marsia'*. 'Aali' expressed his noble qualities and his relations with 'Shad', the last gift of affection to 'Shad'.

Dr Sheela Raj compiled his Ghazals, Rubaiyat and Qataats and published them under the title *'Deewan-e-'Aali'* in 2008.

In the poetry, whatever fragrance of eloquence and perspicuity Raja Narsing Raj 'Aali' has spread through the flowers of his poetry, if they are reviewed, it would become clear that he was a natural poet. He was bestowed with this passion by Nature. He had great interest in Hindi, Persian and Urdu poetry. In his poems, one would get the erudition of passion of both Urdu and Hindi. His poetic name in Urdu (*Nom-de-Plume or Taqallus*) was 'Aali' and in Hindi 'Narsing'. He composed verses in all the genres of poetry, namely *Ghazals*, Poems, Elegies (*Marsias*), quatrains (*Rubaiyat*), *Qataat* (a genre of poetry comprising at least four lines and dealing with the single subject) and *Bhajans* (Hindu rhymes or sacred songs).

If his poetry is reviewed, it can be said that his couplets have elegance, lofty ideas and thoughts, grandeur of imagination and comprehensible approach. On the basis of these attributes, it could be said with certainty that he was a poet of high caliber and esteem. There are many *Ghazals*, which run into 120 to 140 couplets. After reading these *Ghazals* one gets immersed in the novelty of ideas. The evidence of his expertise in language and its expression could be known by studying his *Ghazals*. My pen does neither have the strength nor do I have the appropriate words to throw light on this towering personality. This could be construed as an unsuccessful attempt.

Raja Narsing Raj 'Aali' had a lot of affection for his mother. He considered the service to his mother as felicity.

Jo Ahl Hain Un Se Hikmat Seekho

(Learn wisdom from those who are competent)

Gar Shoukh-e-Saadat Hai To Khidmat Seekho
(If you have the passion for felicity, learn to serve)

Taqat Qudrat Ne Dee Hai Apni Sab Kuch
(Nature has given all its strength)

'Aali' Duniya Mein Maa Se Ulfat Seekho
('Aali' learn in this world, the affection from mother)

Itni Shafaqqat Koyi Kahaan Se Laye
(How can one bring so much affection and kindness?)

Dil Se Laye Ke Ya Zabaan Se Laye
(Should one bring from the heart or the tongue)
'Aali' Betay Ke waste Nemat Hai
('Aali', mother is a blessing for the son)

Maan Mamta Apni Dil Wo Jaan Se Laye
(Mother brings motherly love from her
heart and from her life)

In 1939, the demise of his mother gave him a deep shock. 'Aali' paid homage to the memory of his mother under the title *'Josh-E-Gham'*.

Maan Ke Badle Aaj Hai Aaghosh-e-Gham
(Instead of mother, today, there is lap of grief)

Har Dar Wo Deewar Hai Madhosh-e-Gham
(Every wall and door is intoxicated with grief)

Ghat Nahin Sakta Hai 'Aali' Maan Ka Gham
(The grief of mother's death can't be lessened)

Dekhna Badhta Chala Hai Josh-e-Gham
(See, the fervour of grief has been increasing)

His younger brother, Mahbub Raj was the most favourite of Raja Narsing Raj. In 1930, Mahbub Raj passed away after a brief illness. He expressed the agony of his heart in this manner.

'Aali' Ke Dard-e-Dil Ke Jazbaat Sab Hain Is Mein
(All the passions, pain of heart and sorrows of 'Aali' are in it)

Hai Pesh Dekheiga Yeh Armughaan-e-Mahbub
(It is presented, see, this is the gift of Mahbub)

Dafter Gham Wo Alam Ka Hai Daastaan-e-Muhabbat
(The story of love is the record of agony)

Hai Lafz Lafz Us Ka Aah Wo Fughan-e-Mahbub
(Its every word is the cry of sorrow of Mahbub)

He wrote an elegy in memory of his brother and named it *'Armughaan-e-Mahbub'* and published it in 1931.

Presenting the heart-felt agony of the death of his beloved brother, he said that genuine "brotherly affection" can't be expressed with pen or tongue. Only the heart is the witness that Mahbub was really his beloved brother.

The family of Raja Narsing Raj for generations, remained loyal and well-wisher of Asaf Jahi dynasty and especially the ruler of the time.

M'Aali'k Hain Asaf Zehe Naseeb
(My master is Asaf (VII), it is my good fortune)

Sad Shukr Ke 'Aali' Bhi Un Par Nisaar Hai
(It is hundred times grateful that
'Aali' loves him very much)

He has composed verses eulogizing Nizam-VII on the occasion of his 'Silver Jubilee Celebrations' held in 1936. In these *ghazals*, the element of flattery is not found. He did not demand from anybody any reward for his sincere and unselfish services. His *ghazals* depict the economic prosperity, development and the favours of Nizam-VII.

Mushkiloun Mein Huvi Hai Aasani
(In difficulties, ease has been generated)

Tujh Pe Rahmat Hai Daur-e-Osmani
(It is a blessing, on the reign of Osmani)

Khushk Sahra Bhi Aaj Hain Shadaab
(Even the dry deserts is green today)

Jis Taraf Dekhiye Udhar Hai Aab
(Wherever you see, there is water)

Har Taraf Dekhiye Hai Fun Fun daan
(See every side, there is Art and Artists)

Pad Gayi Jaise Murda Jism Mein Jaan
(As if, the dead body gained life)

Tu Ne Ilm Ko Waqf-e-Khaas Wo Aam Kiya
(You made knowledge devoted to the elite and the public)
Sab Se Behtar Tha Woh Kaam Kiya
(You did what was the best)

Daur-e-Osmani Ke Sab Fidayi Hain
(All are the pledged devotees of the reign of Osmani)

Is Tarah Jaise Bhai Bhai Hain
(As if, they are brothers)

Narsing Raj 'Aali' had a lot of devotion to the then Prime Minister, Maharaja Kishan Pershad 'Shad'. He had not only excellent relationship with Maharaja Kishan Pershad but their relationship and affection were stable and unshaking, which no strongest power of the universe could efface it. This relationship continued with Maharaja till his last breath. Maharaja Kishan Pershad used to call him *'Raja Saheb'* with affectionate and loving appellations. Raja Narsing Raj had the privilege of talking to Maharaja for several hours on many occasions and on different topics. The heartfelt devotion of Raja Narsing Raj 'Aali' with Maharaja could be found in his following couplets.

Un Ka Saani Kaun Tha Ab Hai Kahaan Un Ki Misaal
(Who was his match, is there any one who is his precedent)

Shad Ki Hasti Ghaneemat Thi Deccan Ke Wastay
(The personality of Shad was a boon or blessing for Deccan)

Sakhawat Aur Halawat Mein Murawwat-e-Khalq
Mein Yaksar Talaash-e-Shad

(In generosity and comfort, regard of people,
if you want to search completely in Shad)

Karni Ho To Karlo Rooh-e-Shadaan Mein
(If you want to search, search in the spirit / soul of Shad)

Shad Ke Haq Mein Dua Kar 'Aali'
(Pray for Shad, O' 'Aali')

Tere Mohsin Hain Sochta Kya Hai
(He is your benefactor, what are you thinking ?)

In 1940, Maharaja Kishan Pershad passed away, Raja Narsing Raj 'Aali' was very much aggrieved. He also had the shock that during his illness, before his death, Maharaja remembered 'Aali' in the state of unconsciousness.

Maharaja Kishan Pershad's demise was not only a shock to Raja Narsing Raj but also for all the Hyderabadis, it was a great tragedy. Those who knew him intimately know that the death of the Hyderabad's *'Haatim Tai'* is a vacuum, which is not so easy to fill. Expressing his heart felt emotions, 'Aali' wrote an elegy under the title *'Gham-E-Ahbaab-e-Shad'* (Agony of the friends of 'Shad') which was published in 1940. He has expressed his feelings as "I was always in the sight and memory of the person and whom I revered with my heart. I am perturbed with parting of this personality. In his memory, I am writing this *'Marsia'* (elegy) of grief. This is the last gift of affection".

Aaj Kya Waqia Sitam Za Hai
(What a tragic incident is today)

Maajra Yeh To Rooh Farsa Hai
(This event is very painful for the spirit)

Sab Hain Maayoos Dil Hi Baitha Hai
(All are disappointed heart is dispirited)

Lab Pe Har Ek Ke Yeh Jumla Hai
(On every one's lips, this is the sentence)

Hazrat-e-Shad Ab Kahaan 'Aali'
(Where is Shad now, O' 'Aali')

In the Palace of Maharaja Kishan Pershad, *'Aaiwaan-e-Shad'*, literary sessions and *'Mushairas'* were organised in which noted writers and poets used to participate not only from Hyderabad but from various parts of India as well. Among the poets from Hyderabad, were Josh, Faani, Hairat Badauni, Sidiq Jaisi, Raja Narsing Raj 'Aali' and others were significant. The popularity of the *'Mushairas'* of *'Aiwaan-e-Shad'* reached to very far off places. After the demise of Maharaja Kishan Pershad, the *'Mushairas'* were held in which a set couplet used to be given for composing a poem on the same style. These sets of verses were selected from the poems of Maharaja. Later, such *'Mushairas'* were held at Bansi Raja's palace every year under the *'Sadarat'* of Nawab Turab Yar Jung *'Sayeed'*. These *'Mushairas'* were organised by Raja Narsing Raj 'Aali'. The mannerisms and decorum used to be maintained in these *'Mushairas'*. Regular invitations used to be sent to the poets and the members of audience. The lists of poets were arranged according to their age, status and seniority. There was no discrimination between the Hindus and the Muslims in these *'Mushairas',* since both these communities promoted Urdu language and literature. Initially, the *ghazals* in Persian were presented to the audience and thereafter, the *ghazals* in Urdu language used to be recited. These *'Mushairas'* continued at Bansi Raja's palace till 1957 the year in which Raja Narsing Raj 'Aali' passed away.

Raja Narsing Raj 'Aali' was the disciple of Nawab Fasat Jung 'Jaleel'. After his death, he started consulting his eldest son, Siddiq Ahmed 'Asar'.

Recognising the greatness of 'Jaleel', he wrote many couplets, quatrains and *'Qataats'*.

QATAA

Hain Sukhan Ke Aasmaan Bhi Shayeri Ke Badar Bhi

(He is the Sky of poetry and Moon too)

Shah Ke Ustaad Bhi Hain Faaziloun Ke Sadar Bhi

(He is the teacher of the king and the head
of the learned too)

Is Khitaab-e-Shad Se Ham Sab Hain 'Aali' Munqafar

(For the eloquence of Shad, all of us praise him O 'Aali')

Hain Imamul Fun Bhi Hazrat Aur Jaleelul Quadr Bhi
(He is the Master of Arts and also august)

Lakhon Aa Jaate Hain Mar Jaate Hain
(Lakhs of people come and die)
Haan Kaam Numayaan Koyi Kar Jaate Hain
(But perform some prominent deed)

Kahlate Hain Kaamil Wohi Maanind-E-Jaleel
(Only those are called perfect like Jaleel)

Jo Saath Taqaddus Ke Guzar Jate Hain
(Those who pass away with sanctity)

Jaleel Sa Kohi Ustaad Hai Kahaan 'Aali'
(Where is the master like Jaleel, 'Aali')

Mila Hai Faiz Yeh Mujh Ko Jaleel Manzil Se
(I got this beneficence from Jaleel Manzil)

Rahe Jaleel Ka Aabaad Maikada 'Aali'
(Let the lavern / bar of Jaleel be inhabited)

Ke Har Sharaab Ko Sheerin Bana Ke Peeta Hoon
(I drink every wine making it sweet)

Aap Sa Ab Kahaan Kare Paida
(How can we generate a person like you now)

Hind Ki Sarzameen Fasahat Jung
(The land of India, Fasahat Jung)

In the *ghazals* of "Aali", there are traces of the writings of *'Hazrat-e-Daagh'*. Coquetry in expression and uniqueness of expression of the language could be seen in the following:

Woh Roothe Hain Mere Manaane Se Pehle
(He is sulked before I could reconcile)

Sitam Kar Gaye Naaz Uthane Se Pahle
(He resorted to cruelty before pampering)

Pad Jati Hai Jis Par Use Kar Deti Hai Be Khud
(Upon whosoever it casts, puts him in rapture)

Yeh Aankh Tumhari Hai Ke Jadoo Hai Bala Hai
(This eye is yours, is it magic or evil spirit ?)

Be Rukhi Be Wafayi Be Ahdi
(Headlessness, disloyalty, breach of trust)

Tu Ne Seekhi Hai Kya Jawani Se
(Did you learn these from youth)

Husn Ka Jadoo Tha Ke Afsos Tha Ilahi Kya Tha
(Was it the magic spell or disappointment, O' God !
what was it?)

Kis Ne Kar Diya Dil Chupke Se Musakhar Apna
(Who conquered my heart quietly?)

Dil Liya Mera Jaan Bhi Leli
(Took my heart and also took my life)

Phir Bhi Kyon Tujh Ko Shikwa Hai
(Even then, why do you have a complaint)

Sainkdon Bismil Hazaron Neem Jaan Dekha Kiye
(Hundreds slaughtered, thousands half alive were seen)

Is Gali Mein Ham Qiyamat Ka Samaan Dekha Kiye
(We saw in this street the scene of the Dooms Day)

Husn Mein Kaisa Asar Hai Kya Bala Ki Hai Kashish
(What an effect has in beauty, tremendous attraction)

Jab Nazar Aaya Hasin, Peer Wo Jawaan Dekha Kiye
(Whenever beauty was caught sight, every
young and old saw it)

He has maintained spontaneity in poetry by using simple and easily comprehensible language.

Rafta Rafta Baes-e-Taskeen Huiyeen Betaabiyaan
(Gradually, step by step, restlessness caused consolation)

Dard-e-Dil Itna Badha Ke Madawa Ban Gaya
(The pain of heart increased so much that
it became remedy)

Zameen Pe Rah Ke Tum Khud Ko Na Bhoolo
(Living on the Earth, don't forget yourself)
Abhi Sar Par Tumhare Aasmaan Hai
(Still, there is a sky on your head)

'Aali' Is Buth Ko Bhala Bhulenge Kyon Kar Deke Dil
('Aali', how can we forget this idol after giving heart)

Kab Tadapta Hai Mareez-E-Ishq Darmaan Ke Liye
(When does the patient of love get restless for cure ?)

The loftiness of imagination is the life of his poetry:

Mere Nigaar Ka Saani Koyi Jahaan Mein Nahin
(There is none equal to me in my writing)

Woh Phool Main Ne Chuna Hai Jo Bostaan Mein Nahin
(I have selected that flower which is not there in the garden)

Har Zarre Mein Hai Aur Rag-e-jaan Se Tu Qareeb
(You are in every particle and near to jugular vein)

Paya Hai Tujh Ko Kis Jagah Dhoonda Kahaan Kahaan
(Where did I find you, where did I search for you ?)

Duniya Guzaashtani Hai Yeh Samjhein Makeen Sab
(The world is omissible or proper to be relinquished,
all the inhabitants should understand it)

Tu Hi Nahin To Phir Hai Yeh Tera Makaan Kahaan
(When you are not there, then, where is your abode ?)

Barbaad Dil Hai Is Mein Tamannaon Ko Na Dhoond
(Heart is destroyed; don't search for wishes in it)

Ujdi Huyi Basti Mein Aabadiyaan Kahaan
(In the deserted habitation, where can there be habitations ?)

Narsing Raj 'Aali' was always fond of 'Sufi' Poetry. The poetry of Khawaja Mir Dard, Raja Girdhari Pershad 'Baqi' and Hazrat 'Shad'. His extensive study of *'Vedantha'* philosophy, the companionship of the Muslim Saints and mendicants made this attitude stronger. In his poetry, the influence of mysticism and knowledge of God is predominant.

Poochte Kya Ho Kayenaat-e-Hayaat
(What do you enquire about the universe of life)

Zindagi Khud Hi Ek Muamma Hai
(Life itself is a puzzle)

Jahaan Mein Jo Koyi Dega Hisaab Dega
(Whosoever will give account in this world, he would give)

Teri Woh Dain Hai Yaa Rab Ke Kuch Hisaab Nahin
(Your giving is that gift O' God! Which has
no account (innumerable))

Adum Ke Jaane Waale Der Se Pahunche To Yeh Samjho
(Those who take the path of unknown place,
if we reach late, presume this)

Thake Maande Musafir Saans Dam Bhar Leke Aate Hain
(Tired travellers relax for a while and come)

Qudrat Ka Tamaasha Chaman Wo Daher Mein Dekha
(We saw the show of Nature in the garden and in the world)

Har Phool Ki Khushboo Hai Juda, Rang Juda Hai
(The fragrance of every flower is different and so is colour)

Posheeda Hai Tu Jalwa Tera Ayaan Hai
(You are concealed but your appearance is manifest)

Kasrat Ho Ke Wahdat Ho Nishaan Tera Hai
(Be it plurality or oneness, imprint is yours)

Kis Ke Dil Mein Nahin Hai Tera Maskan
(In whose heart is not your abode ?)

Kis Ke Lab Pe Nahin Bayaan Tera
(On whose lips is not your narration?)

Yaa Rab Jo Kahoon Munh Se Sukhan Tera Hai
(O' God! Whatever I utter from my mouth, discourse is yours)

Sab Jism Tera Hai Dhan Tera
(The entire body is yours, wealth is yours)
Tujh Se Miloon To Hosh Ka Dar Umr Bhar Na Ho
(If I meet you, I will not have the fear of
consciousness throughout life)

Teri Khabar To Kya Mujhe Apni Khabar Na Ho
(Leave alone your whereabouts; even I don't have
any information about my whereabouts)

Raza Ki Manzilat Khaasaan-e-Daawar Le Ke Aate Hain
(Sovereign Saints bring the status of consent)

Wagar Na Sare Insaan Haq Barabar Le Ke Aate Hain
(Otherwise, all the human beings bring the truth definitely)

Shikayat Kya Kare Koyi Tawangar Koyi Muflis Hai
(Who would complain, someone is rich, the other is pauper)

Khuda Ke Ghar Se Sab Apna Muqaddar Le Ke Aate Hain
(All of them bring their fates from the abode of God)

In his quatrains and *Qataat,* there are topics of mysticism and knowledge of God.

Kis Muhn Se Karoon Hamd Ilahi Teri
(With what face should I praise you my Lord)

Deta Hai Har Ek Zarra Gawahi Teri
(Every particle bears your witness)

Bay Mangay Diya Karta Hai Tu Bandoun Ko
(You award your slaves without asking)

Rahmat Hai Mahbub La Mutanahi Teri
(O' beloved, your beneficence is indefinite)

Gar Mujh Pe Nigah-e-Meherbaani Ho Jaye
(If the glance of favour is cast upon me)

Kuch Kaam Ki Meri Zindagani Ho Jaye
(My life would become something of use)

De Mere Gunahoun Ka Sila Yaa Rab
(Give me the reward of my sins, O' God)
Ho Jaye Najaat Meri Javedaani Ho Jaye
(May my salvation be done, eternally?)

All the persons were enamoured of this kind and large-hearted, far-sighted and sincere human being. Raja Narsing Raj's circle of friends was very wide. Besides Salar Jung-III, Sarvar-ul-Mulk, Bahadur Khan, Mandoor Khan etc. were the personalities close in the circle of his friends and were well-wishers. His contemporary poets were Nawab Turab Yaar Jung 'Sayeed', 'Safi' Aurangabadi, 'Fani' Badayuni, 'Josh' Maleehabadi, Hazrat Begum, 'Josh' Alampuri, 'Hairat' Badayuni and others, with whom he had special relations. All of them appreciated his poetry.

Raja Narsing Raj 'Aali' was the running spirit behind the scholars. This veteran personality was manifest in the embodiment of a high rank and distinguished poet. In the literary and poetical world of Hyderabad, his name will always be fresh. His exemplary life was a model for the youths of modern generation, who were leading their lives in the changing environment of the world following blindly the western civilisation and abandoning their own. This worth emulating personality could prove to be path guiding.

Raja Nursing Raj 'Aali' has wrote 'Bhajans' in Urdu. These were compiled by Dr Bhaskar Raj Saxena and Dr Narayan Raj. They are unpublished manuscripts. In these 'Bhajans' 'Aali' prays to various Gods and Saints. He also wrote *'Bhajans'* on *'Ekadashi Mahima', 'Siva Ratri'* and *'Deewali'* etc.

The major attribute of this person was that he devoted all his life for serving Urdu language and literature and for his family members.

The issue of life and death is very important and delicate. 'Aali' was well versed with this reality. After recovering from ailment, he had once said:

Aa Kar Ajal Nikal Gayi Katra Ke Baar Baar
(Death came and passed through avoiding every time)

Aab-e-Hayaat Tha Ke Tera Intezaar Tha
(Was it the elixir of life or was it a waiting for you)

'Aali' has rightly said that this world is like an inn wherein, the travellers continue to come and go.

The transaction of life continues in this manner but a day is fixed for death. No one can escape it. The claw of the same death snatched "Aali" from his well-wishers and admirers.

On 23rd June 1957, Raja Narsing Raj 'Aali' took leave of this mortal world. He had composed in the last couplet (Maqtaa) of one of his *ghazals.*

Rooh Jab Nikli to 'Aali' Rah Gaye Aaza Kamoosh
(When the soul (Spirit) came out, the organs of
'Aali' became silent)

Maalik-e- Khaana Ko Jaate Paasbaan Dekha Kiye
(The people around continued to see passing
of the soul to the master)

In the year 1976, an M.Phil. dissertation in Urdu was submitted to the Osmania University by Pavan Kumari. The title of the dissertation is *"Raja Girdhari Pershad 'Baqi' Aur Enke Khandan Ki Urdu Adabi Khidmaat".* This work was done on Raja Girdhari Pershad 'Baqi', Raja Narsing Raj 'Aali' Mahbub Raj 'Mahbub', Rai Narhar Raj 'Saqi'. The scholar did full justice by discussing the contribution of these poets to Urdu literature. It was published in the year 2009.

A Gold Medal was instituted in memory of Raja Narsing Raj 'Aali' in 'Women's Education' for M.Phil. in Maulana Azad National Urdu University, Hyderabad, India.

A Ph.D. dissertation on Raja Narsing Raj 'Aali' was written in Urdu by Dr Syed Abdul Khalikh Syed under the title *"Raja Narsing Raj 'Aali' 'Ahwal-o-Adabi Khidmaat'* " in 2015 in the University of Hyderabad, Hyderabad, India and Doctorate was awarded.

A book with the same title was published in the year 2017.

The analysis of the contribution made by Raja Narsing Raj 'Aali' to the Urdu literature shows his multifaceted role.

He composed all principal genres of verse of Urdu Poetry, such as *Ghazals, Qasidas, Qata, Rubai, Nazm, Marsia* etc.

Views of different scholars and writers about Raja Narsing Raj 'Aali' :

— Dr Syed Mohiuddin Quadri 'Zore', while writing about Raja Narsing Raj 'Aali' in *Muraqqa-e-Sukhan* - Vol.II, (1937) wrote that most of his *'Ghazals'* are printed in Magazines and Periodicals. In his quatrains and other poems, Sufi ideas are predominantly found.

— Professor Mahender Raj Saxena while writing about 'Aali' in *'Sabras'*, January 1940 wrote that in the poetry of 'Aali', the traces of mysticism are very explicit. It has been deepened by the companionship of Sufis like Maharaja Kishan Pershad 'Shad' and the personal influence of Fasahat Jung 'Jaleel'. In the poetic genres, in *ghazals* and quatrains *(Rubaiyats)* his specific trend is invariably maintained.

— Naseeruddin Hashmi in his book *"Deccani Hindu Aur Urdu"* wrote that 'Aali' inherited poetic taste from his father. He was the disciple of Fasahat Jung 'Jaleel'. He always participated in the *'Mushairas'* organised by Maharaja Kishan Pershad. *'Mushaira'* to commemorate Maharaja Kishan Pershad used to be organised under his supervision.

— In the article Raja Mahbub Nawazwant 'Baqi', Gafoor Ahmed Mujaddadi wrote that "Aali" has an inclination for poetry. He versified mostly *Ghazals* and Quatrains. Spontaneity is found in his temperament. His couplets are the examples of delicate expressions of thoughts, lofty ideas and of a good poet.

— In his article *'Hyderabad Ke Shayar'* published by A.P. Sahitya Akademy, Khaja Hameeduddin Shahed, wrote that "Aali" was the torch bearer of the ancient civilisation of Hyderabad. He maintained it till his last breath.

— In *"Dastan-e-Adab-e-Hyderabad"* (1951), Dr Syed Mohiuddin Quadri 'Zore' wrote that the family of 'Baqi' is distinguished for literary taste. 'Baqi's eldest son, Raja Narsing Raj 'Aali' was the prominent contemporary Urdu poet.

— In the article *"Raja Narsing Raj "Aali" Aur Deewan-e-'Aali'"* in Siasat Daily dated 16th May 2009, Dr Habib Nisar wrote that the torch of Urdu poetry was already lit in the family of Raja Narsing Raj 'Aali' for five generations. During the regime of Nawab Sikandar Jah, Swami Pershad 'Asghar', in the reign of Nasir-ud-Daula and Afzal-ud-Daula, Raja Narhari Pershad, in the period of Nawab Mir Mahbub Ali Khan, Nizam-VI, Raja Girdhari Pershad 'Baqi' alias Bansi Raja and during the period of Nawab Mir Osman Ali Khan, Nizam-VII, Narsing Raj 'Aali' and his brother Raja Mahbub Raj 'Mahbub' continued this torch lit in the court of Asaf Jahi dynasty.

He further wrote 'Aali' was the close confidant and the companion during the last period of Maharaja Kishan Pershad. He also used to love him as his relatives. Any Mushairas of Maharaja Kishan Pershad never used to be without 'Aali'. After the demise of Maharaja Kishan Peshad, 'Aali' continued to organise *Mushairas* every year in commemoration of Maharaja Kishan Pershad. In dignity, appreciation of literary personality, literary taste, he seems to be the successor of Maharaja Kishan Pershad.

— Dr Abdul Khalikh Syed, who did Ph.D. on Raja Narsing Raj, wrote that the poetry was impregnated in the veins of this family 'Aali' was rated as a high ranking poet of Hyderabad. He took the art of Urdu poetry to the higher position and thereby contributed to the promotion of Urdu language. His contribution to Urdu poetry cannot be forgotten.

In his article 'Raja Narsing Raj Bahadur Aali' Sukhunwarane Hyderabad by Dr Mohsin Jalganvi appeared in Eetemad Daily, dated 24th December 2017, wrote that Narsing Raj 'Aali', son of Raja Girdhari Pershad Baqi Mahbubnawaz want, proved to be a proud and envious scion of the family on account of his good upbringing, academic excellence and scholarly by attributes.

He further wrote that being secular to the core, Narsing Raj respected all religions. At the same time he strictly adhered to his own faith and traditions. All through his life, he was known for his hospitality and kindness. He remained a symbol of Deccani Culture and Lofty values. In which ever Government Department he worked, he left the stamp through performance and capabilities.

He was of the view that Narsing Raj 'Aali' gained fame not only on political level but was also popular among the masses. His genial disposition, good manners and considerate nature endeared him to everyone.

NARHAR RAJ

Chapter – Seven

Rai Narhar Raj 'Saqi'

Rai Narhar Raj 'Saqi' was the eldest son of Raja Narsing Raj 'Aali'. He was the grandson of Raja Girdhari Pershad 'Baqi' and the nephew of Mahbub Raj. He was born on 2nd January 1910 in Hyderabad. He received his early education at Kayasth Pathashala, located at the Palace of Bansi Raja, at Hussaini Alam. In this School, his schoolmates were Dr Syed Mohiuddin Quadri 'Zore' and Dr Raghunandan Raj Saxena. Later, he joined New English School, Poona and passed Matriculation examination from Punjab University. He studied Intermediate at Nizam College with Persian as an optional subject. After completing his education, he engaged himself in the affairs of his estate. In 1928, he married the daughter of Rai Murlidhar, *'Mansabdaar'*. His marriage was celebrated with grandeur by his family. The then Prime Minister of Hyderabad, Maharaja Sir Kishan Pershad, attended his marriage. He tied *'Sehra'* to him and honoured him.

Rai Narhar Raj has five sons and two daughters who received higher education. Their details are given in the family tree *(Shajara)*. On account of his popularity among the Kayasth community, he was elected Secretary of Young Men's Kayasth Association. During his period, Boy's Scout was established. His father, Raja Narsing Raj 'Aali', got him admitted into Agriculture College, Poona, especially for getting education in agriculture so that he could make his lands green and fertile. After this experience, he set up a small dairy farm and agricultural farm at Chandrayangutta, near Falaknuma where he promoted agriculture successfully. Due to his experience and capabilities, all the gardens of Sarf-e-Khaas were placed under his supervision where his schemes received applause.

Honouring the wishes of his father, he joined service in 1936 in Excise Department. He was initially posted at Jagtial, Karimnagar District. Later, he was promoted as Assistant Superintendent of Excise. He was sent to Kurnool as Superintendent of Excise in 1958. After some time, he was posted as Incharge General Manager of Govt. Distilleries, Hyderabad. Soon after, he was promoted as Superintendent of Excise and was posted at Nizamabad. Everybody was happy due to his best management.

Rai Narhar Raj got opportunities to participate in *'Mushairas'* and literary sessions along with his father, organised by Maharaja Sir Kishan Pershad. These environments of literary sessions and *'Mushairas'* had a good impact on his personality. As a result of this, he developed passion for composing *'Ghazals'* since he had the opportunities of listening to the famous poets like Josh, Faani, Allama Hairat Badayuni and Hazrat Begum. He also used to attend *'Mushairas'* conducted in memory of Hazrat Fasahat Jung 'Jaleel' at Jaleel Manzil regularly.

In view of his passion for poetry, his father sent him to Fasahat Jung Jaleel. After his demise, his eldest son, Siddique Ahmed 'Asar' accepted him as his pupil.

'Saqi' was an unselfish devotee of Urdu Literature. During his stay at Nizamabad, a memorable *'Mushaira'* was arranged by *Anjuman-E-Taraqui-E-Urdu* on 15th August under his *Sadarat* (Presidentship) which was very successful. In this *'Mushaira'*, his *Ghazal* was applauded very much, by one and all.

During his stay at Nizamabad, he organised many literary sessions of the local Urdu poets. On the occasion of the visit of the then Governor of Andhra Pradesh, Mr. Bhimsen Sachar, a *'Mushaira'* was organised under his supervision which was very successful. The Collector of Nizamabad had entrusted this responsibility to him. Many poets from Hyderabad also participated in the *'Mushaira'*. Governor appreciated his arrangements very much.

On 21st November, he organised an All India *'Mushaira'* to commemorate his mentor, Fasahat Jung 'Jaleel'. It was presided over by Pandit Labbhu Ram Arsh Malsiyani. In addition to the local Urdu poets of Nizamabad, poets from Hyderabad and other places participated in the *'Mushaira'*. Noted among them were Qazi Saleem (Aurangabad), Mahmood Ishaqui (Nanded), Aziz Osman Ali (Mahaboobnagar), Manoharlal Shaarib, Moinuddin Bazmi, Sayeed Shaheedi, Waheed Akhtar, Ibn-e-Ahmed Taab, Suleman Areeb, Shahid Siddiqui, Allama Hairat Badayuni and the son of Jaleel, Anees Ahmed 'Kaleem'.

When 'Saqi' was transferred to Karimnagar, an Urdu Conference was held on 6th May 1962. He was invited to recite a *Ghazal* in the *'Mushaira'*. His *'Ghazal'* was applauded a lot by the audience. When a *'Mushaira'* was organised at Gulbarga on the occasion of the arrival of the noted Poet of Dakhni Urdu, Suleman Khateeb. 'Saqi' was invited to preside the *'Mushaira'*.

Another *'Mushaira'* was organised on 26th May 1962 to provide financial assistance to the young Urdu Poet of Karimnagar, Saber Tawakkali Shaheen. 'Saqi' presided over this *'Mushaira'* also.

Rai Narhar Raj 'Saqi' was bestowed with the heart of a poet by Nature. He was the embodiment of humility and morality. He goes astray to name and fame. He did not participate in normal literary public meetings. His lifestyle was very simple. He was a staunch Hindu. He was the follower of *'Sanatan Dharm'*, as per the family tradition.

He followed religious beliefs meticulously. He respected the veterans a lot. He always wished to be in the company of mendicants like his father. He was also the devotee of Hindu and Muslim saints. He had a firm belief that due to the grace of such saints, his heart feels tranquility. He was always contented with what has been bestowed to him by God.

On account of his contributions to Urdu language, Idara Ishrat-e-Urdu, Karimnagar, selected his poetry for publication. Some of his couplets are presented here.

In the poetry of 'Saqi', there is a glimpse of mysticism and knowledge of God. In his *'Ghazals'*, at some places, there is a clear influence of the famous Urdu poet of Delhi, Hazrat *Daagh*. He also composed *'Naat'* (Poetry in praise of *Prophet Mohammed*) in which he expressed his heart-felt devotion and honour in words. He composed many thoughts in his poems so beautifully and with uniqueness that it can't be described in words.

The element of Godly knowledge is predominant in his poetry. Few couplets are presented here as samples:

Zarre Mein Woh Chhup Kar Bhi Na Pinhaan Ho Saka
(Even after concealing himself in every particle,
he could not remain hidden)

Uska Jalwa Baad Mein Aatishi Mein Aab Wo Gil Mein Hai
(His appearance is in air, fire, water and soil)

Kyon Kar Na Us Ka Shukr Kare Raat Din Ada
(Why not his gratitude be expressed day and night)

Saqi Pe Jis Ka Fazal Wo Karam Beshumaar tha
(Whose innumerable favours are on Saqi)

Kaabe Mein Chale Jao Ya Butkhane Mein Jao
(Either go to Kaaba or a temple of idol)

Juz Naame Khuda Aur Koyi Naam Nahin Hai
(There is no other name except the name of God)

Kyon Bhatakta Hai Tu Aye Saqi Kisi Ke Waste
(Why do you wander for any one O' Saqi)

Kaaba Tere Dil Mein Hai Butkhana Tere Dil Mein Hai
(Kaaba is in your heart, temple of idol is in your heart)

Raat Din Jis Ka Tasawwur Yaad Jis Ki Dil Mein Hai
(His imagination and memory is in the heart, day and night)

Us Ki Rangat Us Ki Boo Duniayae Aab Wo Gil Mein Hai
(His complexion and fragrance is in this world
of water and soil)

Karam Ho Inayat Ho Jis Par Khuda Ki
(Upon whom there is courtesy and favour of God)

Hayat Us Ki Aasaan Hai Mushkil Nahin Hai
(His life is easy not difficult)

Har Lahza Har Ghadi Jo Inayat Huyi Teri
(Every moment every hour the favour which you did)

Saqi Ki Zindagi Ko Darakshaan Bana Gayi
(Made the life of Saqi glittering)

Ab Is Ke Siva Aur Kya Chahiye
(What else is required more than this)

Jise Chahte Thay Use Paa Gaye
(Whom loved, got him)

Ho Kis Tarah Saqi Tera Anjaam Bhi Achcha
(How can your conclusion be good 'Saqi'?)

Masroof-e-Ibadat Saher Wo Shaam Nahin Hai
(Not engaged in worship in the dawn and dusk)

It was the influence of the companionship and favour of the religious sages that he got the passion for the knowledge of God. These couplets are the evidence of it:

Isi Aaqa Isi Maalik Ka Naam Apni Zaban Par Hai
(The name of the same master is on the tongue)

Ke Jis Ka Jalwa-e-Zeba Aasmaan Par Hai
(Whose beautiful appearance is on the Sky)

Zaat Ko Teri Paa Liya Jis Ne
(The one who got your absolute being)

Deen Wo Duniya Mein Us Ki Haar Nahin
(For him, there is no defeat or failure in this world and hereafter)

Maikade Mein Bhi Rah Ke Aye Saqi
(Even being present in the tavern / bar, O' Saqi)

Parsa Tu Hai Mai Gusaar Nahin
(You are a pious person not a drunkard)

In the following two couplets, the oneness of God and his presence in every shape is depicted:

Har Shay Mein Us Ka Jalwa Ayaan Tha Nehaan Na Tha
(In everything, his appearance was manifest, not concealed)

Phir Kaise Ham Kahein Ke Kahaan Tha Kahaan Na Tha
(Then how can we say that where he was and where he was not)

Afshaan Karoon Na Tujh Se To Kis Se Kahoon Main Haal
(If I don't expose myself to you to whom should I tell my condition)

Tere Siva To Koyi Mera Raazdaan Na Tha
(There was no other confidant except you)

Chalo Tan Chorh Kar Saqi Chalenge
(Come on Saqi, let's go leaving this body)

Ke Milna Hai Hamein Is La Makaan Se
(We have to meet this deity who is houseless)

In his poetry, we find both carnal and spiritual love of God. As an example, the following few couplets are presented here which depict his heart-felt passions and feelings:

Betaur Muztarib Tha Ajab Intesar Tha
(Severely impatient and strangely perturbed)

Deedar-e-Yaar Ke Liye Dil Beqaraar Tha
(Heart was anxious for the sight of the friend)

Yeh Bhi Kamaal-e-Jazba-E-Ishq Nigaar Tha
(This was also the extreme form of expression
of passion for love)

Samjha Har Ek Us Ki Taraf Ru-E-Yaar Tha
(Every one thought his beloved is facing towards him)

Zer-e-Itaab Mujh Ko Tu Rakha Tamaam Umr
(You kept me throughout the life in wrath)

Jab Mar Gaya to Kahte Hain Wo Jaan Nisaar Tha
(When died, they say that he was very loyal)

Dam Todta Hai Dekhiye Ab To Mareez-e-Ishq
(See the patient of love is taking his last breath now)

Shayad Qaza Ko Aaj Tera Intezaar Tha
(Perhaps death was waiting for you today)

Aarzoo Yeh Hai Ke Dam Nikle Tumhare Saamne
(It is the wish that I should take the last
breath in your presence)

Muddaa-e-Zindagi Yeh Aakhri Manzil Mein Hai
(The motive of life is in the last stage)

The style of narration is very simple in the following couplets and the language is very clear. One would like to read the second half of the couplet again and again spontaneously:

Rah Rah Ke Bas Khayaal Us Ka Bandha Raha
(Time and again, it was only his thought which remained)

Aa Aa Ke Yaad Har Ghadi Mujh Ko Rula Gayi
(Every time, every moment whenever I remembered, your memory made me weep)

Unhein Dekh Kar Bar Mala Kah Diya
(On seeing him, I told publicly / openly)

Yeh Lo Aagaye Aagaye Aagaye
(Look? He came, he came, he came)

At some places, the influence of Hazrat-e-Daagh is prominent. The impudence of language and its uniqueness, the topic or thought warrants appraisal:

Woh Bigadne Lage Jab Main Ne Kaha Jaane Do
(He got angry when I said, let it go)

Hoon Main Inssan Khata Hoti Hai Insanon Se
(I am a human being and to err is human)

Nigahon Se Teri Huwa Hai Woh Ghayal
(He is wounded by your eyes)

Jo Pahloo Mein Dekha Woh Mera Dil Nahin Hai
(When I looked into the flank that was not my heart)

Mili Mujhe Yehi Daulat Teri Muhabbat Mein
(In your love, I got these riches)

Gham Wo Alam Se Bhara Dil Ka Ek Khazana Tha
(It was the treasure of the heart full of grief and sorrow)

Qafas Mein Haal Yeh Dekha Ghareeb Bulbul Ka
(In the cage, when saw this condition of the nightingale)

Na Boo-e-Gul Thi Muyassar Na Aab Wo Daana Tha
(There was no fragrance of the flower, neither, water nor a grain available)

Na Wo Bahaar Na Wo Gul Na Wo Chaman-e-Sayyad
(There was no spring there, neither flower, nor the garden of the hunter)

Choote Aseer To Badla Huwa Zamana Tha
(When got released from the prison, the time was changed)

Kashish-e-Husn Ka Kya Karoon Main Bayaan
(What kind of narration of beauty should I mention?)

Woh Aankhon Se Dil Mein Mere Aa Gaye
(He entered into my heart through the eyes)

Dukh Dard Sahe Itne Tere Ishq Mein Hum
(We suffered agony and pain so much in your love)

Aaraam Mein Bhi Ab Koyi Aaraam Nahin Hai
(There is also no comfort in the comfort now)

Sometimes, 'Saqi' seems to be vexed up with the world. In his opinion, the world is the place of agony, grief and sorrow instead of pleasure. Here, he doesn't seem to observe even a glimpse of happiness:

Samajhte Thay Duniya Ko Raahat Ka Chashma
(It was thought that the world is the spring of
relief and comfort)

Yahaan Gham Se Khaali Koyi Dil Nahin Hai
(Here, there is no heart, which is free from grief)

Khizaan Ke Baad Jo Badla Tha Naqsh-e-Gulshan
(The situation which was changed after the autumn)

Na Bulbulein Theen Na Gul Na Aashiyana Tha
(There were no nightingales, neither garden nor the nest)

Saqi is of the opinion that those who are truthful, their end is always good.

Marta Hai Sadaqat Pe Jo Mit Ta Hai isi Par
(The one who dies for the sake of truthfulness
and the one that who obliterates for it)

Hota Kabhi iska Bura Anjaam Nahin Hai
(His consequence or end is never bad)

'Saqi' has always been a contented person. He was never after pomp and pride. Whatever he used to get from God, he used to be satisfied with it. He, write thus:

Zar Ki Hawas Na Mujh Ko Hukumat Ki Thi Talab
(I had neither greed for money nor demand for governance)

Banda Bana Raha Yehi Mera Shiaar Tha
(I remained a slave, this was my custom)

Sab Ki Jo Hai Chashm-e-Karam Aaj Jo Mujh Pe Saqi
(Today, whatever benevolent eye of all is upon me 'Saqi')

Ham Utha Sakte Nahin Sar Kabhi Eshsanon Se
(We can't ever raise our head from taking favours)

About the ups and downs of life, he writes:

Urooj Jis Ko Tha Kal Tak Zawaal Aaj Aaya
(Those who had exaltation till yesterday, they
met with downfall today)

Yehi To Dekhiye Qudrat Ka Karkhana Tha
(See, this was the workshop of Nature)

He is the righteous person and he writes that some persons do not have apparent and inner self similar. They have something in their hearts and something else on their tongues:

Ab Khuda Hi Zahir Wo Baatein Ko Samjhe Ham Nasheen
(Now, only God can comprehend their apparent
and inner self, O' companion!)

Muhn Par Meethi Meethi Baatein Aur Keena Dil Mein Hai
(Sweet talks on their lips but malice in their hearts)

He is the bitter complainant of the present era. He writes that during the present time, honesty, nobility and sympathy have altogether disappeared from the world. The life of the noblemen is absolutely impossible in the present period:

Maut Aati Hai Na Jeene Ki Hai Soorath Koyi
(Death doesn't come, there is no way to lead life)

Aaj Kal Haalat Shareefon Ki Badi Mushkil Mein Hai
(Nowadays, the condition of the noblemen is in difficulty)

Koyi Ummeed Nahin Apnon Se Beganon Se
(There is no hope either from our own people or from the strangers)

Ab To Hamdardi Bhi Jaati Rahi Insanon Se
(Now that sympathy or kindness has also vanished from the human beings)

In praise of Maharaja Sir Kishan Pershad, he says:

Ahd-E-Janab-E-Shad Mein Khush Haal Tha Deccan
(During the period of Shad, the Deccan was prosperous)

Khaali Suroor Se Dil-e-Peer Wo Jawaan Na Tha
(The hearts of the young and the poor were not free from pleasure)

About his mentor, Hazrat Fasahat Jung 'Jeleel', he has a lot of praise. At various places, he has expressed himself being his pupil. A few couplets are presented here in this context:

Saqi Ko Apne Fakhr Hai Ustaad Par Bajaa
(Rightly, Saqi is proud of his mentor)

Hazrat Jaleel Saa Koyi Ahle Zaban Na Tha
(There was no speaker of language who was so competent as 'Jaleel')

Jaleel-e-Nukta Daan Ka Faiz Hai Saara Aiye Saqi
(It is all the benevolence of sagacious Jaleel, O' Saqi)

Sadaa-e-Marhaba Aati Tere Tarz-e-Zabaan Par Hai
(The sound of welcome comes upon your style of narration of the language)

Jaleel-e-Sukhanwar Ka Hai Faiz Saqi
(Oh! Saqi – it is the benevolence of great poet Jaleel)

Tujhe Kaun Kahta Hai Kaamil Nahin Hai
(Who says that you are not perfect)

'Saqi' has the passion for service to people. He also has the feeling of patriotism. He wrote in praise of Mahatma Gandhi:

Khidmat Main Mulk Wo Qaum Ki Ho Umr Sab Basar
(Let all the life be spent in the service of the country and nation)

Bapu Ki Zindagani Sabaq Yeh Sikha Gayi
(The life of Bapu has taught us this lesson)

Like his ancestors, 'Saqi' was very much devoted to Muslim saints. He has expressed in words, the devotion, he has for Hazrat Syed Abdul Qadir Jeelani - Ghouse-E-Azam:

Khuda Hi Ke Bande Hain Hum Ghouse-E-Azam
(We are the slaves of the God, O Ghouse-E-Azam)

Usi Ke Hain Dair-O-Haram Ghouse-E-Azam
(The temples and Kaaba are only His O' Ghouse-e-Azam)

Tera Hoon Hamesha Tera Hi Rahoonga
(I am yours and I will always be yours)

Main Khaata Hoon Teri Qasam Ghouse-E-Azam
(I swear by you, Ghouse-E-Azam)

Main Paoonga Manzil Ko Teri Madad Se
(I will achieve destination with your help)

Karam Kar Karam Kar Karam Ghous-E-Azam
(Do favour, do favour, favour Ghouse-E-Azam)

Gunahgaar Saqi Bhi Pesh-E-Nazar Ho
(Saqi, the sinner should also be in front of your sight)

Idhar Bhi Nigah-E-Karam Ghouse-E-Azam
(Cast the sight of favour, this side also Ghouse-E-Azam)

Besides *'Ghazals'*, he wrote *'Bhajans'* in Hindi as well as in Urdu. He compiled two volumes of *'Bhajnawali'* incorporating his *'Bhajans'*, the *'Bhajans'* of his father, Uncle Mahbub Raj and other relatives.

After the death of his father, Raja Narsing Raj 'Aali' in 1957, he organised a *'Mushaira'* in the year 1958 in the memory of Raja Narsing Raj 'Aali' and Maharaja Kishan Pershad 'Shad' at Bansi Raja's palace. The *'Tharah'* (Verse set) was:

Shad Aur Aali Ko Hum Shirin Zuban Dekha Kiye
(We saw 'Shad' and 'Aali' as sweet tongued)

The *Ghazals* of 'Shad' and 'Aali' were read out. Reputed poets of Hyderabad were invited to present their *Ghazals.*

The *'Mushaira'* was considered to be best.

As mentioned earlier, an M.Phil. Dissertation was submitted in Urdu to the Osmania University in 1976, by Pavan Kumari. The title of the Dissertation is *'Raja Girdhari Pershad Aur Inke Khandan Ki Urdu Adabi Khidmaath'* in which a Chapter on Rai Narhar Raj 'Saqi' and his contribution to Urdu literature has been written.

Rai Narhar Raj 'Saqi' passed away on 21st November 1985, after a brief illness.

A Gold Medal has been instituted in his memory at Mahatma Phule Krishi Vidyapeeth, Rahuri, Ahmednagar, Maharashtra State, for Ph.D. in Dairy Science, since Rai Narhar Raj did agriculture course from Poona Agriculture College.

Naseeruddin Hashmi, wrote in his book *"Deccani Hindu Aur Urdu"* that 'Saqi' developed the taste of poetry from his childhood. He was the pupil of Hazrat Jaleel. After his demise, he got his poems corrected from his son Siddique Ahmed 'Asar'.

DR. BHASKAR RAJ

Chapter – Eight

Dr Bhaskar Raj Saxena

Bhaskar Raj was the son of Rai Narhar Raj. He was born on August 1, 1934, in Hyderabad.

He had his early education in Hyderabad in an Urdu medium school. Later, he did his graduation in Veterinary Science and Animal Husbandry, i.e. B.V.Sc. and A.H, and Law (LL.B) from Osmania University. He did his diploma in Marketing from one of the reputed Institutes of Bombay.

He joined government service soon on completion of graduation and continued for almost a decade. Thereafter, he worked with a multinational pharmaceutical company for almost two decades. He was in a senior position. After serving the multinational company, he joined a Public Sector Enterprise in a senior position. After retirement, he was a visiting faculty to the Government Post-Graduate College for Women, at Hyderabad. He also worked as a faculty member for Bharatiya Vidya Bhavan.

Right from the college days and earlier, he participated in various Inter-collegiate Debating competitions. He won number of prizes in various competitions. He was a fluent Orator and writer of repute in Urdu, Hindi and English languages. He was invited by All India Radio, Hyderabad for several years to deliver talks on topics connected with science and culture. He also participated in discussions on TV channels.

He contributed more than sixty articles in English, Urdu and Hindi languages. These articles were based on science, culture, literature, history, religion and other subjects.

He was a staunch follower of *Sanatan Dharm*. He played a very important role in maintaining the temples constructed by his forefathers and improved them.

He wrote the following books:

1. *Hyderabad Ke Bansi Raja* (Urdu).
2. *Hyderabad Ke Adabi Ratan* (Urdu).
3. *Hyderabad-Nizam Kaal Ke Bhakt Kavi* (Hindi).
4. *Narhari Prakash* (Hindi) – He republished this book in 2005. This is the translation of Yog Vashisht from Sanskrit into Hindi by Narhari Pershad.
5. *Yoga Vasistha* - Vedanta Wisdom through miniature paintings (English).

The details about the books are as under:

1. *Hyderabad Ke Bansi Raja - Raja Girdhari Pershad 'Baqi' Ki Hayat Aur Karname.*

   This book was published by Sher-O-Hikmat in the year 1995. Its foreword was written by Professor Jafar Nizam, former Vice Chancellor of the Kakatiya University, Warangal, Telangana and introduction by Mr Muztar Majaaz a renowned journalist of Hyderabad. It has eight chapters which includes the history of the forefathers of Bansi Raja, culture of that era, his role in the formation of the Army and the establishment of Industries, his travels, and a selection of his poems.

   This book also contains photographs and copies of the letters written by Mir Mahbub Ali Khan Nizam-VI to Bansi Raja.

2. *Hyderabad Ke Adabi Ratan.*

   This book was published in the year 2000. It contains chapters on Rai Swami Pershad, Rai Narhari Pershad,

Raja Girdhari Pershad, Raja Keshav Pershad, Raja Narsing Raj, Mahbub Raj and Rai Narhar Raj and the specimen of their Urdu poems. It also has photographs and the letters of Mir Mahbub Ali Khan Nizam-VI addressed to Raja Girdhari Pershad.

There is a special mention of Raja Keshav Pershad '*Hisab*', the eldest son of Raja Girdhari Pershad 'Baqi' from his first wife. He was the classmate of Maharaja Kishan Pershad and Sir Salar Jung-II in *Madar-se-Aaliya*. He was awarded the title of Raja. He was in the Accountant Generals Office in a senior post. He was a poet too and wrote poetry in Urdu. Maharaja Kishan Pershad wrote a chronogram on his death.

This book also contains "TAHKHIKAT-E-SIYAQ-I BAQI by RAJA GIRDHARI PERSHAD BAQI".

3. *Hyderabad Nizam Kal Ke Bhakt Kavi*

   This book was published in Hindi by Narhari Pershad Charitable Trust in the year 2002. It contains chapters on Raja Ram Pershad, Rai Swami Pershad, Rai Narhari Pershad, Raja Girdhari Pershad and Raja Narsing Raj. Dr Susheela Vyapari former Principal, Hindi Maha Vidhyalay, Hyderabad, India wrote its introduction. It also contains the Hindi *kavitas* (poems) of the poets. This book gives the detailed introduction of Narhari Prakash and also its historical importance. *Bhajans* of Bansi Raja and Raja Narsing Raj have also been given. These *Bhajans* are on Manik Prabhu (a renowned saint), *Lord Krishna, Goddess Chandi Devi, Kashi, Durga, Sri Ram* and others. It has Hindi poems also.

4. *Narhari Prakash*

   This book was originally published in year 1856.

   As mentioned earlier, Narhari Pershad was the first to translate *Yog Vashisht* from Sanskrit into Hindi.

   The great saint Swami Ram Tirth, while delivering a lecture in USA in 1904 said "One of the greatest books, most wonderful ever written under the Sun, the *Yog Vashisht* which nobody on the Earth can read without escaping God's consciousness".

It is believed that Valmiki wrote *Yog Vashisht.* Valmiki is the author of Sanskrit epic *Ramayana.* In *Yog Vashisht,* Valmiki narrates in detail the spiritual teachings of Guru Vashisht to Lord Rama.

Yog Vashisht is also known as Maha Ramayan, Argh Ramayan, Vashisht Ramayan, Gyan Vashisht and Vashisht etc. It was first translated in English in 1831 and was published from Calcutta.

Though Narhari Pershad was a author of nineteenth century but he followed the traditions of the writings of sixteenth century '*Bhakti Poets'* i.e., before started writing *Narhari Prakash*, the author has started with 'Ganesh', 'Mother Sharda' and 'Guru' *Stuthi* as Tulsi Das and Kalidas did.

Dara Shikoh, son of Emperor Shah Jahan translated *Yog Vashisht* from Sanskrit into Persian.

Narhari Pershad wrote Yog Vashisht in the form of *Doha, Chaupai, Surta, Chhand* as Tulsi Das wrote *Ramayana.* The presentation is very simple and touches the mind and heart. This can be read from anywhere to anywhere. It has seven chapters which have already been given earlier in detail.

Dr Bhaskar Raj Saxena took great interest in republication of this book. During the process, he faced many problems as the complete original book was not available since it was published more than 150 years ago. As a result, he had to arrange the book by taking out pages partly from different copies of the book. The problem he faced was that in the olden days the books were not serially numbered. The other problem which he faced was the type of script. The original script is different from the script used these days. He could complete this task after spending days and months together. Thereafter, the book was sent for composing. The new edition of the book has 826 pages.

It is the responsibility of all literary personalities and historians that they should recognise the importance of *Narhari Prakash* and give due importance to it. The contribution of the author should also be recognised.

By republishing, such an important book, Dr Bhaskar Raj has done a great service to religion, literature and the readers.

The manuscript of *Narhari Prakash* is in the Salar Jung Museum Library, Hyderabad, India, under the family collection of Raja Narsing Raj.

5. *Yoga Vasistha- Vedanta Wisdom through Miniature Paintings.*

   It is one of the rare books which contains miniature paintings. These paintings depict the stories of *Yog Vashisht* in brief. *Yog Vashisht* is a voluminous epic and has serious philosophy of *Vedanta.*

   Narhari Pershad was a genius, he understood the difficulties of a common man and therefore, he had a novel idea and used creative approach. He has explained the teachings and principles of *Yog Vashisht* through texts and miniatures. There are about fifty five stories and many *upakhyans* but only thirty nine miniature paintings are available.

   Narhari Pershad has selected the stories which will have effect on common man and he benefits from it.

It is a accepted fact that the history of miniature art is from the ancient time. However, the art of miniature paintings was at its peak when caves of Ellora were painted during the second century A.D. Every painting conveys a message and tells a story. However, a person should have a sharp eye and a brain to see and understand it.

The theme of each painting in *Yoga Vasistha* is based on different principles of *Vedanta*. There is no evidence as to who has painted these paintings as there is only one painting which has a signature of Rai Narhari Pershad with a date mentioned. However, these paintings are based on Hindi version of *Narhari Prakash*. Therefore, there is a strong possibility that these miniatures were painted by Narhari Pershad but it cannot be said with certainty as there is no concrete evidence. In about twelve to fifteen paintings, the gist of the paintings is given in Persian and Hindi as well. The hand writing and inscription appears to be similar to the hand writing of Narhari Pershad.

These paintings are unique because for the first time in Hyderabad an artist attempted to portray the paintings based on the philosophy of *Vedanta* and that too during the Nizam's period. This clearly indicates that there was a liberty to express one's feelings and views and also freedom from the rulers of that time.

Yoga Vasistha has six chapters. They are :

Chapter-I :

Vairagya Prakaran (The Divine Disinterest), The Story of *Recesions*.

Chapter-II :

Mumukshu Prakaran (The Divine Seeker), The Story of *Suka*, The story of *Vasistha*.

Chapter-III :

Utpatti Prakaran (The Origin), contains The Story of *Akasaja*, The Story of *Lila*, The Story of *Karkati*, The Story of *sons of Indu,* The Story of *Indra* and *Ahalya* and The Story of *Lavana*.

Chapter-IV :

Stithi Prakaran (The sustenance). It contains the Story of *Sukracharya*, The Story of *Dama*, *Vyala*, *and Kata*,

The Story of *Bhima,* and Drdha, The Story of *Dasura* and The Story of *Kaha*.

Chapter-V :

Upasama Prakaran (The Quiescence). It contains the Story of King *Janaka*, The Story of *Punya*, and *Pavana*, The Story of *Bali*, The Story of *Prahlada*, The Story of *Gadi*, The Story of *UddaLaka*, The Story of *Suraghu*, The Dialogue between *Bhasa* and *Vilasa*, The Story of *Vitahavya*.

Chapter-VI :

Nirvana Prakaran (The Final Liberation), The Story of *Kag-Bhusunda*, The Story of *Deva Puja* (Worship of God), The Story of *Arjuna*, The Story of *Bhagiratha*, The Story of *Chudala and Sikhadhvaja*, The Story of *Kaca*, The Story of *Bhiringhisa*, The Story of *Iksvaku*, The Story of *Hunter* and a *Sage*, The Story of *Vidya-Dhara*, The Story of *Manki*, The Story of *Mind,* The Story of *Vipascit*, The Story of *Sata-Rudra*, The Story of *Indra,* The Story of a *Block of Stone*.

These paintings narrate the story briefly as mentioned under each Para.

The artists of the eighteenth and nineteenth century painted the rulers, the style of living during that period. These paintings have Islamic influence limited to some extent on costumes and male characters. No doubt, there were some other artists concentrated on religion and mythological themes based on *Bhagwat Gita* and *Ramayana*. They depicted their Hindu deities like Lord Rama and Krishna.

The fact cannot be ignored that there are large number of mythological miniatures all over the country which are mostly based on Ramayana, Mahabharata and *Puranas* but *Yoga Vasistha* is based on the paintings concerning the stories of *Yog Vashisht*.

But probably this is the only set of the paintings based on *Yog Vashisht* which have been depicted in *Yoga Vasistha*.

These paintings were displayed every year on the fifth day of Kartik month at the Devi Temple at Chanderayan Gutta Hyderabad, India, for the benefit of the public to get themselves acquainted and benefited with the stories of *Yog Vashisht* which continued till 1957, till such time selected guests were also invited. The above dates also commemorate the completion of the book *Narhari Prakash* by Rai Narhari Pershad.

Dr Bhaskar Raj Saxena has done a great service to religion and literature by presenting *Yoga Vasistha* in the year 2008.

Dr Bhaskar Raj passed away on August 2, 2012 after a brief illness.

A Gold Medal has been instituted in his memory at the University of Hyderabad, Hyderabad, India for Ph.D. in Hindi.

Mahbub Raj

Chapter – Nine

Mahbub Raj 'Mahbub'

The forefathers of Raja Girdhari Pershad Mahbub Nawazwant 'Baqi' alias Bansi Raja arrived in the Deccan and settled down in Hyderabad permanently. The favours and courtesies of Asafia Dynasty made them rich and distinguished. They were great writers. They composed verses in various genres of poetry and got acclamation of their knowledge and art.

Bansi Raja held many important positions. He was treated as the close associate of Nawab Mir Mahbub Ali Khan, Nizam-VI. He spent most of his life during the period "The Golden Era of the History of the Deccan", in which the Hindus and the Muslims were far from prejudice and narrow mindedness. Mutual contacts and unity had erased the difference of duality between the two communities. It is evident that in such an environment, poetry and literature written by the distinguished writers and poets were the mirrors of independent thoughts and the manifestation of unity.

The effect of this environment made Bansi Raja a broad-minded and sincere human being. He was a famous poet and a writer of high repute. He composed verses in Persian and Urdu.

Bansi Raja had two sons: Raja Narsing Raj 'Aali' and Mahbub Raj 'Mahbub'. The former was the Superintendent of

Saving Bank of Postal Department. He occupied high positions in other departments besides Posts and Railways. Right from childhood, his passion for poetry, made him a poet of high repute. He was the pupil of *Fasahat Jung Jaleel.* He had simplicitly and plainness of language. Mysticism was predominantly found in his poetry. He was the intimate companion of the then Prime Minister of the erstwhile State of Hyderabad, Maharaja Sir Kishan Pershad. He was the protagonist of the Ganga-Jamuni civilisation of Hyderabad.

Mahbub Raj was born in 1894 A.D. At the behest of Nawab Mir Mahbub Ali Khan, he was named after him as Mahbub Raj.

Tera Naam Mahbub Jisne Rakha Tha
(The one who had named you Mahbub)

Woh Mahbub Tha Jaan-e-Mulk-e-Deccan Ka
(He was Mahbub, the beloved of the country of the Deccan)

When Mahbub Ali Pasha stepped into the Palace of Bansi Raja, as a Royal favour, he took Mahbub Raj on to his lap. That day became memorable in his life. He was so overwhelmed with joy with the arrival of the king that he cast his pleasure in these words:

Ba Qasr-i-Past-i-Baqi Qaiser-i-Aali Muqam Amad
(Into the lowest Palace of Baqi, the highly
esteemed king arrived)

Zehe Izat Afzayi Pushtaini Ghulam Amad
(This ancestral slave is very fortunate that
his honour is increased by his arrival)

In 1896, Bansi Raja expired. At that time, both of his sons were very young.

Aakhri Waqt Do Lakht-e-Jigar Chorh Gaye
(At the last moment, he left two parts of liver (dear children)

Raja Narsing Wo Mahbub Pisar Chorh Gaye
(Left the sons, Raja Narsing and Mahbub)

Chaar Chhe Saal Ke Masoom Shajar Chorh Gaye
(Left four and six years old innocent plants (sons))

Dekhne Paye Na The In Ke Samar Chorh Gaye
(He had not seen the fruits of their
accomplishments, left them)

The early stages of the lives of both the brothers, were very hard and troublesome. With the orders of the king, the estate was given under the special control of Court of Wards of Sarf-e-Khaas. (The private estate of the Nizam).

The tiny shoulders of the mother fulfilled this responsibility nicely. She made them exemplary personalities of civilisation and mannerism by providing them education and training. With their abilities and capabilities, both these brothers inhabited the garden of 'Baqi' once again.

Mahbub Raj got his primary education at Madrasa-e-Aaliya. He was very intelligent and quick-witted. He was always popular among his classmates and teachers. Later, he passed Matriculation examination from the Punjab University.

Mahbub Raj was very self-respecting, high minded and by nature, a free thinker. He never liked improper praise and flattery of the people. This was the reason that he always kept himself away from government service. About his nature and sense of honour, he writes:

Ajeeb Ghuyur Tabiyat Hai Teri Aiy Mahbub
(O Mahbub! You have a strange sense of
honour by your nature)

Kisi Ki Tujh Ko Khushamad Zara Nahin Aati
(You don't know even a little how to flatter any one)

Initially, he was attracted to cultivate lands. The difficulties faced in the field of agriculture, made his temperament, hard working and stable. He believed that a human being can pass through different stages with genuine desire and hard work. He had interest in industry and handicrafts. He laid the foundation of textiles factory "*Sanna-*

E-Deccan" wherein he made many innovations and created new designs. He himself used to look after all the managerial affairs of the factory for its development. He used to say:

Kaam Achcha Ho to Kyon Wakht Bura Ho Apna
(If the work is good, why should our fate be bad?)

Sach Hai Hum Aap Hain Qismat Ke Banane Wale
(It is true that we are the makers (Architects)
of our own fortune)

It would not be wrong to say that Mahbub Raj is termed as the founder of the domestic handicrafts. He organised the exhibition of domestic handicrafts under his supervision on the occasion of the *'Jatara'* (Annual religious congregation) of Keshavagiri and later at the wish of Maharaja Kishan Pershad, on the occasion of the *'Jatara'* of Alwaal.

The nobles, the rich, the elite and the European officials who visited these exhibitions praised about the good management of Mahbub Raj. Nizam of Hyderabad himself visited the exhibition and expressed his delight.

In 1924, on the insistence of his elder brother, Raja Narsing Raj, he initially joined *'Bab-e-Hukumat'* (Government Secretariat) and later held the post of Superintendent of Octroi Department in 1928. Besides government service, he always worked as *'Sarishtedaar* of *Sarf-e-Khas Mubarak'*, *'Peshkaar'* of *Zafargarh Court*, Warangal. He had the honour of getting the *'Mansab'* (monthly pension given to nobles) as per the hereditary tradition. He was also the Secretary of Kayasth Sabha and member of the co-operative society of the Kayasths known as *"Anjuman-e-Imdaad Bahami-e-Kayasth Sahibaan"* for a long period.

He knew horse riding, wrestling, bennout (South Asian martial art of fighting with cudgels or chubs). He was an expert in gun shooting, a good photographer and swimmer. He was trained for motor driving. He was very hospitable.

Mahbub Raj had a very compassionate heart. He was disgusted with the bad status of the community:

Aaj Kal Bigdi Huyi Qaum Ki Haalat Kyon Hai
(Why is the status of the community ruined these days ?)

Dil Mein Hai Bughz Dikhawe Ki Muhabbat kyon Hai
(There is grudge in heart, why is love ostentatious)

He was grieved with the situation of the community that it is shrunk in the *Jagirs, Mansabs* and government services only since lack of education deprived them of trying their luck in other occupations. He wanted to introduce new trends in the community. It was his earnest desire to elevate the status of the community from its low level:

Mere Dil Ki Agar Hai Aarzoo Ya Rab To Itni Hai
(If there is any heartfelt desire of mine, it is this)

Ke Nek Anjaam Ho Khoobi Se Meri Zindagani Ka
(That the end consequence of my life be virtuous)

Fortunately, he got such opportunities, very soon. As the Secretary of the Kayasth Sabha, he made many reforms. He made an attempt to abandon old and outdated traditions to bring about changes. He persuaded the Kayasths to take interest in business. He made them aware of the importance of industrial education in industry. In order to fulfill his objectives, he told his colleagues:

Qaum Ke Shaida Bano Aur Qaum Hi Par Jaan Do
(Become infatuated with the love of the community and sacrifice life for the community only)

Kuch Na Kuch Aasaar Chorh Jao Apne Naam Ke
(Leave some impressions of your name)

The area of operation of his reformative efforts was not confined to the Kayasths or the Hindus. He gave the message of working together and earning bread through hard work to his Muslim brethren also:

Ek Hi Maan Ke Do Atfaal-e-Watan Hain Jab Yeh
(When both of them are the children of the same mother land)

Kis Liye Jhagde Hain Aapas Mein Yeh Nafrat Kyon Hai
(Why are these conflicts among them and
why is this hatred?)

Khana Jungi Ke Nataij Ko Zara Sochein To
(Think for a while the consequences of internal conflicts)

Apni Barbadi Ki Is Qaum Ko Aadat Kyon Hai
(Why does this nation have the habit of its own ruination ?)

Like Bansi Raja, Mahbub Raj was also the well-wisher of his master. He always prayed for his master and remained eulogist for him:

Raahat Naseeb Hogi Na Mahbub Kyon Tujhe
(Why not you get relief Mahbub, since you have)

Osman Sa Badshah-e-Deccan Hukumraan Hai Ab
(Since a king like Osman is the ruler of the
Deccan these days)

He had special contacts with the family of Maharaja Sir Kishan Pershad. He was always his companion and sincere to him. Most part of the life of Mahbub Raj was spent in the companionship of Maharaja Kishan Pershad. Maharaja also had specific affinity for him. In his poems, Mahbub Raj mentioned the love, favours and beneficence of Maharaja many a time. He always used to pray for Maharaja:

Khuda Shad Ko Rakhe Shadaan Vo Farhaan
(May God keep Shad delighted and cheerful)

Nahin Aiysa Achcha Zamana Kisi ka
(No one has good time like this)

Wohi Shad Ki Shakal Mein De Raha Hai
(He is giving us in the form of Shad)

Ke Hai Rizq Ko Bhi Bahana Kisi Ka
(Livelihood also has someone's pretext)

Deccan Ko Fakhar Ho Kyon Kar Na Apne Sadre Azam Par
(Why shouldn't Deccan feel pride of its Prime Minister?)

Bane Hain Sainkdon Muflis Tawangar Shad Ke Ghar Se
(Hundred beggars have become rich from the house of Shad)

Dua Un Ke Liye Mahbub Ke Dil Se Nikalti Hai
(Prayer emerges from the heart of Mahbub for him)

Rahein Phoolen, Phalen Bagh-e-Jahan Mein
Fasle Dawar Se

(Be prosperous in the garden of this world
with the harvest of justice)

His passion for poetry was promoted by Majaraja Sir Kishan Pershad. He says:

Baat Karne Ka Na Tha Tujh Ko Saleequa Mahbub
(You had no decency or decorum of conversation, Mahbub)

Sohbat-e-Shad Se Ab Tu Sukhandaan Nikla
(With the companionship of Shad, you turned
out to be the one who understands poetry)

Jaah Vo Izzat Badhi, Taukheer Badhi, Shaan Badhi
(Dignity and honour enhanced, reverence
increased, grandeur increased)

Shad Ki Tujh Par Hain Mahbub Atayein Kya Kya
(Mahbub! What kind of favours of Shad you have on you?)

Mahbub Raj used to recite his *Ghazals* in those *'Mushairas'* organised by Maharaja Sir Kishan Pershad at Aiwan-e-Shad.

These Mushairas not only used to provide enjoyment to the audience but were the best sources of teaching the decorum of the congregation, reverence and respect for the elders, not only to the poets but also to the audiences. It was obligatory on the part of every one to maintain the decorum and decency of the session. There was no discrimination between the Hindus and the Muslims.

It is very regrettable that it is being practiced quite the opposite in the poetic gathering (*Mushaira*) that are held these days. Setting aside the decorum of these literary meetings, slogan shouting and hooting has become the common practice. The poets do not get appreciation on the basis of their age or merit of their poems but are viewed on the basis of their religion. The members of the present generation are not aware of the fact that on a par with the Muslims, the Hindus also contributed to the promotion of Urdu language and literature. The fact is that the status of Urdu language and literature which enjoys today would not have been possible without the participation of the Hindus. During the progressive era of today, the importance of the old traditions of Hyderabadi Civilisation has been lost. Decency, decorum, sincerity, affection and unity have been lost in the haziness of the past.

Mahbub Raj had the privilege of being the pupil of Maharaja Sir Kishan Pershad. Later, on the advice of Maharaja Kishan Pershad, he requested Nawab Fasahat Jung 'Jaleel' for correcting his poems. Seeing the progress of his poetry under the experienced and reputed poet like 'Jaleel', he said:

Kya Ho Mahbub Rakham Midhat-e-Ustaad-e-Jaleel

(What eulogy could be written about mentor
Jaleel O' Mahbub !)

Chand Dinon Hi Mein Rangi Khoob Tabiyat Meri

(Only in a few days time, my temperament
got coloured very nicely.)

He preferred Urdu than Persian for composing verses:

Sadqe Tere Aiy Zaban-e-Urdu

(I sacrifice my life O' Urdu language !)

Jamta Nahin Rang Farsi Ka

(The colour of Persian does not suit firmly)

Mahbub Raj was very much devoted to the sages and mendicants. He used to visit temples and Dargahs. He visited the *Samadhi* of Manik Prabhu, located at Manikpur in Raichur

District of Karnataka and paid homage to their spiritual guide Markhand Prabhu:

Jo Hain Mashhoor Martand Guru

(The famous mentor is Martand Guru)

Jin Ki Shohrat Hai Aaj Kal Har Soo

(Whose fame is everywhere these days)

Aur Musiqi Ke Hain Mahir-e-Fun

(He is an expert in the art of music)

Ajar Hai Unka Jo Kare Darshan

(There is reward for those who are blessed with his sight)

Pakke Murtaaz Janiye en Ko

(Consider him to be the matured ascetic)

Hain Yeh Avataar Maniye en Ko

(He is the vicegerent of God, recognise him)

In the grandeur of his father, Girdhari Pershad, Mahbub Raj writes:

Bansi Raja Jise Sab Ahle Deccan Kahte Hain

(Bansi Raja, whom the people of the Deccan call)

Apne Maalik Ke Wo Masroof-e-Sana Rahte Hain

(He kept himself engaged eulogizing his master)

Neech Aur Oonch Zamane Ki Sab Hi Sahte Hain

(Ups and downs of the time, everyone endures)

Chashma-e-Faiz Wo Ata Rahte Thay Aur Sahte Thay

(He used to get benefit from the spring of favour and reward)

Saare Ruoosaa-E- Deccan Ne Maana Hai Loha Jin Ka

(All the rich men of the Deccan have appreciated his talents)

Woh To Baqi Na Rahe Naam Hai Baqi in Ka

(He is not existing but his name exists)

Unke Ausaaf Ko Har Ahle Jahan Jaanta Tha
(Everyone of this world knew his attributes)

Woh Liyaqat Thi Ke Har Ahl-e-Qalam Maanta Tha
(His capability was such that every writer used to recognise)

He used to consider his mother as divine blessing of his life and the service of his mother as felicity and duty:

Maan Hi Ek Nemat-e-Uzma Hai Har Ek Jaan Ke Liye
(Mother is the only the greatest blessing, for everyone)

Baghbaan Jaise Ho Darkaar Gulistaan Ke Liye
(As gardener is required for the garden)

Bayis-E-Sabar Woh Tasalli Hai Pareshan Ke Liye
(Is the cause of consolation for the worried?)

Wohi Maawa Wohi Malja Har Inssan Ke Liye
(She is the only refuge for every human being)

Every couplet, which came out of his pen in praise of parents, is the testimony that he was rightly proud of his ancestors. He used to act on their deeds and follow instructions. He used to advise his progeny also to follow it:

Mahbub Jis Qadar Bhi Karo Naaz Hai Baja
(Mahbub to whatever extent you indulge in
coquetting, it is befiting)

Tum Unki Yaadgaar Ho Jo Naam Kar Gaye
(You are their memorial who earned name
and became famous)

He had a lot of affection and respect for his elder brother Raja Narsing Raj 'Aali'. He established the precedent of love and affection for his brother such that he was referred to as a *"Kalyugi Lakshman"* as a simile.

Apart from his personality as a common man, if we view the poetry of Mahbub Raj, it would be known that his verses are highly rich in imagination written in simple and comprehensible language. His poetry is filled with the topics on love and affection. His impudent writings have enlivened Ghazals. In his poetry, the use of similes and metaphors are also less. He expressed his heartfelt passions in his poetry in a plain and pleasant style. Simplicity is the backbone and the life of his poetry, which highlights his style of narration and depicting truthfulness:

Apne Aamaal Ki Kharabi Ko
(The defaults of our actions)

Ham Ne Gardan Jhuka Ke Dekh Liya
(We saw bending our neck)

Is Bazm Mein Kaun Kis Ko Pooche
(Who would ask whom in this gathering)

Matlab Ki Har Ek Ko Padi Hai
(Everybody is worried about his motive)

Uth Uth Ke Shad Hain Sadr-e-Azam
(Get up, get up, Shad is the Prime Minister)

Qismat Soyi Kahaan Padi Hai
(Where is the luck lying asleep)

Mahbub Tujhe To Yaad-e-Dilbar
(Mahbub, your memory of your beloved)

Har Dam Har Lehza Har Ghadi Hai
(Every breath, every moment, every hour)

He has no dearth of topics or imagination. His couplets always reflect his nature of innovation and flight of fancy. The following couplets represent his impudent narration:

Tod Kar Ise Pachchtayega Aiy Mast Adaa
(You will repent after bursting it, O person of Elegance)

Dil Par Aabla Hai Khosha-E-Angoor Nahin
(Heart is blister, not a bunch of grapes)

Khwab Mein Aate Ho Phirte Ho Nigah-e-Shauq Mein
(You come in dreams and wander in the sight of fondness)

Kaisa Parda Hai Ke Chupte Ho Nikal Kar Saamne
(What kind of veil is this that you hide in exposure)

Dhoonda Saara Jahaan Magar Tujh Ko
(Searched for you in the entire world but)

Dil Ka Parda Utha Ke Dekh Liya
(Lifted the curtain of heart and saw)

Do Roza Husn Aur Fikr-e-Do Aalam Sakht Mushkil
(Beauty for two days and worry about two
worlds is very difficult)

Idhar Duniya Udhar Uqba Karein Ahle Jahaan Kya Kya
(This side is the world and that side is the next world
hereafter what should the inhabitants of the world do)

Discussions on beauty and love are the life of any poetry. Along with the descriptions of beauty, love, philosophical and mystical topics, counsel and admonition also found in his poems. He has laid stress on the thought of the Doomsday and remembering God, he wrote:

Buzdil Hain Past Himmat Jo Duniya Chorh Baithe
(They are cowards, low spirited who relinquished the world)

Mahbub Sab Mein Rah Kar Yaad Us Ki Kar Rahe Hain
(Mahbub, living among all of them, is remembering Him)

Aamaal Ka Samra Hai Mahbub Na Kar Shikwa
(This is the fruit of your deeds, Mahbub, don't complain)

Achcha Jo Kiya Hota Achcha Hi Hota
(Had you done good, good would have happened)

Khayal-e-Ghair Se Ho Pak Dil Mahbub Ka Maula
(Heart of Mahub should be free from the
thought of the other, O' Master)

Agar Tehre Mere Dil Mein Tasawur App Ka Tehre

(If any concept is established in my heart it should be yours)

Ajal Taale Nahin Talti Yahaan Majboor Hai Insaan

(Death cannot be postponed, here human being is helpless)

Maseeha-e-Zamaana Ho, Arastu Ho Ke Luqmaan Ho

(Whether he is the Messiah of the era, Aristotle or Luqmaan)

He believed that in every worship and obedience, sincerity of heart and truthfulness of intention is essential:

Hazaron Saal Ki Tait Se Kahin Behtar Hai

(The obedience of thousand years is far better than)

Khuloos-E-Dil Se Agar Sajda Ek Bar Kiya

(Prostration of one time if performed with sincerity of heart)

In Mahbub Raj's verses, there are less difficult thoughts or structures. Whenever, he composed verses in difficult areas, he exhibited the maturity of poetry and the force of narration:

Sainkdon Teri Jafayein Sainkdon Tere Sitam

(Hundreds of your atrocities and cruelties)

Yeh Bhi Socha Hai Kabhi Hai Roz-e-Mahshar Saamne

(Have you ever thought that there is Judgement Day ahead)

Ishtiyaq-e-Deed Se Dariya Ka Toofan Badh Gaya

(Craving for sight enhanced the storm of the river)

Kashtiy-e-Ummeed Ja Pahunchi Jo Saahil Ke Qareeb

(When the boat of hope reached near the seashore)

In his poetry, at many places, he said :

Kya Ghazal Tum Ne Kahi Mahbub Dil Khush Ho Gaya

(What a Ghazal you composed, O Mahbub! Heart felt delighted)

Yeh Asar Paya Nahin Hum Ne Kisi Tahreer Mein

(We did not find its effect in any movement)

Bazme Shora Mein Hum Charcha Hi Sunte Hain
(In the gathering of poets, we continued
hearing only his fame)

Hai Qabil-e-Sad Tahseen Mahbub Ki Goyayi
(The eloquence of Mahbub is praiseworthy hundred times.)

Shair Kahne Ko To Sab Mahbub Kahte Hain Magar
(Apparently, everyone calls poet Mahbub but,)

Shaaz Hi Hoga Koyi Jadoo Bayan Meri Tarah
(Rarely, someone may be eloquent like me)

The poetry of Mahbub Raj is not confined to *ghazals* only. He also composed quatrain, *Qataa (*Genre of Urdu poetry comprising at least four lines and dealing with one subject/ topic) *musaddas* (A poem comprising six line stanzas) and *bhajans* (Hindu hymn or sacred song).

Persons possessing commendable qualities and innumerable attributes are rarely born. His every act was specific and each quality was distinct. He was an example of pious character. For the nation and the country, he was the source of inspiration and instruction. His personality was equally popular with the poor and the rich, relatives and friends. The popularity and affectionate behaviour not only affected the human beings but also God. This is the reason that he expired at the young age. He died on 4th Aaban, 1340 Fasli (1930) after a brief illness:

Makaan Ko Chorh Jaata Hoon La Makaan Ki Taraf
(I leave the house, going towards the homeless (Deity))

Hai Maqsad Jane Ka Maabood-e-Do Jahaan Ki Taraf
(The purpose is to go towards the deity of both the worlds)

It is more than 75 years after his death; that his poetry was confined only in his notebooks. Being the grand-daughter-in-law of Mahbub Raj, Dr Sheela Raj took up the task of compiling and publishing the collection of his poetry *"Deewan-e-Mahbub"*. In the present day context wherein the literary values are changing, it is the era of progressive writers, the objective of publication of the verses of a large-hearted, far-sighted and a sincere person is to enlighten the dark and narrow minds to liberate them from prejudices and narrow-mindedness in order to inculcate the atmosphere of national integration.

As Mahbub Raj has established his authority in the hearts of the people through affection, in the same manner, the collection of his poems will also become popular and memorable. As he himself hinted that:

Jahaan Mein Yaadgaar-e-Shayeri Mahbub Rahne Day
(O! Mahbub let your poetry remain memorable in the world)

Kabhi Bhoole Se Yaad Aaye Kisi Ko Yeh Sukhan Apna
(Sometimes, someone may remember my
poetry inadvertently)

Mahbub Raj was a man of taste and had a big circle of friends. He had excellent manners and always respected others. He had three sons and six daughters.

As has already been mentioned, an M.Phil. has been done on *"Raja Girdhari Pershad 'Baqi' Aur Inke Khandan Ki Urdu Adabi Khidmat"* in the year 1976 by Pavan Kumari in Osmania University, Hyderabad. In this dissertation, a chapter on Mahbub Raj was written.

Mahbub Raj passed away at the age of 36. Even then his contribution to Urdu literature is outstanding.

Views of the different Writers:

In the article *'Hyderabad Ke Chand Kayasth Shohra'* appeared in *'Sabras'* January 1940, Prof. Mahender Raj Saxena wrote that the main characteristics of the poetry of Mahbub Raj is that his language is very simple. He writes chaste language. He uses small meters and the construction of his couplets is much organised. He is good in narrating the love story in a very effective and piercing language.

Naseeruddin Hashmi in his book entitled *"Deccani Hindu Aur Urdu"* wrote that Mahbub Raj had interest and passion for the poetry right from his childhood. In the beginning, he used to show his poem to Maharaja Sir Kishan Pershad. Later, he became the pupil of Hazrat Fasahat Jung 'Jaleel'. He used to participate in the *'Mushairas'* hosted by Maharaja Kishan Pershad.

Prof. Fatima Parveen in her lecture on the occasion of the release of *'Deewan-e-Mahbub'* said that while reading the poetry of Mahbub Raj, one does not feel that these couplets are hundred years old. The feeling and passion presented in these couplets seem to be the voice of our heart. There is a deep impression of mysticism in the poetry of Mahbub Raj.

Dr. Sheela Raj

Chapter – Ten

Dr Sheela Raj

Dr Sheela Raj was born and brought up in a Kayasth Saxena family of Hyderabad. Her father Late Rai Prithivi Raj was the Director of Agriculture in the Government of Andhra Pradesh.

Dr Sheela Raj did her Master's degree in Urdu Literature and later M.A. in History and B.Ed. from Osmania University-Hyderabad. She was awarded a Doctorate in History by Shrimathi Nathibai Damodar Thackersey Women's University, Bombay. For her Doctorate, she was given prestigious "Shrimathi Prameela Thakersey" award.

She was married to Dr Narayan Raj, the great grandson of Raja Girdhari Pershad Mahbub Nawazwant 'Baqi'. 'Baqi' was a luminary of the family. Raja Narsing Raj 'Aali', the son of 'Baqi' was the grand father-in-law of Dr Sheela Raj. 'Aali' had profound knowledge of Persian, Urdu, Hindi and Marathi languages. As mentioned earlier, Quartrain (Rubayi) was a special field of his poetry. Dr Sheela Raj was the daughter-in-law of Rai Narhar Raj, who was also a poet.

After completing her postgraduation in Urdu literature she was appointed at Mahbubia Girls Junior College, Hyderabad. After her marriage, she was shifted to Bombay, from where she did her Ph.D. in History. Her topic of research was 'Socio-Economic and cultural developments in Hyderabad from 1869 to 1911'. Incidentally, this was the period when Mir Mahbub Ali Khan Nizam-VI was the ruler and Sir Salar Jung was the Prime Minister of Hyderabad. Impartial historians will agree that Nawab Mir Mahbub Ali Khan Nizam-VI and Sir Salar Jung–I, acquired the distinction as 'men of destiny'. Even today the people of Hyderabad take their names with respect. Mir Mahbub Ali Khan was the beloved of the people and Sir Salar Jung-I had a versatile personality, a renowned administrator and reformer of great caliber.

Dr Sheela Raj was a distinguished historian dealing with history of Hyderabad of the nineteenth and early twentieth century. Her work presents a comprehensive picture of Social and cultural life of Hyderabad. Her books forms an important and valuable part of the historical source material for the history of Hyderabad.

She is considered to be an authority on the cultural and social history of the erstwhile Hyderabad State.

Her scholarly articles numbering more than forty in different disciplines including academic, literary, historic and religious contribution during the reign of Mir Mahbub Ali Khan Nizam-VI and Mir Osman Ali Khan Nizam-VII are testimony to the fact that she was a prolific writer. These articles were published in Urdu and English newspapers, magazines and research journals. She was not only a writer but an orator too. She was invited by several academics and research institutes to deliver lectures in and out of Hyderabad. She was invited to deliver H.E.H. Nawab Mir Osman Ali Khan, memorial lecture in the year 2007.

She translated unpublished and published books from Persian into Urdu and Urdu into English.

She was a firm believer in the Hindu-Muslim unity. She was influenced by the policies adopted by Mir Mahbub Ali Khan, Nizam-VI. The people of Hyderabad even today respect Nizam-VI as a secular ruler. She was of the view that the religious tolerance and respect for each other's religion is the need of the hour.

Dr Sheela Raj was the life member of the many Historical Institutes and Societies. She was the member of the executive committee of Maulana Azad Oriental Research Institute Hyderabad-India. She was also the member of the Executive Committee and Advisory Board of the Society for Promotion of Tolerance-Hyderabad, India.

She published nine books out of which four are in English and five in Urdu. Most of these books are on Social and Cultural History of Hyderabad.

The books published by Dr Sheela Raj are:

1. *Toosha-e-Akhebath - 1984*
2. *Medeiavalism to Modernism - 1987*
3. *Shahi-Shadi - 1992*
4. *Portrait of an Era -1996*
5. *The Legacy of The Nizams -2002*
6. *Diwan-e-Mahbub -2007*
7. *Shahan-e-Asafia ki Ravadari Aur Hindu- Muslim Riwayat -2007.* This book was later translated on public demand into English under the title 'The Religious Tolerance of the Asaf Jahi kings and Hindu–Muslim Traditions'.
8. *Diwan-e-Aali-2008*
9. *The Profile of Secular and Transparent Hyderabad Under Nizam-VII -2014.*

1. Toosha-e-Akhebath: Raja Girdhari Pershad 'Baqi' travelled extensively throughout India. He recorded his travel details in Persian. Some of the places he travelled along with Mir Mahbub Ali Khan Nizam-VI. In all, he has recorded the details about twelve travels out of which three were with Nizam-VI. He visited places like Alampur, Malkarjun, Maniknagar, Tuljapur, Pandarpur, Kanakgiri, Madras, Tirupati, Kanchipuram, Aurangabad (along with Nizam-VI),

Nasik, Trimbakeshwar, Allahabad, Gaya, Kashi, Ayodhya, Mirzapur, Poona (along with Nizam-VI), Delhi, Mathura, Brindavan, Gulbarga, Aurangabad, Poona (along with Mir Mahbub Ali Khan Nizam-VI), Benaras, Calcutta (along with Nizam-VI), Jwalamukhi, Kanpur, Amritsar, Pushkar Raj etc.

While recording the details of his travels, Raja Girdhari Pershad mentioned about the historical background of the place, social, cultural and economic life of the people he visited and the important events which took place during his travels. He gave prime importance to the events which took place while he was with the Nizam. For instance, when he was passing through Benaras, Kashi Naresh did not come to the railway station to receive Nizam but he sent his nephew. The nobles of Hyderabad who accompanied Nizam were upset. Later, Kashi Naresh visited Nizam and explained Nizam his genuine inability to come at the first instance. Similarly, when Nizam visited Delhi to attend the *Darbar* in 1877, Bansi Raja has given a complete sketch of the seating arrangement in the *Darbar*. He also mentioned that he wrote a poem entitled *Lateef-e-Darbar*. Criticising the policies of the British and distributed about 500 copies of his poem to different dignitaries who were invited to attend the *Darbar*. These details of travel were written in Persian and translated into Urdu by Dr Sheela Raj in a book entitled *Toosha-e-Akhebat* which was published in the year 1984. The foreword of the book was written by Padma Shree Bilkees Latif, wife of Air Chief Marshall Idris Latif, the then Governor of Maharashtra.

This book was published by Rai Narhar Raj 'Saqi' and released by Shri Ram Lal, Honorable Governor of the Government of Andhra Pradesh at Raj Bhavan, Hyderabad.

2. Mediaevalism to Modernism: Socio-Economic and Cultural History of Hyderabad from 1869 to 1911.

Dr Sheela Raj wrote this book in which she discussed about the Societies in Hyderabad, Status and power of the Nobility, Social life, Customs and Traditions, Land Settlement and Rural Development, Economic Life and Occupations in Rural and Urban areas, Modern Communication, Emergence of Modern industry, Trade, Growth and Spread of Education, Literature and Performing Arts.

The history of the rise and growth of the erstwhile Hyderabad State under the Nizams had several phases. The multifaceted progress of the late nineteenth century in the field of administration, industries, commerce, trade, communication and education brought Hyderabad from dusk to dawn.

The second half of the nineteenth century was significant from the point of view of administrative changes, restoration of peace and tranquillity and improvement in the crippled finances of the state, the challenges faced by the architect in the development of Hyderabad who did not even bother to see the rising power of the British paramountcy. This is a period when these architects pulled the erstwhile Hyderabad State from an old antiquated feudal structure into a more free and modern era.

This study on Hyderabad undertaken by Dr Sheela Raj in the modern style of the annals school covers all aspects of society: political, social, cultural and economic and examines their interdependence on each other. In this study, Dr Sheela Raj has shown really a historical sense and can rightly be claimed a place among the modern historians.

Sheela Raj described the progress during the period from 1869 to 1911. During this period, the history of Hyderabad State under the Nizam-VI made outstanding progress due to socio-economic development coupled with educational and cultural achievements. It gave new dimension of reforms for the growth of industries. In this book, she furnished a vivid picture of life of the people and also their composite culture made up of Telugu, Kannad, Urdu and Marathi cultural heritage, presenting a colourful society of Hindu-Muslim unity in diversity. She also displayed the linguistic pattern of the state and its class structure which changed from mediaeval stagnation to modern attainment. During this period the State produced towering personalities like Sir Salar Jung-I-Prime Minister, Statesman and Regent for almost thirty years. After his demise, Mir Mahbub Ali Khan, Nizam-VI took the reigns and brought tremendous changes in the economics, social and cultural life of the people of Hyderabad. He was in the real sense, a *'Mahbub'* (beloved) of the people. Dr Sheela Raj who was well versed with Persian and Urdu languages and Persian being the official language of that time and most of the official documents were in Persian, she made use of them.

Mir Mahbub Ali Khan was the most enlightened ruler who was so passionately committed to work for the good of the people. His efforts to alleviate the sufferings of his people during the famines especially in the year 1897 and the floods of 1908 were an indication of his sincerity. When he saw the sufferings of his people during the floods of 1908 tears rolled out of his eyes. The great poetess Sarojini Naidu described this incidence in her poem *'The Tears of Asif'*.

Based on Persian and Urdu manuscripts and records, and secondary English sources this historical work deserves full appreciation.

This book was published by Popular Prakashan Private Limited, Bombay in the year 1987, was released at Hyderabad by Prince Muffakham Jah, the grandson of H.E.H the Nizam-VII.

3. *Shahi Shadi* : Raja Girdhari Pershad 'Baqi' wrote in detail about the marriage of Najeeb Unnisa Begum, the sister of Mir Mahbub Ali Khan Nizam –VI with Imam Jung, son of Khursheed Jah which was performed in the year 1891-1892. The details of the marriage were written in Persian and it was in the form of manuscript. Dr Sheela Raj translated this manuscript from Persian into Urdu.

It was a tradition in those days that when a marriage was performed in the family of Nobles, it was customary to perform the marriage of a poor girl also. The marriage ceremonies in those days were performed over a period of four to six weeks. The intention behind this was to get acquainted with the families of the bride and bridegroom intimately so that the two families know each other intimately. Their behaviour, attitude, likes and dislikes and temperaments are intimately known to each other. Probably, this was the reason that the divorce rate at that time was almost negligible.

In *Shahi Shadi*, Dr Sheela Raj furnished complete details about the marriage, ceremonies including cultural customs followed at the Bride and Bridegroom houses and their dresses. At that time the jewellery was not only worn by ladies but even the gents. Jewellery of the ladies and gents were of different kinds and also made in different ways. During nineteenth century, in Hyderabad gents used to wear jewellery in Darbar, on the occasion of *Eid* and on the occasion of Hindu festivals.

At the end of this book an exhaustive Glossary provides valuable information about the nobles, their titles, customs, traditions, palaces of the Nizam, dresses, different kinds of jewellery, musical instruments, different kinds of eatables etc.

This book will be of interest to the present day generation as it narrates the customs and traditions of the past.

This book was published by H.E.H the Nizam's Urdu Trust Hyderabad in the year 1991. The book was released at Hyderabad by Mr M.A. Hadi, I.A.A.S. (Retd) the then Secretary H.E.H the Nizam Jewellery Trust.

4. Portrait of an Era: It is a known fact that books based on personal diaries, notes, letters, reports and other relevant documents, provide not only interest with iota of truth but also serve as valuable sources of information for social, economic and cultural history of a particular era.

Dr Sheela Raj, in this book, portrays the Asaf Jahi Dynasty of Hyderabad when Mir Mahbub Ali Khan Nizam-VI was the ruler and Sir Salar Jung was the Prime Minister of

Hyderabad. Dr Sheela Raj took great pains in collecting source material from the personal records like diaries, notes and reports with documentation coupled with evidences of Raja Girdhari Pershad alias Bansi Raja.

The book discusses various aspects of the life of Bansi Raja who held important positions like tutor, mediator, writer, poet, commandant of the army and also a close confidant of the then Nizam Mir Mahbub Ali Khan.

The book has not only been well documented but systematically distributed in eight chapters. It talks of the multi-coloured life and many fold activities. It throws light on magnificent personalities working for peace and welfare of the State through unity in diversity. It throws light on community, creed, cast, colour, culture, language and religion.

The author has given the details of the ceremonies performed in the royal palace, *Darbar*s and various interesting instances.

Dr Sheela Raj has mentioned that nineteenth century Hyderabad was a shining example of Hindu-Muslim unity and tolerance. She further wrote "it should not be forgotten that culture and tolerance can form the strongest pillar for national integration."

This is a well written and thoroughly researched and incisive piece of socio-historical analysis which makes use of factual data to arrive at some fresh and illuminating conclusion about its subject.

This work is of high quality: it provides a reader with lively, informed and well balanced study of the society and culture of nineteenth century Hyderabad.

This book was published by Minerva Press 195, Knightsbridge, London in the year 1996. The book was released by Prince Muffakham Jah at Hyderabad.

5. *The Legacy of The Nizams:* It was published in the year 2002. Two volumes of *Mamlakat-e-Asafia* in Urdu were translated by Dr Sheela Raj into English. During the past

five decades considerable historical research was carried out concerning the erstwhile Hyderabad State. Unfortunately, some of the writers in the recent past did not portray the facts as they did not had the basic knowledge of Persian and Urdu languages. Some of them projected the history of Hyderabad with a biased mind. The impartial historians will record the facts free from prejudices and biased mind. The fact should not be forgotten that historical works are the part of the national heritage for the present and future generations.

The translation of two volumes of the book *Mamlakat-e-Asafia* into English was a gigantic task. However, Dr Sheela Raj, took into consideration all the facts and added new dimensions to the translation. She has tried to unearth and add material in many areas where additional information was felt necessary. In this book, she highlighted Hindu-Muslim unity in the erstwhile Hyderabad State.

As a result of these additions, the first volume is about 620 pages and the second volume is of about 810 pages. These two volumes are available in the library of Salar Jung Museum under the collection of the family of Raja Narsing Raj.

These two volumes have been edited and abridged by the H.E.H Nizam's Urdu Trust Hyderabad under the title "The Legacy of The Nizams" and published in the year 2002. It contains 310 pages.

6. Deewan-e-Mahbub: This is the poetic collection (collection of ***Ghazals***) of Mahbub Raj. Dr Sheela Raj compiled this book and published in 2007.

Mahbub Raj 'Mahbub' was a poet of eloquence. He got his taste of literature and poetry right from childhood and later under the patronage of Maharaja Kishan Pershad. He used to attend literary sessions and *Mushairas* organised by Maharaja Kishan Pershad regularly.

In his poetry, besides poems on love subject there are a number of couplets in which the passion of true love, morals mysticism have been presented in the effective manner.

Dil Wohi Achcha Hai Jo Khoogar Ho Dard-e-Ishkh ka
(That heart is good which is addicted to the pain of love)

Dard Achcha Hai Wohi Jis Ki Dawa Kuch Bhi Nahin
(That pain is good, for which no remedy is available).

Mahbub made a journey from mundane love to divine love very fast.

Hum Ko Paida Kiya To Gharz Itni Thi
(When we were created, its purpose was only this)

Jaanne Wala Koyi Dekhne Wala Ho Jaye
(Someone who is a knower should become the seer)

Aap Karte Hain Justaju Apni
(He quests for Himself)

Aap Hi Bayis-E-Judai Hain
(He himself is the cause for separation)

In these couplets, the heart of a mystic seems to be throbbing. It is not simply a task, it is ecstasy. In these couplets all topics pertaining to motives of creation, unity of existence, observation of reality, obliteration and immortality have been penned down.

He also expressed his humility with the ruler of that time, Mir Osman Ali Khan in his couplets and appreciated his statesmanship.

Mahbub Yeh Hikmat Yeh Siyasat Yeh Fazeelat
(Mahbub this wisdom, politics, this excellence)

Zeba Shahe Osman Ali Khan Ke Liye Hai
(Is graceful for king Osman Ali Khan)

The poetry of Mahbub Raj remained in diaries and notebooks for about 75 years. Dr Sheela Raj took pains and laid hands on this valuable treasure. She arranged all the Ghazals systematically and published it. Diwan-e-Mahbub is a great contribution to Urdu literature.

This book was published by the Narhari Pershad Charitable Trust, Hyderabad in the year 2007. The book was released by Mr Zahid Ali Khan, Editor of Siasat Urdu daily, Hyderabad.

7. *Shahan-e-Asafia Ki Ravadari aur Hindu Muslim Riwayat :*

Dr Sheela Raj was invited to deliver lectures by Abul Kalam Azad Oriental Research Institute, Hyderabad. She agreed to deliver the lectures on the following topics.

(i) The Religious Tolerance of Mir Mahbub Ali Khan Asaf Jah - VI.

(ii) The Religious tolerance of Mir Osman Ali Khan Asaf Jah - VII.

(iii) Asaf Jahi Kings and the Hindu-Muslim traditions.

It is a fact that during the period 1724-1948 when the Asaf Jahi rulers were ruling the erstwhile Hyderabad State neither the mosque were demolished nor the temples were looted. Holi was played with water and not with the human blood. Asaf Jahi rulers considered themselves as the guardians of the people and did not discriminate between the Hindus and the Muslims. The rights of the people were protected and they were treated in a decent manner. As far as the living style is concerned, they bore in mind to make people happy. The Hindus and the Muslims adopted each other's customs, traditions and costumes. It was difficult to differentiate between them as most of their costumes were similar.

Once, Mir Mahbub Ali Khan Nizam-VI said that the Hindus and Muslims were his two eyes. Asaf Jahi rulers never imparted justice on the basis of religion. Bribery was not in practice.

The architectural features of both the Hindus and the Muslims were manifested in the construction of Osmania University. The doors of Hospital and Educational Institutions were open to both the communities without discriminating the caste and creed.

The Hindus occupied the key posts in the government. For instance the post of *Peshkar* was always with the Hindu family. The revenue department was always with Malwalas, a Kayasth Mathur family. The finance of the State was with the family of Raja Ray Rayan a Maharashtrian.

Dr Sheela Raj while delivering the above three lectures highlighted the historical facts. The process of research was a laborious exercise as Mahmood Bin Muhammad former Ambassador of India to Saudi Arabia rightly wrote in his foreword to the book entitled *'The Religious Tolerance of the Asaf Jahi Kings and the Hindu-Muslim Traditions'*. It is like the peeling of an onion layer by layer, until you reach the core, the essence.

The lectures were well attended by the cross-section of the people. On demand, it was decided to publish the three articles in the form of a book. The book is entitled *Shahan-e-Asafia Ki Rawadari Aur Hindu-Muslim Riwayat* was published in the year 2007. The book highlights many aspects of socio-cultural life of that period. It discusses the religious linguistic and racial variations, harmony and mutual tolerance. It also discusses the traditions followed by the two main communities and their extra ordinary tranquility among the privileged and unprivileged class. The book became very popular among the readers. It was the earnest desire of Dr Sheela Raj to present the articles/papers in English but on the insistence of the organisers the papers were presented in Urdu. To fulfill the desire of Dr Sheela Raj, the book *Shahan-e- Asafia Ki Rawadari aur Hindu-Muslim Riwayat* was translated into English under the title *Religious Tolerance of Asaf Jahi Kings and Hindu- Muslim Traditions* which was published in the year 2010, unfortunately, after the demise of Dr Sheela Raj.

8. *Diwan-e-Aali :*

The ghazals of Raja Narsing Raj 'Aali' a renowned poet of Deccan were compiled by Dr Sheela Raj. Raja Narsing Raj 'Aali' composed verses in all the main genres of Urdu poetry, such as, *Ghazals, Qataa, Nazm, Rubai, Hamd, Marsia, Qasida, Masnavi, Salam* etc.

The book highlights the fact that he had expertise in expressing his passion for love, temperament, pleasant nature and colourful thoughts.

Dekha Tha Usko Aankh Ne Dil Ho Gaya Figar
(Eye had seen him but heart got wounded)
Kis Ki Khata Thi Aur Chala Kis Pe Waar
(Whose fault was it and who got the attack)

In the couplets of *Ghazals* at some places, he had laid stress on the communal harmony since the benefit of both the Muslims and the Hindus lies in it.

Saaf Rakhte Hain Ham Aine Ki Surat Dil Ko
(We keep clean our heart like a mirror)
Hinduon Se Na Gila Hai Na Musalmanoun Se
(There is no complaint either with the
Hindus or the Muslims)

When 'Aali' saw that the Hindus and the Muslims were going astray and their brotherly relations are getting affected, he tells them in a painful style:

Dil Dukhane Mein Kya Bhalai Hai
(What is the virtue in hurting the hearts)
Jab Har Insaan Apna Bhai Hai
(When every human being is our brother)
Roh Rahaa Hoon Mai Sun Ke Yeh Aali
(I am weeping O' Aali after listening to it)
Hindu Muslim Mein Ab Judayi Hai
(There is separation between the Hindus and
the Muslims now)

'Aali was a large-hearted, farsighted and an enlightened person who did not discriminate between human beings.

He paid tribute to Pandit Jawahar Lal Nehru in the following words:

Jo Apna sab Luta De Mulk Par Aur Jaan Se Khele
(The one who has sacrificed for the country
and risked his life)

Jawahar Lal Ki Manind Sardaar Ho Jaye
(Would become leader like Jawahar Lal)

'Aali' had great regard for the Seventh Nizam Nawab Osman Ali Khan, Maharaja Kishan Pershad and his mentor Nawab Fasahat Jung 'Jaleel' Manikpuri. He wrote :

Maalik Hain Asaf-e-Saabe Zehe Naseeb
(Master is Asaf Saabe Nizam-VII, it is my good fortune)

Sad Shukr Hai Ke Aali Bhi In Par Nisaar Hai
(It is hundred fold gratitude that Aali is
also devoted to him)

'Aali' expressed his emotional attachment to Maharaja Kishan Pershad in the following couplet which lasted for many decades till the death of Maharaja Sir Kishan Pershad.

Shad Ke Haq *Mein Kar Dua Aali*
(O' Aali, pray in favour of Shad)

Tere Mohsin Hain Sochta Kya Hai
(He is your benefactor, what are you thinking)

'Aali' was the pupil of Hazrat Fasahat Jung 'Jaleel'. He wrote about him:

Ab To 'Aali' Dil Hamara Aur Bhi Maghmoom Hai
(In the memory of our mentor, I am restless)

Diwan-e-Aali is a masterpiece contribution. Dr Sheela Raj has taken lot of pains to compile 'Aali's ghazals.

The book was printed and it was released by Prince Muffakam Jah Bahadur after the demise of Dr Sheela Raj.

This book was published by Narhari Pershad Charitable Trust, Hyderabad, in the year 2008.

9. The Profile of Secular and Transparent Hyderabad Under Nizam-VII

Dr Sheela Raj extensively worked on the socio-economic and cultural development during 1869-1911. As a result, she decided to write a book entitled 'Emergence of a new era-Socio-economic and cultural developments in Hyderabad during 1911-1950', with a view to complete the study on the socio-economic and cultural development in Hyderabad during 1869-1950.

She worked extensively on the project and collected source material from primary and secondary sources. She classified the proposed book into thirteen chapters which are:

Chapter-I: Introduction.

Foundation of the Asaf Jahi rule- major features during 1911-1950.

Chapter-II: The Nizam.

Nizam-a man of complex mind-personality as a ruler and a person.

Chapter-III: Structure of the Society – Hyderabad and Hyderabadis.

The growth of population, languages, caste and class components.

Chapter-IV: Social Life of the people.

An examination of the society. The new administration and the westernising society had any impact on the social life.

Chapter-V: Reorganisation of finance and modern concepts.

Principle sources of income measures taken to improve finances, currency and exchange.

Chapter-VI: Economic life of the people.

The main sources of land revenue, classification of the land assessment, pricing policy etc.

Chapter-VII: Secular Policies.

An examination of society with reference to communal and religious integration.

Chapter-VIII: Modern means of communications.

Purchase of Railways, Railway extension, Air services, introduction of bus services, extension of post and telegraph.

Chapter-IX: Emergence of modern industries.

Growth and development of industries during 1911-1950. Emergence of new industries and control of the government on major industries.

Chapter-X: Trade.

British policies hampered trade in general in Hyderabad Nizam's government to exhilarate.

Chapter-XI: Progress of Education.

Free primary education, establishment of Osmania University and other technical and professional colleges like engineering and medical colleges, priority to women education, impact of changes in educational pattern.

Chapter-XII: Cultural Renaissance.

Growth of literature and literary activities. How far these literary activities flourish during the first half of the twentieth century, role of journalism and press. Archaeological Department, Position of their performing arts like music, dance drama and paintings.

Chapter-XIII: Conclusion.

(**Note:** The details of the chapters have been given in brief).

Dr Sheela Raj could complete only four chapters out of the thirteen she proposed, she passed away in the year **2008** after a very brief illness.

Thereafter, number of historians and academicians were requested to complete the work of writing the remaining nine chapters. Unfortunately, none came forward to undertake this gigantic task. It was, therefore, decided that the four chapters written by her should be published in two parts.

PART-I : Economic life of the people of Deccan.

Chapter-I: Geographical, Geological and Climatic features and economic conditions of Rural and Urban Deccan.

PART-II: Secularism, Education and Communication during the reign of Nizam-VII.

Chapter-II: Secularism under Mir Osman Ali Khan Nizam - VII.

Chapter-III: Progress of Education during the Nizam-VII.

Chapter-IV: Development of Communication during the period of Nizam-VII.

This book was published in the year 2014 by Narhari Pershad Charitable Trust, Hyderabad.

List of the Papers, Published, Presented in Various Conferences and UGC Workshop by Dr Sheela Raj

1. *R.S. Sharma as a Historian.*

   Paper presented at the UGC Workshop held at S.N.D.T. Women's University in 1977.

2. *Society in Hyderabad During the Second Half of Nineteenth Century.*

   Paper presented at the 39th Indian History Congress held in Hyderabad in December, 1978.

3. *Development of Education in Hyderabad During Second Half of the Nineteenth Century.*

   Paper presented at the 40th Indian History Congress held at Waltair in December, 1979.

4. *Development of Communication in Hyderabad During the Second Half of the Nineteenth Century.*

   Paper presented at the UGC Workshop held at S.N.D.T. Women's University in 1979.

5. *Famine Havoc in Hyderabad During the Second Half of the Nineteenth Century.*

   Published in the Quarterly Review of Historical Studies, Calcutta, Volume xxxvi, No. 3, p. 37.

6. *The Role of Woman in the Development of Education and Society in Hyderabad During the Second Half of Nineteenth Century.*

   Published in the Essays in Indian History and culture, proceedings of the Annual Conference of Indian History and Cultural Society, New Delhi in January, 1986.

7. *Hindu-Muslim Integration in Hyderabad During the Second Half of the Nineteenth Century.*

   Published in the Quarterly Review of Historical Studies, Calcutta.

8. *Religious Tolerance and Nizam VI.*

   Paper presented at Parbhani (Maharashtra) during "Bahadur Yar Jung" Celebrations on 16-17th January, 1988. It was later published in Subras, Urdu, Monthly Journal of Idara-e-Adabiyat-e-Urdu, Hyderabad in November, 1989.

9. *Development of Women's Education in Gujarat During 19th and the First Half of the Twentieth Century.*

   Paper presented at the Seminar on the "History of Women in India", 24-26th March, 1988 held at Maniben Nanavati Women's College, Bombay.

10. *"New Approach to Research in History*

    "Paper presented at the seminar held at S.N.D.T. College of Arts, Bombay from 28th March-2nd April, 1988.

11. *Legacy of the Past-Kishen Pershad and Salar Jung-III.*

    Paper presented at the Seminar on the Last Phase of Asaf Jahi Rule held at Hyderabad from 10-12th March, 1989 at the Andhra Pradesh Archives.

12. *Hyderabad- Floods of 1908 and its Aftermath.*

    Paper sent to the XV Annual Conference of Indian History and Culture society held on16-18th December, 1991 at Bhopal.

13. *Progress of Education in Hyderabad State During 1911-1948.*

    Paper published in Islamic Culture- An English Quarterly, Special 75th Anniversary Issue, Volume LXXVII, No. 2, Hyderabad, April 2002.

14. *Development of Communications During Nizam-VII.*

    Paper presented at the Seminar held by Dept. of Islamic Studies and Urdu, Osmania University, Hyderabad on October 30th – 31st, 2002.

15. *Religious Tolerance and Nawab Mir Mahbub Ali Khan Asaf Jah Sadas.*

    Paper presented at Abul Kalam Oriental Research Institute, Hyderabad, on April 28th, 2007.

16. *Secularism Under Mir Osman Ali Khan Nizam VII.*

    A Memorial Lecture on the 125th Birth Anniversary of H.E.H. Nawab Mir Osman Ali Khan, Nizam VII, held at Nizam's Jubilee Pavilion Trust, Purani Haveli on 16th July, 2007.

17. *Economic Life of the People in Deccan (Rural & Urban) 1924-1948.*

    Chapter written for History of Modern Deccan Vol. II, by Abul Kalam Oriental Research Institute, Hyderabad.

18. Development of Education in Hyderabad During The Second Half of the 19th Century.
19. Religio-Cultural Harmony-Our Goal.

List of Articles Published in English Newspapers by Dr Sheela Raj

1. *A Remarkable man.*

   Published in Deccan Chronicle (Magazine Section) A Daily Newspaper dated 11th October, 1981 of Hyderabad.

2. *An Artistic Monument.*

   Published in Deccan Chronicle – Hyderabad, dated 12th September, 1982.

3. *The Beloved Ruler.*

   Published in Deccan Chronicle (Magazine Section) – Hyderabad dated 10th October, 1982.

4. *Communal Peace During the Nizams.*

   Published in Deccan Chronicle, dated 6th February, 1983.

5. *His Generosity Was Legendary.*

   Published in Deccan Chronicle (Magazine Section) dated 8th January, 1984.

List of the Publication in Urdu Newspapers by Dr Sheela Raj

1. *Mirza Ghalib*

   Published in Siasat, Urdu Daily, Hyderabad, dated 1st July, 1966.

2. *Jigar Muradabadi*

   Published in Siasat, Urdu Daily, Hyderabad, dated 1st August, 1966.

3. *Nawab Sir Viqar-ul-Umara Bahadur*

   Published in Siasat, Urdu Daily, Hyderabad, dated 1st November, 1982.

4. *Hyderabad ki Tehzeeb*

   Published in Siasat, Urdu Daily, Hyderabad, dated 31st March, 1983.

5. *Dudh-Mai-Siasat*

   Published in Hindustan - Mumbai, dated 11th January, 1984.

6. *Dr Kurien ki Na Kabhil-e-Faramosh Kidmat*

   Published in Hindustan - Mumbai, dated 11th February, 1984.

7. *Delhi Darbar-1877*

   Published in Siasat, Urdu Daily, Hyderabad, dated 22nd July, 1985.

8. *Hyderabad Mein Guzista Teen Sau Sal Mein Barish Ke Liye Duain*

   Published in Siasat, Urdu Daily, Hyderabad, dated 21st July, 1986.

9. *Nawab Imad-ul-Mulk*

   Published in Siasat, Urdu Daily, Hyderabad, dated 6th October, 1986.

10. *Raja Shiv Raj Dharamvant Bahadur*

    Published in Siasat, Urdu Daily, Hyderabad, dated 6th December, 1987.

11. *Mazhabi Rawadari Aur Daur-e-Asaf Jah Sadas*

    Published in Mahanama Sabras, Hyderabad, in November, 1989.

12. *Ornaments*

    Published in Siasat, Urdu Daily, Hyderabad, July, 1993.

13. *Falaknuma Palace*

    Published in Siasat, Urdu Daily, Hyderabad, dated 28th August, 1994.

14. *Purani Haveli*

    Published in Siasat, Urdu Daily, Hyderabad, dated 8th October, 1984.

15. *King Kothi*

    Published in Siasat, Urdu Daily, Hyderabad, dated 9th October, 1994.

16. *Hindu Muslim Riwayat Ka Amin-Part-I*

    Published by Munsif Daily, Hyderabad, dated 19th November, 1998.

17. *Hindu Muslim Riwayat Ka Amin-Part-II*

    Published by Munsif Daily, Hyderabad, dated 26th November, 1998.

18. *Hindu Muslim Riwayat Ka Amin-Part-III*

    Published by Munsif Daily, Hyderabad, dated 3rd December, 1998.

19. *Bahadur-E-Yar Jung Number-Tafsira*

    Published in Siasat, Urdu Daily, Hyderabad.

20. *Tariq Khandan Paigah- Part–I*

    Dr Sheela Raj Ki Tariqi-O-Adabi Kidmath-2014.

21. *Tariq Khandan Paigah- Part-II*

    Dr Sheela Raj Ki Tariqi-O-Adabi Kidmath - 2014.

Gold Medals, Fellowship, Memorial Lectures instituted and organised in the memory of Dr Sheela Raj.

The University of Hyderabad instituted a Gold Medal in memory of Dr Sheela Raj during the year 2008, for the candidate who is awarded Ph.D. in History.

The Asiatic Society of Mumbai instituted an Annual Fellowship in History in memory of Dr Sheela Raj in 2008. The fellowship is awarded to the candidate who carries out research in History.

Shrimati Nathi bai Damodar Thackersey Women's University Mumbai instituted a Gold Medal during the year 2008 in memory of Dr Sheela Raj. The Gold Medal is awarded to the candidate who is awarded Ph.D / M.Phill / M.A. in History.

H.E.H. The Nizam's Jubilee Pavilion Trust, Hyderabad, has been organising an annual 'Dr Sheela Raj Memorial Lecture' since 2009.

A Ph.D. has been done on Dr Sheela Raj in the Department of Urdu, Osmania University, Hyderabad, on the topic 'Dr Sheela Raj Life And works' by Mr. M.A. Aziz in year 2014.

Views of different Historians, Scholars and Writers about Dr Sheela Raj's contributions:

Mr. Z.A. Ali Baig while reviewing the book *Toosha-e-Akhebat* in Siasat Urdu Daily wrote that Dr Sheela Raj reminded the culture and tradition of her forefathers to the present generation.

In the foreword to the book *Medievalism to Modernism* by Dr Sheela Raj, Prince Muffakham Jah Bahadur (Grandson of Nizam-VII) wrote "Dr Raj's picture of the State of Hyderabad is Socio-Economic and cultural". It is valuable not in one but in two respects. In the history of the 'premier' of the former Indian Princely States, she has made a significant contribution towards the better understanding of a critical and a vibrant period. In the history of our nation, she has thrown light on an underlit part of our past, the immediate past, with a special and useful attention to the political and personal framework of an Indian State.

There was a need for such a work on the subject. Because of her accomplishment, Dr Raj merits great appreciation".

On 05.11.1982 under title "Research into City's past" the Deccan Chronicle Hyderabad wrote that the book Medieavalism to Modernism, the choice of her topic for research was very apt. She belongs to the famous family of Bansi Raja, it was the time when well known Nizam Mir Mahbub Ali Khan was the ruler.

While expressing the views on the book entitled *Medievalism to Modernism* (October 10th, 1987) by Dr Sheela Raj, Professor Mani P. Karmerkar, Director, College Development Council, S.N.D.T. Woman's University Bombay wrote that Dr Sheela Raj has shown a real historical sense and can rightly claim a place amongst modern Indian historians. She has set a pattern for the study of modern history, which should be emulated by other young writers to enrich and bring out the faceted development in the Modern India.

While writing about the book *Medievalism to Modernism* under the title 'Uncovering Progress' in Deccan Chronicle, Hyderabad dated 17.04.1988 Shri Pratap Kishore wrote "Sheela Raj, a scion of the family which also played no meanless role in the modernisation of the Hyderabad State by providing able and dedicated administrators, has its objectivity and insight, with a plethora of interesting and fascinating incontroversial fact wrote a lucid account as to how the changes from Mediaevalism to Modernism were brought about without harming anyone in the process".

Dr Syed Dawood Ashraf while writing in *Siasat,* Urdu Daily, Hyderabad, on 23.01.2010 about the book *Medievalism to Modernism* wrote that the research work on Hyderabad and its culture carried out by Dr Sheela Raj is very valuable. Many books and articles have been published on Hyderabad of that period in Urdu and English. Her book '*Medievalism to Modernism*' written in English is a research work.

Professor Nizamuddin S. Gorekar while reviewing the book *Medievalism to Modernism* by Dr Sheela Raj in Indica-Vol. 27 (1990) No. 1. wrote "Dr Sheela Raj has given a good account of progress made during the period of nearly forty years (1869-1911). It may be stated that Hyderabad State under the Nizam made immense progress and obviously due to socio-economic development coupled with the educational and cultural achievement. It gives a new dimension to the sweeping reforms in the domain of exchequer for the growth of business and industrial activities".

Professor David in his article 'The rulers and the rule'-socio-economic and cultural history of Hyderabad 1869-1911 by Dr Sheela Raj in Times of India on 04.12.1985 wrote "Dr Sheela Raj, while providing well researched analysis of the development of Hyderabad wrote a comprehensive and readable account of this epoch making era in the annals of the State".

Mr. Abid Ali Khan, Editor of *Siasat* Urdu Daily, Hyderabad, while reviewing the book '*Shahi Shadi*' written by Dr Sheela Raj in the year 1984 wrote that Dr Sheela Raj is worth congratulating for translating valuable Persian treatise into Urdu. As a daughter-in-law of the family, she made an attempt to kindle the torch of Urdu Literature once again.

He further wrote, "An educated lady of Hyderabad has transformed the version of '*Shahi Shadi*' (Royal marriage) into Urdu. Although, it is a translation done by Dr Sheela Raj, it excels the original. It is a major addition to the treasure of Urdu literature. It is hoped that it will be received well. I hope that the pains taken by Dr Sheela Raj in translating the book from Persian into Urdu will be appreciated".

Professor Nizamuddin S.Gorekar while reviewing the book entitled *'Portrait of an Era'* by Dr Sheela Raj in Journal of Asiatic Society of Bombay 1998 wrote "Dr Sheela Raj has taken great pains in collecting the source material from the personal records and diaries, notes and reports with documentation coupled with the evidences of Girdhari Pershad alias Bansi Raja. The most influential personality of the Asaf Jahi dynasty of the second half of the Nineteenth Century".

He further wrote, "The book is well presented with attractive get up of printing. The author as well as the publishers deserve hearty congratulations as this will help the future writers in general and historians in particular to emulate the writer and follow the track of unity and integrity for creating harmony and peace in the country".

While reviewing the book *'Portrait of an Era'* by Dr Sheela Raj, Bhavani Shankar Shukla editor of 'Manav' Lucknow (52.4-page 400-1999) wrote:

"Bansi Raja's forefathers were in military and administrative service of the Nizams and his family occupied an important place in the nobility of his time. Born in 1828 A.D. Bansi Raja was brought up in the atmosphere where the royalty and the nobility interacted and intermingled with each other. His father Rai Narhari Pershad was a scholar of Hindi and Sanskrit and was a staunch religious person. The literary, cultural and religious atmosphere of the family must have had great impact on Bansi Raja in the early days."

He further wrote "the fact that the author of the 'Portrait of an Era' is the great grand daughter-in-law of Bansi Raja and therefore she was likely to be indulgent and biased in portraying the image of our hero has no basis. Her relationship with Bansi Raja should not be seen as weakness of the book but taken as its strength. Sheela Raj has taken pains to do a lot of research and has done full justice to her scholarship. Her tremendous capacity to sift genuine research material from the mass of personal and public document and to her quality of being detached and unbiased observer in writing a book like this. At times the book enumerates many facts and even stand their corroborative evidences with reference to Bansi Raja and this hampers the flow of narration and the pleasure of reading this biography. None the less, the 'Portrait of an Era' is good, readable, interesting, well documented and purposeful book deserving welcome".

While reviewing the book *'Diwaan-e-Mahbub'*, Rasheed Ansari wrote in Sabras of 2007 that as in the past, even today Hindus are playing an important role in the promotion of Urdu language and literature. Those who claim that Urdu is the language only of the Muslims are misleading the world. They won't be successful in their attempts, provided people like Dr Sheela Raj are the members of the caravan of Urdu.

He further wrote that Dr Sheela Raj has written the preface with great care and hard work. It is worth reading. Like the traditional daughter-in-law, she had made an attempt to prove herself the protector of family traditions and values. She compiled poetic collection of Mahbub Raj and got it printed.

Professor Sulaiman Ather Jaweed while writing about *'Shahan-E-Asafia Ki Ravadari Aur Hindu-Muslim Riwayat'* in *Siasat,* Urdu Daily dated 02.02.2008 wrote that Dr Sheela Raj by her temperament and literary taste is basically a historian. She has a passionate association with the Asaf Jahi rulers. She has carried out research on various aspects of Asaf Jahi period on governance covering Social, Economic, Cultural and Administrative aspects.

Mr. Syed Mohammed Abdul Quader 'AZM' while reviewing the book *'Shahan-E-Asafia Ki Rawadari Aur Hindu-Muslim Riwayat'* in Siasat Urdu Daily dated 29.02.2008, wrote that this book is a tribute to the large heartedness of tolerance of the Asaf Jahi Kings. For her valuable book the people of Hyderabad will always remain indebted to her.

Mr. Mahmood Bin Muhammad, Former Ambassador of India to Saudi Arabia wrote in his foreword of the book *'The Religious Tolerance of Asaf Jahi Kings And Hindu Muslim Traditions'* that the process of research is indeed a laborious one, it is like peeling of an onion, layer by layer until you reach the core. It calls for the right attitude unlimited patience, unremitting hard work, objectivity, good communication skills, training and, not the least of all funds. Dr Sheela Raj is well equipped for the task and has done commendable job. Her books are bound to attract the interest of historians, academicians, researchers, public, students and scholars.

Professor Ashraf Rafi, Vice-President, Abul Kalam Azad Oriental Research Institute Hyderabad, in her introduction of the book, *'Religious Tolerance of the Asaf Jahi Kings And Hindu-Muslim Traditions'* wrote that Dr Sheela Raj on account of her profound scholarship and prolific analytical perspective is considered to be an authority on cultural and political history of the erstwhile Hyderabad State.

In the foreword of the book '*Diwan-e-Aali*' Zahed Ali Khan, Chief Editor of *Siasat* Urdu daily, Hyderabad wrote "In the Kayasth family, there are a number of reputed poets of Urdu. One of the dignified poets was Raja Narsing Raj 'Aali'. The compiler of '*Diwaan-e-Aali*' herself is a dignified, capable and competent writer whose writings are read by the readers of *Siasat* Urdu Daily with great interest". He further wrote "I congratulate Dr Sheela Raj from the depth of my heart that she has compiled this valuable literary treasure in the form of a book. I personally honour such persons from the depth of my heart who engage themselves in the preservation of literary and cultural heritage of their ancestors.

Professor Suleman Ather Jaweed, while writing about '*Diwaan-e-Aali*' in *Siasat* Urdu Daily dated 21.02.2009 stated that Dr Sheela Raj deserves congratulations as she has enlivened the poetic collections of her ancestors with great interest and curiosity. She compiled '*Diwaan-e-Aali*' on the same lines as she did for '*Diwaan-e-Mahbub*'. Her efforts would be appreciated with reverence.

Fazalullah Mukarram wrote in *Sabras* in 2009 that 'Diwaan-e- Mahbub' and 'Diwaan-e-'Aali' the poetic collection of Mahbub Raj and Raja Narsing Raj respectively, if studied, reveal that how much affinity she has with the literary and cultural deeds of her family. Dr Sheela Raj has explored the deeds of her ancestors. She has given eternal life to their poetic collection.

Professor Ashraf Rafi said (Siasat 21.02.2009) that Dr Sheela Raj was a good teacher. She had a good insight in History, Urdu language and literature. She was the countenance of Hindu-Muslim unity. She led her life as an educationist. She was an expert in English, Urdu, Hindi and Persian languages.

Allama Ajaz Farukh said about Dr Sheela Raj (*Siasat* Daily, dated 21.02.2009) that she was the example of civilisation. Her demise is not the death of a person but of a civilisation of an era.

Mehmood-Bin-Mohammed, Former Ambassador of India to Saudi Arabia while reviewing '*Diwaan-e-Aali*' published in Siasat Urdu Daily, Hyderabad, dated 21.02.2009 wrote that Dr Sheela Raj was the representative of Hyderabadi civilisation. Such persons are a blessing. She led the life of a scholar. She had devoted her life for preservation of history.

He further wrote "Dr Sheela Raj is not with us now but she has contributed a lot to History and Urdu literature. Her contribution would be remembered in the realm of Urdu language and poetry".

Dr M.A. Azeez in his Ph.D. thesis submitted to Osmania University, Hyderabad, entitled '*Dr.Sheela Raj-Life And Work*' wrote that Dr Sheela Raj has made it a motto to highlight Religious Tolerance of the Asaf Jahi period. She was an enlightened writer. By consolidating the history and civilisation of the Asaf Jahi period, Dr Sheela Raj has done an outstanding service, as a result of which her name would be remembered in the history of Urdu language forever.

Dr Sheela Raj passed away on 17th July, 2008.

Chapter – Eleven

Conclusion

While writing about the family of Rai Daulat Rai, I have not only made an attempt to project its literary contribution but also tried to project its close association with the Nizams, its loyalty towards the rulers, socio-economic life of that era, and religio-cultural approach covering two hundred years. This will stimulate the minds of the present and future generations to think in terms of national integration and communal harmony.

The fact cannot be ignored that communal harmony and national integration are the essential tools which help in winning the heart of the people.

When we study the past, the future gets benefited. The present can be understood only when past is studied, and understood in its true perspective. Historical events are important to understand the future.

Asaf Jahi rulers and the nobility of the erstwhile Hyderabad State maintained communal harmony at all cost and never took religion to the streets as being done by the present day politicians for their selfish benefit. It is a established fact of history that the rulers and nobility of Hyderabad maintained religio-cultural integration, communal harmony and religious tolerance. As a result, they were respected by all irrespective of caste and religion.

The family of Rai Daulat Rai served the Nizams sincerely and honestly for many centuries. They were loyal to the rulers. The Nizams too had great faith and confidence in this family.

Rai Daulat Rai's family was given important responsibilities by the Nizams to handle the tense situations. The members of the family too proved their efficiency and loyalty not only to the Nizams but also to the State as well by handling such situations efficiently.

Some of this family members served three successive Nizams which itself is an indicative of the fact that they were honest and efficient persons. For instance, Rai Narhari Pershad served three successive Nizams. Bansi Raja served two Asaf Jahi rulers and five successive Prime Ministers.

This family consists of philanthropists, industrialists, scholars, poets and philosophers of repute who achieved distinction in every sphere of life.

The family members of Rai Daulat Rai played a major role in the management of the Royal Palace for decades. The Royal Kitchen was under their charge for many years. The *Mashaal Khana* was also under their charge. During the reign of Mir Mahbub Ali Khan Nizam-VI, all the royal ceremonies in the palaces including social and religious, the royal marriages were organised under the supervision of Bansi Raja. The family had the honour to present *Pan* and *Itr* at both the English and *Mughlai Darbars.*

The family of Rai Daulat Rai is a staunch Hindu family. They are the followers of *Sanatan Dharm*. The family had a wide concept of religion and believe in communal harmony, tolerance and unity between various religions. The members of the family constructed temples and visited pilgrimage centres. They also visited the Tombs and *Mazars* of the Muslim saints. They had the firm faith in the saints of both the Hindus and the Muslims religion. Bansi Raja donated generously in cash, jewellery and clothes at the temples. He was immensely generous, good at heart, benevolent.

Charity was his second nature. It is proved beyond doubt that this family was a family of philanthropists.

The family of Rai Daulat Rai always worked for the welfare of its rulers and the State. It always looked after the interests of the State and contributed to the Military and Administration of the State. The family was always sincere in the task assigned to it and handled delicate situations tactfully. It upheld the traditions of the Asaf Jahi rulers with great care, specially, *Darbars*, royal marriages, social and religious functions in the palace. To manage the royal kitchen was not an easy task, it was also managed efficiently by the members of the family. The responsibilities assigned to them were successfully carried out by them skillfully.

Bansi Raja's arms and ammunitions factory posed a serious threat to the British. He maintained that he can be a successful industrialist and can establish many factories and run them successfully. But for the vested interests of the British, the industrial growth of the erstwhile Hyderabad State was hampered. His services for the development of industries in erstwhile Hyderabad State cannot be ignored. When the history of the industrial development of Hyderabad is written, the name of Bansi Raja would definitely appear as the pioneer industrialist.

In 1861-62, when Sir Salar Jung decided to form Reformed Troops, he entrusted this formidable task to Bansi Raja. After the formation of Reformed Troops, Bansi Raja was appointed Head *Sarishtedar* of the Regular and Irregular Troops.

As mentioned earlier, during the reign of Asaf Jahi rulers, not only many renowned poets emerged in Hyderabad but flourished due to the patronage of the rulers, such as, Raja Chandu Lal 'Shadan', Hafiz Shamsuddin Mohammed 'Faiz' etc. The poets like Dagh 'Dehlvi', Amir 'Minai' etc. came from Northern India and flourished in Hyderabad. In fact, the generosity of the Nizams attracted many poets. Persian and Urdu poetry flourished under the Nizams. The royal magnanimity inspired literary activities. This was a unique period of literary development. Many books were written and published on different topics in different languages.

However, amongst these activities there was also a Hindu Kayasth family of Rai Daulat Rai which played an important role in contributing to literature. This family has not only contributed to Persian and Urdu literature but also to other languages, such as, Hindi, Braj Bhasha, Awadhi and Sanskrit.

This family produced literary figures and renowned poets. They were men of merit and master of languages.

The members of this family wrote books not only in poetry but also in prose. These books are of literary merit. One of the family members Rai Narhari Pershad translated the famous *'Yog Vashisht'* from Sanskrit into Hindi. This is considered to be the first translation of *'Yog Vashisht'*. Narhari Pershad was a renowned scholar of Sanskrit and Hindi. His contribution to Hindi literature is noteworthy. Besides Hindi, he had mastery over Braj Bhasha, Awadhi language and Persian. He also wrote *'Bhagwat Puran'* in Awadhi language and in another *'Bhagwat Puran'* he wrote some *Skands* which were in Persian and Hindi. Rai Narhari Pershad's father Swami Pershad composed poetry in Hindi, Urdu and Braj Bhasha. His pen name was 'Swami'. Swami Pershad's father, Raja Ram was the scholar of Hindi and Persian. He translated Persian books into Hindi. He wrote 'Chitragupt Mahatm' in Hindi and Braj Bhasha.

Raja Girdhari Pershad 'Baqi' the son of Rai Narhari Pershad, was a renowned scholar of Persian. He ranked amongst the great Persian poets and scholars. He is considered to be a poet of high caliber in every sense of the word. He composed in all major genres of verse recognised in Persian poetry. In whichever form he wrote, he wrote with distinction. He rendered great service to the Persian and Urdu literature.

'Baqi' wrote in Hindi as well. His nom-de-plume in Hindi is 'Girdhari'. He also wrote *bhajans* in Urdu language. One of his unpublished books *'Shiv Puran'* in Urdu poetry has been transliterated into Hindi and was published in 2017.

Raja Narsing Raj 'Aali', the son of Raja Girdhari Pershad composed poetry in Urdu and Persian languages. He was a poet of repute. He wrote in all the major genres of verse recognised in Urdu poetry. He organised annual *'Mushairas'* (poetic gatherings) for several years in memory of Maharaja Kishan Pershad, who was also a poet of repute.

Rai Narhar Raj 'Saqi' son of Raja Narsing Raj was also a poet. He was the disciple of Fasahat Jung 'Jaleel'. His *Ghazals* are neat and composition is interesting to read. He too wrote *Bhajans* in Urdu and Hindi. He also organised *'Mushairas'* (poetic gathering).

Dr Bhaskar Raj, son of Rai Narhar Raj 'Saqi' was not a poet but wrote five books in three languages i.e. Urdu, English and Hindi. His book *'Yoga Vasistha-Vedanta wisdom through miniature paintings'* is a great contribution to literature and religion. His efforts to republish the book *'Narhari Prakash'* are commendable which is also a great contribution to Hindi literature and religion.

Mahbub Raj 'Mahbub' the second son of Raja Girdhari Pershad was a poet. He passed away at the prime age of his life. He left behind a large number of *ghazals* which were compiled by Dr Sheela Raj and published. His *ghazals* are interesting to read.

Dr Sheela Raj, the daughter-in-law of the family, is a historian and scholar of repute. By compiling *'Diwaan-e-Aali'* and *'Diwaan-e-Mahbub'* she has done a great service to Urdu literature. Her book *'Shahan-E-Asafia Ki Rawadari Aur Hindu-Muslim Riwayat'* is an outstanding contribution to the history of Asaf Jahi Dynasty and Urdu literature. She wrote several books on the history of Asaf Jahi Dynasty in English as well.

The family of Rai Daulat Rai is a unique family whose seven generations have contributed to literature

in six languages. Probably, this family has no parallel in the literary field.

I consider it as an honour to be the member of this illustrious family. I am grateful to my forefathers for giving me strength and courage to write about them which itself is an honour. The lovers of Literature and the Kayasth community should be proud of this family.

References

Raja Girdhari Pershad collection.

Private papers and miscellaneous manuscripts.

Letters:

His Highness The Nizam Mir Mahbub Ali Khan.

Raja of Sandela.

Literary figures from North India.

Distinguished personalities of Saxena community from North India.

Miscellaneous manuscripts.

Daily Diaries of Raja Girdhari Pershad - Urdu only.

Register containing the details of the marriage of Najeeb Unnisa Begum, sister of Nizam-VI - Persian.

ENGLISH BOOKS

Chhabra, Hari Sharan, *Hyderabad Personalities, A Unique Authentic And Comprehensive Biographical Directory of Hyderabad and Its People*, New Publishers, New Delhi, 1954.

Leonard, Karen Isakew, *Social History of an Indian Caste, The Kayasthas of Hyderabad,* London, University of California Press Ltd., London, Berkeley, Los Angeles, 1974.

Mudiraj, K. Krishnaswamy, *Pictorial Hyderabad-Vol. II,* Chandrakant Press, Hyderabad, 1934.

Raj, Narayan, *Khoob Chand's Urdu Book Entitled "Kayasth Kul Nirnay", Select Genealogies of Renowned Kayasths*, Under Publication.

Raj, Sheela, *Medievalism to Modernism, Socio-Economic and Cultural History of Hyderabad-1869-1911*, Popular Prakashan Pvt. Ltd, Bombay, 1987.

Raj, Sheela, *Portrait of an Era - Hyderabad in the Days of Nizams, 1828-1896,* Minerva Press, London, 1990.

Raj, Sheela, *The Religious Tolerance of Asaf Jahi Kings and Hindu-Muslim Traditions,* Narhari Pershad Charitable Trust, Hyderabad, 2010.

Raj, Sheela, *The Legacy of The Nizams,* Vani Prakashan, New Delhi, 2002.

Saxena, Ram Babu, *A History of Urdu Literature*, Allahabad, Ram Narayan Lal, 1927.

Saxena, Bhaskar Raj, *Yoga Vasistha -Vedanta Wisdom Through Miniature Paintings,* Rupa & Co, New Delhi, 2008.

The Chronology of Modern Hyderabad from 1720 to 1890 A.C. – Published by the Central Records Office, Hyderabad Government, 1954.

URDU BOOKS

Akbar, Jalaluddin, *Hyderabadi Shora*, S.A. Graphics, Hyderabad, 2009.

Kumari, Pavan, *Raja Girdhari Pershad Baqi Aur En-Ke Khandan Ki Urdu Adbi Khidmath*, S.A. Graphics, Hyderabad, 2009.

Hashmi, Nasir Uddin, *Deccani Hindu Aur Urdu*, Taarikhi Urdu Barani, Delhi, 1958.

Pershad, Girdhari, *Baqi, Baqa-i-Baqi*, 1890.

Quadri, Syed Rafiuddin, *Ifadaat-E-Zore*, Vol.-IV, Educational Publishing House, New Delhi, 2017.

Raj, Narsing, *Josh-E-Gham*, 1349 F.

Raj, Narsing, *Dard-E-Baqi-O-Durd-E-Saqi*, Sardar Press, Hyderabad, 1342 A.H., 1922 A.D.

Raj, Narsing, *Armughaan-e-Mahbub,* Etemaad Press, Hyderabad, 1359 AH, 1931 A.D.

Raj, Narsing, *Gham-E-Ahbaab-E-Shad*, Hyderabad, 1940.

Raj, Narhar, *Gulhai Sadrang,* Idara-E-Ishat-e-Urdu, Karimnagar, 1962.

Raj, Sheela, *Shahi-Shadi,* H.E.H. The Nizam's Urdu Trust, Hyderabad,1991.

Raj, Sheela, *Tosha-E-Akhebat,* Hindustan Printers, Bombay, 1984.

Raj, Sheela, *Deewan-e-Aali*, Narhari Pershad Charitable Trust, Hyderabad, 2008.

Raj, Sheela, *Deewan-e-Mahbub*, Narhari Pershad Charitable Trust, Hyderabad, 2005.

Raj, Sheela, *Shahan-e-Asafia Ki Rawadari Aur Hindu-Muslim Rewayat,* Abul Kalam Azad Oriental Research Institute, Hyderabad, 2007.

Saxena, Bhaskar Raj, *Hyderabad Ke Bansi Raja,* Sher-O-Hikmath, Hyderabad, 1995.

Saxena, Bhaskar Raj, *Hyderabad Ke Adbi Ratan*, Sher-O-Hikhmat, Hyderabad, 2000.

Shahid, Khaja Hamiduddin, *Hyderabad Ke Shayar,* Andhra Pradesh Sahitya Academy, Hyderabad, 1958.

Salah, Laeeq, *Shamsuddin Faiz - Hayat Aur Adabi Karname*, National Faheen Printing Press, Hyderabad, 1980.

Zore, Mohiuddin Quadri, *Dastaan-i-Adab-E-Hyderabad*, Hyderabad, 1951.

Zore, Mohiuddin Quadri, *Farkhunda Buniyad, Hyderabad*, Hyderabad, Turage Barqi Press, Hyderabad, 1951.

Zore, Mohiuddin Quadri, *Muraqqe-i-Sukhan, Vols. I & II*, Azam Steam Press, Hyderabad, 1935.

PERSIAN BOOK

Ufakh, Munshi Dwarka Pershad, *Hayat-E-Baqi*, Lucknow Press, 1310 AH. 1892 A.D.

HINDI BOOKS

Pershad, Girdhari, *Keshav Mahatm*, Bharat Jeevan Press, Kashi, 1853.

Pershad, Narhari, *Narhari Gyan Updesh.*

Pershad, Narhari, *Narhari Mal.*

Pershad, Narhari, *Chitragupt Ki Katha*, Narhari Pershad Charitable Trust, Hyderabad, 2015.

Pershad, Raja Ram, *Chitragupt Mahatm*, Manuscript.

Saxena, Bhaskar Raj, *Hyderabad Nizam Kal Ke Bhakt Kavi*, Narhari Pershad Charitable Trust, Hyderabad, 2002.

Saxena, Bhaskar Raj, *Maha Kavi Narhari Pershad 'Narhari' kritik Narhari Prakash*, Geeta Prakashan, Hyderabad, 2005.

DISSERTATIONS

Azeez, M.A., Dr *Sheela Raj Life and Work*, Ph.D. Thesis, Osmania University, Hyderabad, 2014. Urdu.

Begum, Najiba, *Raja Girdhari Pershad 'Baqi' Shaksiat Aur Urdu Shayari*, M.A. Dissertation, Osmania University, Hyderabad, 1967. Urdu.

Kumari, Pavan, *Raja Girdhari Pershad 'Baqi' Aur En Ke Khandaan Ki Urdu Adabi Khidmath*, M.Phil Dissertation, Osmania University, Hyderabad, 1972. Urdu.

Sharma, Umesh Kumar, *Narhari Pershad Ki Rachnaon Ka Mulayankan*, M.Phil. Dissertation in Hindi, Maulana Azad National Urdu University, Hyderabad, 2008. Hindi.

Siddiqui, Quader, Mohiuddin, Mohammed, *A Critical Study of The Persian Poetry of Raja Girdhari Pershad 'Baqi'.* Ph.D. Thesis submitted to Maulana Azad National Urdu University, Hyderabad, 2016. Persian (Result awaited).

Syed, Abdul Khalikh, *Raja Narsing Raj Aali Ahwal-O-Adabi Khidmath*, Ph.D. Thesis, University of Hyderabad, Hyderabad, 2015. Urdu.

JOURNALS / MAGAZINES

ENGLISH

Asian Affairs, *Glimpses of an era*, Publisher, Minerva Press, London, December, 1998.

Indica - Vol. 27, No.1, Nizamuddin S. Gorekar, Heras Institute of Bombay, 1990.

Indian History And Culture, Bombay, 1990.

Journal of the Asiatic Society of Bombay, Nizamuddin S.Gorekar, Asiatic Society of Bombay, Bombay, 1998.

The Eastern Anthropologist, Bhavani Shankar Shukla, 59.4, p. 219, Lucknow, 1999.

URDU

Sabras, Monthly Journal, Mahender Raj Saxena, January 1940, Hyderabad.

Sabras, Monthly Journal, Rasheed Ansari, August 2007, Hyderabad.

Sabras, Monthly Journal, Sayed Fazalulla Mukkaram, Hyderabad, 2009.

Index

T

U

V

W

Y

Z